Sarah Case

Sarah Case read Drama at Manchester University, then trained and worked as an actor during the 1980s and '90s. She later retrained in Voice Studies at Central School of Speech and Drama, and within a year of graduating was appointed Head of Voice on Italia Conti Academy's BA (Hons) Acting course. During that time she began to develop the notion of collaboration between differing disciplines and, over the course of more than fourteen years there, expanded the integrated approach to voice. She continued to learn and work with a number of international practitioners in voice, largely through the Giving Voice Festivals at Aberystwyth and at the International Centre for Voice. These included masterclasses with Iegor Reznikoff (Sound Therapy) and Nellie Dougar-Zhabon (Breath and Impulse); extended workshops with Patricia Bardi (Physical Voice in the Moving Body); Voic(e)motion with Guy Dartnell; Lamentation with Marya Lowry; Ancient Choral with Tomasz Rodowicz of Gardzienice Theatre; The Voice of Violence with Lise Olson; Improvisation with Katarzyna Deszcz; and Butoh theatre techniques with Katsura Khan. She later returned to the ICV at Central with the movement director Simone Coxall to present and explore work on the integration of voice and movement. She now works as a freelance voice tutor and coach. Her other interests besides theatre and music include equal rights and defending freedom of speech, yoga, cycling and comedy.

The *Integrated Voice*

A Complete Voice Course for Actors

Sarah Case

NICK HERN BOOKS
London
www.nickhernbooks.co.uk

A NICK HERN BOOK

The Integrated Voice
first published in Great Britain in 2013
by Nick Hern Books Limited,
The Glasshouse, 49a Goldhawk Road, London W12 8QP

Copyright © 2013 Sarah Case

Sarah Case has asserted her moral right
to be identified as the author of this work

Cover designed by Nick Hern Books

Typeset by Nick Hern Books
Printed and bound in Great Britain by
T.J. International, Padstow, Cornwall

A CIP catalogue record for this book is available
from the British Library

ISBN 978 1 84842 184 4

Contents

Preface

Another voice book? What this book aims to do is to show a methodology for developing a vocal instrument that is integrated into body and mind/thought; it shows how body work is aided and enhanced by the application of the breath and the voice, and how voice work aids movement into acting; it looks at the progression of voice through a two-year period; and includes a section on one of the most misunderstood areas of actor training and the working actor – the warm-up.

It is aimed mainly at training actors (at drama school or those working on their own), and it will also be useful to tutors, to trained working actors, and to others who may want to develop their own voice. When I refer to the first or second year, therefore, this can apply to people working on their own as much as it refers to students at a drama school.

I consciously and purposefully do not always explain what an exercise is for – sometimes it is obvious, quite often it is not – as, in my experience, it is very often better for students to discover the point for themselves. Of course I do not want trainee actors to be in a fog of misunderstanding, but in writing this, I began to feel quite tied by too much explanation. This would be a different book, and so I hope that this 'try it and see' approach will be useful. Likewise, I do not give exercises conclusions, or explain why and how they work. There are already many voice books that do that very successfully, and this is a different approach. More importantly, I feel that giving an explanation would a) be very repetitive, due to the integrated nature inherent in this work, b) potentially cause students to 'end-game', and c) limit the possibility of the exercises. In other words, if you expect it to do this or that, you may not discover the other!

Most of the people using this book will be in training and will therefore begin to understand it as they work alongside their own particular school of thought; and if something is unclear or difficult to understand, then the tutors in institutions will be able to guide you through. If working on your own, it is highly likely that you may want to have some occasional private coaching to help you on your way, and I think that probably applies to other books on the subject too.

There is a DVD with the book, showing the fundamental principles of how to work with the voice and body, with some key exercises, which will hopefully clarify the basics of the work. There is detail on simple techniques such as how to work on the floor and move freely and easily with the voice, including advice on how to apply your breath and voice work to movement. These elements are inherent in the workout routines. The main section on the DVD is intended to help you do a warm-up or workout on your own, with the help of a guided session and other voices to sound along with; and shorter warm-ups that show how to tailor your warm-up to a particular requirement.

Acknowledgements

In my development as a voice teacher, many practitioners have helped and guided me, and I owe a debt of gratitude particularly to the work and writings of Cicely Berry, Kristin Linklater and Patsy Rodenburg. I would like to thank David Carey, who trained me as a voice teacher at Central School of Speech and Drama; he has been a great influence. Thanks also to Jane Boston for her wisdom and support, and to Barbara Houseman for both her work and kind words of support; they have long been an inspiration.

Thanks go to Annie Morrison for her generosity and permission to quote the usage of the Morrison bone prop; to Lise Olson for permission to quote from her work on heightened vocal states; to Patricia Bardi for permission to include some of her exercises on the skeleton and organs; to Harriet Whitbread who gave me a lot of help in my early career, particularly in my understanding of text and rhythm; and to Carol Fairlamb and Richard Ryder for their support and encouragement.

A huge thank-you to Alex Bingley for his knowledgeable reading of the manuscript and invaluable suggestions, and above all for his great and rock-solid support over the years we worked together.

I would like to thank the director Lawrence Evans for his perspectives on the actor's process, and Simone Coxall, whose understanding of how the body works and creative application of movement were a profound influence and help. Thanks also to Angela Gasparetto for her support. I would also like to acknowledge my yoga teacher, Julia Moore, for her inspired approach and whose teaching has informed particular elements of this work.

Many thanks to a lovely crew for filming, sound and editing on the DVD, and special thanks to Andrew (Cube) Dickinson for all his help with it.

My thanks go to students and graduates of the Acting degree course at Italia Conti and elsewhere, who taught and inspired me over the years, and a very big thank-you to the actors on the DVD.

Thank you to Nick Hern for his warm and encouraging support, and to my wonderful editors Matt Applewhite and Jodi Gray for their great help, guidance and judicious suggestions.

Finally I would like to thank Rikki Blue for proofreading, all his help with the DVD, and for his encouragement, patience, and unending support; the intelligence and calm when I needed it most.

*

The author and publisher gratefully acknowledge permission to quote extracts from the following:

Beowulf translated by Seamus Heaney, published by Faber & Faber Ltd.

Under Milk Wood by Dylan Thomas, copyright © 1952 by Dylan Thomas. Reprinted by permission of New Directions Publishing Corp. in the USA, and David Higham Associates in the UK (published by Orion Books Ltd.)

Thebans by Liz Lochhead, published by Nick Hern Books Ltd.

Introduction
A Philosophy of the Voice

A lot has been written about the how and why of voice training, and whilst the list of textbooks is relatively short, those
volumes that are widely used and referred to are in some ways
definitive. It strikes me that there are fundamentally only a
small number of exercises to do with voice, although expressed
in many different ways. It is, then, how you apply those basics
that has myriad variations.

Ultimately there are a finite number of aspects to work on
because the vocal anatomy has a finite number of parts. What
I think is most important to remember is that a single approach
won't help everyone. If we are working on breath support, say,
we can choose to do it in very 'technical' ways or more abstract,
'image-based' ways, but the ultimate aim and achievement are
generally the same. In the same way that, when I am working
on a part as an actor, I choose whatever 'method' or 'way in' I
need to access a character, a similar process applies to voice. I
do not reject anything out of hand. There are some very 'old-
fashioned', even archaic exercises, that really do work for me. I
still use some W.A. Aikin[1]/Clifford Turner[2] articulation exercises, as do so many current voice practitioners, because they
work – but I don't use them in isolation. Different methods
work for different students/actors; differing methods can work
for the same person but at different times during their training
and, of course, beyond that training into working. I find that
using very different ideas or methods *simultaneously* can have

1

extraordinary effects. And the great thing about this work is that, as you repeat it, coming back to it time and time again, even the simplest of things just keeps going deeper – if you allow yourself to go there and give in to the experience.

The aim is to empower you from the outset to see the voice as being an outward expression of your inner world, and to be able to use the voice without judgement. So we need to introduce voice and the notion of the whole body; the principle of breath and truth, and the importance of truthful thought; and how voice and your thoughts are affected by the breath.

Know Your Starting Point

Have you any preconceptions or thoughts about what voice training is, and why it is so important? How long does it take to train a voice? The simple answer is that it takes a lifetime, but in the short term, you will have acquired the basic skills of voice, speech and text during your first year of training, and will have consolidated and expanded into a strong and flexible instrument after two years, which is then developed and given body, weight and far greater flexibility throughout your third year. After about five to ten years, your voice will be in very good shape. It takes a long time, but it is amazing how quickly it responds in the early stages to good, solid and creative work, so let that be your impetus. It doesn't just happen in sessions, though, you have to do a lot of regular, self-directed training. It's muscle!

What is Voice?

What is a voice for? In order to say something! What do you *want* to say? – as a person, as an actor; how you feel now, in this moment; a subject that you want to say something about, for example, political, personal, artistic. What does it cost to say that, and what do we mean by 'cost'? Making a statement about something you hold dear can be very exposing – it costs you something to put yourself on the line, as a person in company, and as an actor on the stage. It costs us to talk in front of strangers – perhaps embarrassment or joy. There are wider costs

– for example, putting yourself on the line and peer pressure. So voice is a powerful force.

Breath and truth have to be about making statements. We are not asking for big, bombastic declamations, just simple truths. Keep coming back to simplicity as you do this work: less is more. It is about removing the clutter of frantic gestures and facial contortions, which we think make us more convincing but in fact make us less so.

So, how are you feeling physically, mentally and emotionally right now? This is the start of your awareness of self, and awareness of the body and voice. You need to work entirely through the breath. Think about the free breath and free body and what that means to you – how does your breathing feel? How does your body feel?

What Parts of the Body Are Used to Create Voice and Speech?

I don't go into great detail about the anatomy and physiology of the voice, as there are already some excellent books to guide you on this – this book is much more about the doing and learning through experience than intellectual understanding. I will, however, give you a basic outline of what is involved, and introduce information as we go through.

First of all, let's look at all the parts of the body involved in making voice and speech sounds. Jot down or make a mental note of all the parts of the body you think go into speaking. You can see the whole list of parts in detailed diagrammatic form, with a brief explanation of what they all do, in Appendix (i) – 'Bodyworld'. You can take a peek now, so you can see how much of the body is involved, but it will make more sense later on as you progress through the work. Use the detail in the Appendix for little reference points along the way.

All those parts are involved in creating vocal sound. It is a surprisingly long list! A basic knowledge will help you understand *what* is happening, leading to *why* we do certain exercises, and *how* you can identify any problems that may arise. Students and actors also feed back that knowing the basics of the mechanism empowers them and interests them. The point is that voice is very physical, and we will do a lot of work through movement, through the body – it's fundamental, it is about making those integrated connections. And so there is necessarily some repetition in the book, to allow the work to both settle and go deeper. What I mean, for example, is that, by using the breath and an easy sound, you get more air into the body and you begin to make the breath–voice–body *connection** (see the Glossary), which is what integration is all about. And by repeating the exercise, that connection grows stronger and stronger.

Possibly the biggest hurdle we face, however, is not in the achievement of a well-supported, balanced and articulate voice, but in the application of those skills to the craft of acting. Getting a voice to be a usable and flexible instrument is not that much of a mystery, if we are prepared to put in the work. That is not to say the voice is not mysterious – it is, and the more we explore it, the more mysteries we discover, and the more we are left to wonder at its marvels and infinite possibilities. It does, of course, take longer in some people than others; I believe that most if not all students these days accept the idea that the training never stops (whether they/we do anything with that information is another matter!).

It is the transfer of skills that seems to be so easy to understand in principle and yet so difficult in practice. In class work, there is always application to text, and every exercise is put in context by a process of shared learning that works both ways – from tutor to actor and vice versa. What is often surprising is that marvellous work in a voice or movement class seems to go out of the window during the pressure of rehearsal and other classes. How to address this integration is a question that we need to keep asking – and here is a crucial part of our philosophy. We must constantly talk to each other, share ideas, and develop, not just a coherent philosophy that is neither rigid nor too all-encompassing, but one that does service beyond our own ideas. We can achieve this through observation and collaboration. Tutors are often constrained by time and busy schedules, but these experiences feed back into the work, and the partnerships I have been able to enter into (particularly in the early stages of my teaching when I was fortunate enough to work in a genuinely collaborative environment), helped formulate the notion that voice, movement and acting are not a hierarchy but inter- and codependent. This guided me towards the integrated approach. For students, I think it helps them see that one skill is in no way separate from another. Voice is acting, acting is movement, movement is acting, is voice, and so on. This may be stating the obvious but that is no bad thing. So, state the obvious. And keep it simple.

The Structure of this Book

Part 1 deals with the first year of training, and is divided into chronological sections. Part 1a comprises Sessions 1–5, the first five weeks, laying the foundations of release, relaxation, breath and gentle sounding. It also applies the work to speaking, right from the outset. Breaking for a short 'Interval', we look again at applying breath and voice to movement. Part 1b is the next few weeks, Sessions 6–9, continuing with those fundamentals, with a reminder to do self-led practice – keeping it going during your break. Part 1c is a consolidation of the work so far. After a recap and time for a break, we go into the last part of first-year training, Part 1d, Sessions 19–27, the culmination and fruition of nine months of practice. At the end of this part I give a summary of the first year of voice.

Part 2 has a slightly simpler structure, but takes the work into much deeper areas. Part 2a consists of Sessions 1–9, increasing stamina and muscularity, greater capacity and thought. After a break, you go on to Part 2b, Sessions 10–17, for work on deep resonance and vocalising through the structures of the body, further integrating and strengthening the voice–body–text connection. The culmination of the main thrust of vocal training is to be found in Part 2c, Sessions 18–24, in which we look at extreme vocal states, such as shouting, anger and screaming.

Part 3 provides a recap of textual exploration, as well as new ideas for working on text, and Part 4 focuses on the warm-up.

In order to find exercises more easily, and for when I refer back to something, each one is numbered. For example, 1.1.1 is Part 1, Session 1, Exercise 1; 2.3.3 is Part 2, Session 3, Exercise 3. Part 3 is slightly different in structure, so that 3.4 means Part 3, Text Exercise 4; 3.6b is Part 3, Text Exercise 6b, and so on.

Finally, I provide a glossary of the most commonly used terminology throughout the book (where a word appears in the glossary, it is followed by an asterisk in the text), key concepts are explained, and an appendix with a brief description of vocal anatomy and physiology as a quick reference point. There is also a series of extras from which you can create handouts on articulation exercises.

The accompanying DVD includes workouts or warm-ups that you can join in with, and includes separate sections on specific exercises (these are indicated by a ☙ in the text).

The key is simplicity.

Less effort, more effect – and this is where it all starts.

Part 1

Less Effort, More Effect

Part 1a

'Less effort more effect.' What does this mean? At the start of voice training, perhaps the most important aspect to deal with is the restricted and unhappy body. So many people are walking around with their shoulders up at their ears, hunched in a state of tension that goes right through the body – and directly into the voice. When we start to un-tense, to release the body, there is a tendency to want to 'get it right' and push for results. So, in the beginning, work with diligence and the desire to change and improve, but *without effort* – the more you push, the less you get out of it. A pushed voice is strident, usually over-loud, and almost always disconnected from a thought; that is to say there is no truthful engagement with the thought because you are working from a position of tension. Try a line of text and push it out. Now relax, release and try again. (You will find this quick check even more effective when you have a few weeks or months of voice training under your belt.) You are giving yourself the time and the opportunity to share your voice and your thoughts with someone, instead of hitting them over the head with it – and your voice will love you for the time you took to care about it.

Let's start with release. What does that mean? Simply put, it means letting go.

Try this simple demonstration – let your arms hang by your sides, and then clench your fists. Hold this and notice what happens to your arms, shoulders, neck and breath. Let the fists go, shake out a bit, and then take note of your body and your breath. Repeat several times, and you may notice things are getting easier. Hold your shoulders tightly or tense them slightly too, and see the effect that has on how you feel. And then let go.

Now try this (it's good to do this with someone else, or to do it near a large mirror, but don't watch yourself doing it just yet):

The Shake

- Stand easily with both feet equally distributing the weight. Imagine the head floating up at the same time.

- Shake the right hand/wrist easily but quite vigorously.

- Keep it going, but bring in the elbow and shake it around. (Leave the left arm alone.)

- Bring in the shoulder, gently at first, and gradually more vigorously, until the whole arm is shaking and moving around. Keep this going for about a minute.

- Take the shoulder out of it, let it go, and keep the elbow and wrist moving.

- Take the elbow out so just the wrist/hand are moving.

- Stop that too and be still. Notice how you feel.

- Now take a look in the mirror. You might see that one arm is considerably longer than the other! It can be quite a shock. This will show you just how much you hold on to, unnecessarily. If you don't have a mirror, float both arms out in front of you and bring the palms together – you might see that the fingers on the right hand extend way beyond those on the left.

- You need to balance yourself, so go through it all on the left side.

- Repeat, but this time, shake and release the breath on a gentle 'f' or a 'sh' – this makes the movement easier and go deeper. The deepening of the experience is that the relaxation and easing of tension will be greater, more profound, and that ease will actually go further into the muscles as more oxygen is brought in. More 'stretching' will occur without effort because the releasing on an easy 'f' or 'sh' helps the muscles relax.

- It works with the legs too. Stand evenly and easily. Notice how your legs and feet feel. Now gently shake the right ankle and do a few slow rotations, first one way and then the other. Do this with the right knee. Now do it with the hip joint – gently at first, then getting more adventurous, but keep breathing and be easy. Shake the whole right leg and foot. Place it down again, shake it all again, and rest it down. Notice the difference in how it feels. Notice what the left leg feels like. You may well feel lopsided and that the left leg is a bit 'dead' – again, the result of tension or lack of ease and release. All this directly affects the voice.

- Do the left leg, in order as before.

- Repeat with a continuous 'sh' as you do it.

If you repeat this with a 'sh', you will, without realising it, be breathing more easily and in a more centred way (the breath will be dropping into your centre, lower down, in a much more natural way than if you consciously or with tension breathe into the upper chest. The shaking action takes your attention away from breathing in and so that becomes much easier). You are therefore already integrating simple techniques. You can't rush this work, but you can help it go in more easily if you integrate as you go.

That simple exercise proves how effective repetition is, and just how much tension we hold on to. New first-year students laugh at the difference between one arm that's been shaken and the other that is still a bit tight, and shorter. After a year's training, people are amazed at the fact that the exercise still produces clear changes in the body; and after a few years, the exercise *still* keeps on working for you. Imagine what can happen with repetition and rediscovery of all the many more advanced voice and speech exercises you will acquire. From the outset I will include an introduction to the physicality of sound and break-down of words using abstract physical movements.

An Introduction to Voice, Breath and Truth

I am now going to formalise a series of sessions, like a progressive series of lesson plans. These sessions equate roughly to 'terms' and 'weeks' as if following an academic year in a UK drama school. The semester system will fit into this, because there are, for example, twenty-seven sessions for a first year, twenty-four for a second year. Each block has a gap of a few weeks to give you a break, but with guidance on how to maintain the work during less formalised periods. This is intended to be a useful guide if you are in drama-school training, but also a model if you are working outside of an institution.

Session 1

Keywords: *Effortlessness: less effort, more effect*

Release the skeleton and prepare the body   `1.1.1`

- Focus, stand easily noticing your alignment* – release the skeleton up and down and out, just using your imagination to let it all feel open. I'll explain that – if you stand freely and avoid slumping, you can encourage the spine in particular to elongate by breathing and imagining that there is space between each of the vertebrae. The breath aids this process, so by thinking your breath into the spaces between, the spine can actually lengthen as the discs float a bit more. You can imagine and feel your head floating on top of the spine like a balloon, creating a sense of space, and the spine lengthening down through to the tail bone and out and away from you. The spine cannot physically widen, of course, as it is bone, but if you *imagine* it widening you can get a great sense of space and feel the whole back widening with the breath. Another idea is to think of the vertebrae becoming fat, wide and open, as if there were space increasing on the inside of each vertebra.

If you find this difficult at first, it can help to think of the spine in three or more sections, perhaps concentrating on the lower back/sacrum and lumbar region, then the middle and upper back, and finally the cervical spine (neck). You can fill in more detail and link it all as you get more experienced.

Allow the body to follow your mind's instruction.

- Massage your feet. Sit on the floor and give your feet, toes and ankles a good massage. Take your time over this, at least five minutes. Stand again and notice how much more 'grounded'* you feel.

- Loosen your joints – release, shake and gently stretch.

- Gently roll your shoulders and free up the arms and hands, letting the neck be free.

- Raise your right arm from the shoulder blade out to the side on an easy in-breath, extending it out all the way through to the fingertips, then lower it on a easy out-breath, etc. Then repeat with the left arm. Do this several times. Watch that the top of the shoulder doesn't rise up or tighten.

- Patting and tapping the body – pat your arms, torso, legs, going up and down and all over your body. Feel a tingle and sense of ease when you have done this.

- Loosen and massage the lips, tongue, and jaw – start this easily by giving it all a good but gentle massage, working lips and tongue with your fingers and massaging and stroking gently down the jawline.

1.1.2 **Release and prepare using breath and 'f'**

- Repeat all the above, but as you do so, allow a breath to come in and send it out through the body on a continuous little 'f'.

- Imagine that little feathers are coming out onto your lips – lots of little 'ffff's as you go through the patting, tapping, massaging, etc.

Release and prepare using breath and 's', 'sh' and 'v'

1.1.3

- Repeat all the above, but allowing a breath to come in and send it out through the body on a little 's' and/or a 'sh' of continuous breath/sound.

- Go through this with a gentle continuous 'v' – imagine that the little feathers are coming out onto your lips with a bit more impetus.

- Let this sound go right through the body.

Move the body with these sounds – arm swings

1.1.4

- As you go through, start to bring in some easy arm swings with those voiceless sounds of 'f' and 'sh', and add intention – be happy, be a bit annoyed, etc.

- Do the same with easy, effortless leg swings.

- Notice what happens to your breath and sound when you add intention – by giving it a bit more conscious thought you are beginning to integrate your work, even the simplest of exercises, with a breath connected to a thought. This will go into the next stage: bring in some voiced sounds such as 'v' and 'z' and some hums.

- Swing your limbs very easily with humming.

Note: let me briefly explain the terms 'voiced' and 'voiceless' – some sounds use the voice and some just use the breath. Place your fingers across your larynx pressing lightly on the 'adam's apple', and make the sound of 'v', letting it go on for a few seconds. You will feel vibration from your larynx into your fingers. Do it a few times. Now make a little 'f' sound, just using the breath to pass over the lips between your upper teeth and lower lip, so that it is like a whisper. You should feel no vibration from the larynx. Flip between the two – between 'f' and 'v' – and you will feel the sound turning on and off. Do the same with an 's' (voiceless) and a 'z' (voiced), and then with a 'p' (voiceless) and 'b' (voiced).

1.1.5 **The silent 'ah'**

- Try the silent 'ah': stand freely and easily (this should be
  very free by now) and *let* the breath into your body through
  your mouth. If you gently smile, this will allow it to be even
  easier. The idea of this is to help release the jaw and
  tongue, and also to ensure a good opening of the mouth
  and pharynx. The 'ah' is the shape of the gently open
  mouth (as if saying 'ah'), and the silent bit is just that. In
  other words, breathe in and out through an open mouth
  with as silent a breath as possible.

- Try this again and think of something funny, which helps lift
  the soft palate (and clear any constriction in the mouth).
  Put your tongue tip behind the lower-front teeth so that
  the tongue stays forward (which also helps eliminate
  constriction through bunching or retraction of the tongue).
  As the mouth drops open a little, the breath just comes in
  and out very easily.

- See how quietly you can let the breath flow in and out. We
  will come back to this in later sessions, but right from the
  outset see if you can just let the breath in silently. This is
  more efficient, it takes less effort, and starts you on the
  path of not getting in your own way.

By now you should have a feeling of space in the body, in the air
passage and mouth – take time to really notice the effect.

1.1.6 **Patting with sound and word**

- Go back to patting, tapping your body, and moving freely
  with 'f', 'sh' then 'v', and then into a hum 'mmm'. Then take
  it on to a very gentle 'mmaaa', just letting the sound pour
  out of you.

- Now try letting the breath in and then out on a 'Hello, how
  are you?' and answer yourself, or each other, 'Mmm, I'm
  fine, thanks, how are you?', so that you are now bringing
  the work onto words.

This might seem very simplistic, and it is. The point is to do very little at the start. Some voice tutors advocate only doing release and breath work without any voiced sound at all in the first few sessions. However, because you *are* going to be speaking on a daily basis, you may as well learn to start doing it right now! And by starting with the kind of 'Hello, how are you?' type of spoken word, you learn from the outset that this is all designed and intended to give you a voice to speak with at any time, anywhere. We come on to written text a bit later, but for now bring it right into your own life and experience first.

Making a statement – bring in the word

1.1.7

- Let a breath into your body and make a statement of fact 'My name is... and I love cats' or ' My name is... and I am from York...'

- Notice how easy it is to speak this into the space. Own your name and your voice, it's as simple as that.

- Now apply this to alignment/posture – doing it with erect and/or collapsed body and spine, with your arms relaxed by your side or with folded arms – and see and hear the effect on both speaker and listener.

- Let another breath into the body and make a statement about sensation and/or emotion: 'At the moment I feel...'

- If you are working with others, move on to comments about each other. Start with facts, and then commit to a (non-judgemental) opinion about another person. As David Mamet says, the point is to invent nothing, deny nothing. In other words, do it without comment, just say 'You are tall,' 'You have green eyes,' 'You seem happy,' and so on.

The physicality of words

1.1.8

I will show you how to take any word and break it down:

- Let the breath in and sound out on a 'v' and let it go on continuously for as long as is comfortable for you.

- Repeat this 'vvv' sound and start moving around the space, bending a little, stretching up or out to the sides, just play around with it.

- When you have played with 'vvv' for a while, try out an easy, gentle 'oy' (as in 'boy') sound (speaking it, not singing it).

- With an easy breath, play around with 'oy' and, as before, move your body around with your 'oy'.

- Begin again with the 'vvv', taking it into 'oy' – so as you are moving around the space, you are stretching and moving to the sound 'vvv-oy', again sounding the 'vvv-oy' many times.

- Now try out the sound of 's' – there is no sound other than the breath and a slightly hissy 's' sound, like a little snake. Repeat, again moving it through the space with your body involved.

- Try out the 'vvv', which you take into a long 'oy', into a long 's', and you will find you are saying 'voice'.

Do this with another word:

- Try out a delicate little 'p' sound. Don't voice it – all that should happen is that you let in a breath and then make a 'p' sound with your lips. It is a tiny little sound which you can play with by imagining you have a little 'p' in your hand, and you toss it lightly up into the air and catch it again – don't let it go too high! Just let the 'p' jump up and down onto your upturned fingers. The movement is light and delicate and so is the sound – it won't travel very far.

- With the other hand, play with an 'uh' sound, just patting it a little way away from you (this is the vowel sound in 'the' or the first vowel sound in 'ago').

- Here's another one. Pat away a little 't'.

- Then put them together and you get 'p-uh-t'.

- Try out an 'ey' sound (as in 'hey!') and play around with it.

- Go back to a 't' jumping around in your fingers.

- Then add in an 'oh'.

- Put it all together, with the body involved too, of course, and you are saying (and moving) 'p-uh-t-ey-t-oh'. 'Potato!'

The idea is to get not just the breath, thought, voice and body all involved together, but the imagination too – and above all, I want you to let yourself be taken by surprise.

Now think of your own word and try it out. Say it first, then work out bit by bit how it's broken down into discrete units of sound, as we did with 'v-oy-s' and 'p-uh-t-ey-t-oh'.

Session 2

Keyword: *Effortlessness (get used to this!)*

1.2.1	**Bubble walk**

- Find your focus, stand easily feeling your alignment – release the skeleton up and down and out, just using your imagination to let it all feel open. Allow the body to follow your mind's instruction.

- Walk around the space and imagine you have bubbles of air in your body.

- Do this quite methodically, from the top of your head, putting in a bubble of air where your brain once was, then imagine bubbles of air in your jaw joints and in your mouth, down through the neck, putting bubbles into the shoulder joints, elbows and wrists, and into the joints of the hands and fingers.

- Continue down the spine in your mind's eye, imagining you have a bubble between each of the vertebrae. As the vertabrae get bigger the lower down your spine you go, those bubbles of air will have to seem bigger too, until you get to the pelvic girdle or pelvic bowl, which is now a huge bowl of air.

- Put bubbles into the hip joints, into the knee and ankle joints, and then between the bones of the feet and toes, many bones, many gaps, many tiny little pockets of air.

- Come to a halt and stand still, close your eyes, and sense the bubbles through your body.

- Open your eyes. You may feel very light, and possibly taller.

- If you repeat this over the coming days, you will almost certainly gain lightness, height, and a sense of space in the body.

If you feel a bit too 'spacey' then imagine stepping in clay to make an imprint, and making lots of gentle but firm images in the soft clay or earth with your feet and toes. This will bring you back to the ground.

Body tapping

1.2.2

Repeat from Session 1 (1.1.1 and 1.1.6).

Feathers

1.2.3

- Loosen the lips, tongue and jaw by giving them all a gentle massage, using when possible a gentle 'f' and 'v', or 'sh' or an easy hum. Integrate right from the start – if you use the breath and the voice to work those parts of the body you are preparing for the work, it all goes in more easily and helps your mind to make the connections of the work through the body.

- Let a breath into your centre (imagine it coming into the area inside you just behind your navel) and release it out on a series of little 'f's, imagining that they are feathers being blown out into the space.

- Allow lots of little feather 'f's come onto your lips, and bring your fingers to your lips to feel them dancing around there.

- Then let the feathers of 'f' go out into the space again, imagining that they are coming from your centre – around your tummy/navel, up through the body, onto the lips. Then let them be guided by your fingers out into the air, into the space.

- This is light, easy and gentle work. Don't force those feathers out, just *let* them out into the room. This is very important. Never force this work, be patient – and you will have a lot of fun with the breath, your sound, and your imagination.

1.2.4   More feathers

- Start to move around the room. Extend the idea of feathers of 'f' coming out of your mouth, going into an 's' sound and onto extensive playing with 'sh'.

- Begin to take this onto voiced sounds, playing with 'v'.

1.2.5   The body and centre of the body start to get more involved – sound your body!

- Stand easily and freely with your weight distributed evenly, so that your alignment is flowing from the feet, grounding through the floor and at the same time flowing upwards towards the air. Let the arms hang freely for a moment before you begin to move.

- Imagine and let a breath come into your tummy, your centre, and then let a 'v' sound come into your right side, imagining it running around your middle as you gently sound it out.

- You may feel the impulse to move – do so, move around with the 'vvv' playing around your body, around the right side of your waist.

- Imagine the 'vvv' is running down your right leg, tracing it as you do so with your hands – this helps you both imagine and feel as if the 'vvv' is really sounding down your leg.

- Stand easily again, and letting in a breath, feel a 'zzz' sound emitting itself from your centre into your waist on the left-hand side.

- Let the 'zzz' go down your left leg – and as with the 'v' down the right leg, trace this sound with your hands all the way down the leg and through the foot.

- Do this several times on each side.

- Come back to upright, and now let the 'vvv' sound out from your centre, going internally down the inside core of your right leg – so you make this sound and imagine it is now going down inside the leg. Because you had traced it with your hands externally, it should now be much easier to imagine that the 'vvv' is vibrating right down the core of your leg.

- Repeat the same process with 'zzz' inside the left leg.

- You can now let a breath into your tummy, your centre, and gently commit to sounding a 'vvv'. This time, you trace it with your hand(s) up your body, through the chest, along the arms, up the neck, and up through the head.

- Repeat with 'zzz'.

- Do this several times, and you should be able to start to do this without the help of the hands. Imagine those sounds are travelling from your centre, up through the body until the 'v' or 'z' comes out along the arms and right out through the fingertips, and/or travelling up until the sound comes out of your mouth or the top of the head.

It is very important that, while you are doing this, you are relaxed – this does not mean collapsed! What I mean by that is that you are not slouching or slumped, but standing up in as relaxed a manner as possible. When you are free and easy, the sounds are easy and gentle. Don't ever push your sound. Less is more.

- Repeat the same process with humming through the body.

The body gets more involved – sound some text 1.2.6

- When you are ready, try this out with an easy line of text. If you can't think of one, try a bit of Shakespeare: 'Now is the winter of our discontent' or 'To be or not to be'. Also try something of your own, like what you had for breakfast this morning.

In other words, you bring it back to you, and the mundane and the everyday. This helps you integrate your process early on in your vocal development. It won't be that easy to start with, but the sooner you get the idea that this is not just for 'text', but for the everyday, the sooner you will own a centred, supported and free voice.

Session 3

As you will have seen, the work is quite abstract and image-based at times. I'm including some parallel 'technical' exercises, so that if you do one creative and abstract session, and then one that is much more obviously literal, you get the best of both worlds. And different people respond to different types of work – do both, and eventually you will find you can incorporate the one into the other very easily. Just go with the flow and see what happens.

Bubble walk

1.3.1

Repeat from Session 2 – 1.2.1.

Bubble walk with 'f'

1.3.2

- Repeat the whole lot, and as you go through each body part, let in a breath and allow a gentle little 'f' to come out of you. Imagine it going into each part you are thinking of, so that you have little bubbles of 'f' in your head, your jaw joints, down your spine, and so on. This simple exercise can have a profound effect on how your body feels, and *is*, as well as on the breath going into the body, and establishing the breath–thought connection. This concept will become increasingly clear, but for now, just see it as thinking what you want to say as you breathe in, then speaking that thought on the out-breath simultaneously – so that you are linking your thought to the breath stream.

- If you then repeat it all with a 'vvv' sound, you get even more.

1.3.3 Blow bubbles of 'f'

- Let the breath into your centre, around your tummy, and then, using your hands to guide it, start to blow little shaped bubbles of 'f' – bring your hands down to your navel area, let the breath in, and then on the out-breath, bring your hands gently to your lips and start to shape little bubbles with an 'f' sound.

- Begin to shape those bubbles of 'f' with the hands extending out into the space a little more.

- Play with 'sh', so you have lots of 'sh'-shaped bubbles going out into the space, from your centre, out of the lips and into the room.

- If these bubbles now begin to extend and grow into different shapes and sizes, you will feel your breath extending further each time.

- Try all this with 'v' and 'z' and then onto 'bubbles of hum'!

If you do this with a group of people, try splitting into two groups, and watch the other half of the group doing this.

Ask them to do some 'stretches' – you will see 'gym stretches', the kind you see people doing before an aerobics class or running session. This is explained and shown in a bit more detail in the interval section, 'How to stretch without "stretching"', following Session 5.

Get them to repeat the shaping of bubbles of 'f' and hum – they will still be stretching but the difference is enormous. They move far more freely – quite simply, they will be moving MORE – but the body, and therefore the breath and voice, are far easier and the sounds are easier to extend. The exercise integrates breath, sound and body. What could be simpler?

Floor work – positioning and the tide of breath

First of all, let me explain the 'semi-supine' or Alexander Technique* floor position. Lying down on the floor is important in voice, it helps you to relax and release, and make different and new discoveries about both the breath and the voice. Get a book to put under your head. The thickness will depend on you – try a few to see what feels right. Get someone to help you too, looking at your alignment*.

- Sit down on the floor, and get your knees, legs and feet all in alignment with your pelvis, and then lie down with your head on the book. Your knees are up and feet are flat on the floor. Rest your arms easily by your sides for the moment, and allow your spine to lengthen and widen. You may need to adjust so your feet are closer to or a bit further away from your bottom. There is a natural hollow in the lower back. Don't try to flatten it.

- Don't *do* anything. Use your imagination to let the spine release into the floor, and see it in your mind's eye lengthening all way up the spine, and out of your head towards the wall behind you, and all the way down the spine, out through the coccyx (tail bone) towards the wall in front of you. At the same time, imagine the spine widening towards the walls on either side of you. Let go.

- Bring your hands to your centre. Let them rest easily around your navel area. Do not rest them too low – don't place them down towards the groin. This is very important, particularly at the start of training. I have observed that if people place their hands *too* low in the body, it actually causes more strain, can overextend the arch in the back, and consequently cause the breathing to rise in the chest or be in some way restricted, which defeats the point of the exercise. We want the breath to come deep into the body, but by concentrating and placing the hands on the central tummy/navel area, you get a deeper breath than if you place them way down.

- So you are now lying easily, simply noticing the breath rise and fall beneath your hands. Again, don't *do* anything just yet, simply observe. As the breath comes into the body, your hands rise, and as it leaves the body as you breathe out, your hands fall. This is normal and natural, and the way we want to encourage breathing at all times. So, the chest doesn't rise much on the in-breath. It may do so at first, but quite soon your body will realise that breathing into the centre is what it does 'naturally' (for example, when you are asleep) – in other words, when you can't interfere! (Note: you do, of course, breathe into the upper chest as well as lower down into the body, but it is not the main area of focus and it shouldn't 'heave up'.)

The tide of breath

If you are already in training or have had some lessons, you may have come across the notion of the breath as a tide – sometimes called the 'tidal breath'. It's a very good image to work with – go through this sequence and you will discover why. (I always ask people to do first and think later; to experience first and question afterwards, when necessary. This way, you are more likely to 'get it' without intellectualising the process. That comes later, and is more effective for having physically experienced something first, because this is a physical process we are working on. It's not a PhD!) It is a very good way to discover ease of breath, and is a great image that just makes sense.

- Lie in the Alexander position, with your hands resting lightly on your tummy, either side of the navel (so that they are not clasped – this helps open up the back ribs). Really begin to take notice of the rise and fall of the breath. As the breath comes into the body, imagine it as a very gentle tide rippling up the beach. As you breathe out, the tide goes out – and you see your breath as a tide, going easily out towards the sea.

- Allow the body to settle into a relaxed yet energised state. As you continue to lie there, you will find the spine lengthening and widening, and the whole body gives in to gravity and softens (for a reminder on how the spine can 'do' this, see the first exercise in Session 1).

- Begin to notice your breath. Without changing it or 'doing' anything to it, place a hand on your tummy, and after a few seconds you will notice something. The hand rises as you breathe in, and falls as you breathe out. This is what happens when you are asleep – the breath always takes care of itself.

- As your breath comes in and out, start to notice its rhythm – as it comes in, it goes deep into your lungs. (This will go deeper as you relax, as the whole breathing mechanism will slow down. Don't force this, it will just come. Different pace of breath will come later.) Once the breath has come in of its own accord, it will naturally go out again. Imagine this coming in and going out as if it were the tide.

- Place yourself on an imaginary beach. There is a gentle and easy tide, on a warm and calm day, and you can hear a very gentle tide coming in and going out. As you breathe in, the tide is coming in, easily, fairly quickly, and gently running up the beach.

- As you breathe out – and this is the important part – the tide goes out. When the tide goes out to the sea, you will notice that it appears to pause for a tiny moment; there is a little hiatus at the end of the tide, before it rushes back up the beach again. Of course, the tide never stops moving, but it does appear to suspend for a moment before coming back in. And the point is, it does come back in when it's good and ready. This brings me to a very important aspect of breath work – concentrate on the out-breath and the in-breath will take care of itself.

- Notice your own breath – after *you* have breathed out, there is a little momentary pause, like the sea. This is perfectly natural. Your body will breathe *you* – you don't have to think about it, it just happens.

- Bring this tide onto a more focused breath – let the tide in, and then on the out-breath, let the tide out on a little 'f', a continuant and easy sound, just touching the 'f' out of your body from the centre.

- The tide comes into your centre, just around your navel, it goes out from your centre. Keep seeing it around your middle, inside your middle, and emanating from there.

- Let the tide out on a gentle 's' and do this several times. This process needs to be given time. Enjoy the peace and pleasure of being on a beautiful beach, with your tide just flowing in and out of its own accord. As you keep going with this, the tide becomes easier and easier, and as a result, it goes deeper and deeper into your being.

- Do this several times and then let the tide go out on a gentle 'sh-shhhhhh' sound – the longer you do this, the more gentle and easy it will be. It sounds like the tide. It *is* the tide.

- Repeat for as long as you like. It could be one minute, it could be five minutes. Really *see* the tide coming in of its own accord, and then going out on sound.

- When this is truly established, you can make some voiced sound – let your tide out on a continuant 'v' sound. Really see it and feel it going out on that sound. If you like, you can begin to colour the sea too. See and feel what happens. Let the sound be around, or just above, the middle of your pitch range – it is too tiring on the voice if you warm up on low notes.

- After doing this for many breaths, take it onto a 'z', and then a 'zh' (as in the middle sound of the word 'leisure' or 'measure', the 'zh' is a very pleasurable sound).

- You can now begin to hum your sea, hum your tide, and you will find the sound warm and easy. This is warming up your voice, it is connecting you to your centre, it is connecting your breath to your centre, your thoughts and imagination. It is integrating mind, breath, voice and body.

- After humming the tide for a while, let it go out on a hum releasing into a 'mah'.

- Take your tidal hum, when it is really easy and established, onto an easy open vowel – perhaps 'mmaaahh' or 'mmmoooo', whichever feels good and gentle and focused. Try both sounds.

- After a few minutes, take it back into a hum and use the tidal hum to stretch out your body – this will be incredibly easy, luxurious and free, because you are so relaxed and the voice has now found its way throughout the body, whether your conscious brain realises it or not.

- With the hum (or 'mmaaahh', if you prefer), roll over to one side. Very slowly and gently, hum yourself to a sitting position, *leaving your head until last*. This is so that you are really working through the spine and neck, lengthening in the back of the neck in particular. This helps establish a good head–neck relationship, prevents any sensation of lightheadedness, and also protects the lower back from any jolting.

- Once you feel 'present', keeping the hum and/or 'mmaaahh' going, you bring yourself to standing. This practical exercise of humming or sounding whilst moving not only keeps your voice going, it helps to bring it into standing without jolting voice or body. You can practise using text, once this more abstract and free sound is easily established. You may also find it's a lot easier getting up whilst sounding! The voice aids movement, no doubt about it, and it aids the whole integration process.

- All of that can take anything from a few minutes to maybe fifteen or more. It's up to you. But the more often you repeat this, as with all the basics in voice work, the more effect it will have. The effect will be to deepen and lengthen your breath, and to encourage a smooth, consistent and even sound – and on top of that you get the benefit of a very relaxing and rewarding experience.

- Sleepy? You may find that you start to fall asleep when doing this, particularly when guided by someone (so that you don't have to concentrate on what you are doing), and this is perfectly okay at the start of training. It is usually a sign that either you are simply tired, or more likely, that you are simply not used to letting go. So give in to it and gently bring yourself back to the present. When you have been doing this for a few weeks or so, you will be able to give in to the work and be very conscious. Conscious relaxation is a great place to get to, just be patient.

1.3.5   The tide of breath – standing and moving into speaking

- Standing freely and easily, rediscover the notion of the breath tide, letting your breath drop in, coming up the beach, and let the tide out on a 'sh' for a few seconds.

- Once established, having done this for some time on the floor, you can very easily bring it onto sound, so hum or 'mah' your tide whilst standing.

- When that is easy, walk around the room, with your tidal breath and tide of sound. If you are still thinking of the beach, so much the better, because if you engage your imagination, you may well integrate the sound into body and voice more quickly, and at the same time awaken your imaginative processes which will help you move on to text.

- Think of a short piece of text (the first line of a poem or nursery rhyme, or what you had for breakfast), and try it out – text as the tide going out to sea. Why not?!

Hopefully you will find yourself both sounding and speaking easily, freely, and without even realising it you are most likely supporting your voice and the words.

Speaking it – active engagement

- Give your lips, mouth and cheeks a rub, massaging them all on the outside. Again, do this freely and gently, and after all that floor work, this should happen easily and quite quickly – your whole face will feel very malleable and flexible.

- Now think of a line of text, and letting the breath into your centre as usual, let that line of text out from your centre, up through your body, and it will flow like a tide out of your mouth. It really is that easy. Trust to it and do it. Let your voice and speech out.

- Try it with some everyday phrases – what you are going to eat later on; what you watched on television recently and what was good about it. In other words, connect all this to your everyday voice, and to something that you personally care about or have an interest in.

- Try again with a line of text, with the same sense of connection and caring.

Taking it onto text – political rhetoric

Rhetoric is the study and use of language to persuade other people (or a speech used to persuade other people to your point of view); it is the art of public speaking and debate. Rhetorical skills are used in political life, but also in private. We will look at political debate here, and go on to rhetoric in dramatic text in the second part. For now, if you can, get hold of a famous speech (e.g. 'I have a dream' by Martin Luther King, a speech by Emmeline Pankhurst – or anyone you have an affinity with or even vehemently oppose). The reason for using rhetoric is that you have a personal connection to it either because you passionately agree with the writer/speaker, or because you are absolutely opposed to their view and want to try it out. The speech must not be from a play (we go on to rhetoric in Shakespeare in the second year) but from 'real life' – which also helps you integrate your voice into a text that is about making a truthful statement, as there is no character to hide behind. You are going to do this as you.

- Get hold of a speech, and then reduce it down to about two minutes' worth of speaking, so it's a manageable chunk. This is a very good exercise in itself, because it will make you look for what is really important. Find the key issues or statements.

- Read through your speech, quietly but aloud. Read it to another person, and listen to theirs too, and notice what the person is saying, and also how they are saying it. Is it very academic in style or very chatty? Is it about world issues or something more personal? Have a look at these elements and then try it out again.

Taking it onto text – parallel idea 1

- Look at a short nursery rhyme or children's poem, and read it through aloud a few times.

- Look at the important word in each line – what really matters, what is the key word?

- Play around with that text, move it with your body round the space, and find its rhythm. I am not going into detail about this yet, just see if you can find it for yourself.

- Look at key words again and play with them in your mouth and through the body. Be truthful, however simplistic or childlike the language is.

- Speak the whole rhyme or poem.

Taking it onto text – parallel idea 2

- You can also get together in pairs or in a group and just talk about something that interests you. Listen to each other, and start to notice how another person speaks.

- What are their stress patterns – which words do they seem to stress more, what becomes their pattern of intonation and stress? How much do they go up and down in pitch, or how little? Don't be judgemental, just notice it – listening is a fundamental part of being an actor, and if you start to listen and notice people's patterns of speaking, then when you come on to text, you are more open to different possibilities.

Session 4

At this very early stage in training I introduce the modern bone prop. These implements went right out of fashion for quite some time, and perhaps for good reason. The old props were very large (you can still get the big, old-fashioned ones) but I have a problem with those – because they make the jaw open so wide, they can cause a lot of jaw and tongue tension. This is the last thing you want for a free voice and speech. The new prop, certainly the one I would recommend, was designed and developed by Annie Morrison,[3] and its two key issues are that a) it is quite small, and b) it has a little groove so that it rests easily between the front teeth without having to be gripped. You can try these exercises with a piece of cut-down rawl plug, but this is not a great substitute in the long run.

What does the bone prop do? When I was training, we used big old props, sometimes even large pieces of cork. I remember it being merely an aid to 'good' articulation, but one that created jaw tension. It could be that I was a lousy student, but my jaw became pretty tense, and I also used to think of props as just a way of getting 'clear speech'. But this modern prop does a lot more than that. Because the space it creates at the front of the mouth is small, it opens up the oral space at the back of the mouth. Having space here creates a more open sound. Later on in training, you will find that this enhances oral resonance, which will be explained more fully as we come to it, so when you learn to use it properly, you get a better vocal sound. The prop also makes the lips much more mobile, which helps you to get the sound forward. It may feel odd at first, but then breathing consciously made you feel odd for a bit! You are changing the habits of your lifetime. Be prepared to change. Of course, the bone prop *does* help enormously with articulation – I have noticed really startling effects quite early on in the training. Not only do people start to articulate discrete speech sounds more clearly, but they also start to feel and use words much more physically, and sooner into the process.

The prop does not replace all the articulation exercises and drills you need to do, it is an extra tool that just happens to have a lot of other added benefits, if you use it in the right way. The 'right way' involves very careful release of the jaw in particular – bone props have often been rejected by professionals because they caused that jaw tension I mentioned. I have found that the only way to use it effectively is to start out by being so floppy it falls out – thereby discovering an essential and very effective way into jaw-release work.

The Bone Prop is Not a Chew!

It is very easy to get overly attached to your prop. It shouldn't sit in your mouth unattended – so don't use it as a chew or 'sweet'. If you chew it you could damage it, and because you are not paying attention to its function, you can get jaw tension from sitting idly even with it just resting in your mouth.

Here's a simple demonstration of *what not to do with your bone prop*: stand or sit and place your little finger (the 'pinkie') between your front teeth. Just rest in that position, leaving it there as you read this. What I do to demonstrate this is to simply let students stand or sit with their little fingers held between their teeth whilst I chatter for a minute or so. That is probably enough, and by now you may begin to notice something. Are your teeth now beginning to bite into or press slightly uncomfortably down into your finger? The longer you leave it (and it really doesn't take long to notice), the more you will feel that pressure. This is just the weight of your upper jaw relaxing down and pressing on your finger. So imagine what happens if you leave your prop in there for ages – it will build up pressure and create tension. If you haven't already done so, take your finger out! Now try that with the prop – you will realise very quickly that it is to be used for talking, not silence. Use it as you speak, keep checking it's nice and loose, but with *just enough* light grip for it to stay upright and useful to you.

1.4.1   Clean-hands exercise (i) – the lips and mouth

So called because you need clean hands to do this preparatory work! This is a variation on a theme that you will come across quite often – basically massaging the mouth. From now on, I will do the clean-hands exercise at the start of every session. Firstly, because once you have been rolling around on the floor, you really won't want to do this, and secondly and more importantly, because the exercises really open up the oral space and have a great effect on the following breath and voice exercises. It is a progressive and connected process that you are learning.

- Stand freely and easily with even weight distribution. Notice how your mouth feels.

- Lick your lips and then put all the fingers of each hand into your mouth. Give the cheeks a massage with your fingers on the inside of your mouth, and your thumbs on the outside. *After just a few seconds*, remove your hands and rest. Shake out.

- Repeat, and this time check that the shoulders haven't gone up for the ride. Relax the shoulders, let the shoulder blades rest on the back of the ribcage, and soften in the arms and hands as you do this mouth massage. After twenty seconds or so, stop, remove your hands, shake out and rest for a couple of seconds.

- Repeat, and do for another thirty seconds or so.

This series of very short massages, with a rest in between, is incredibly important. It is far, far more effective than doing one long massage of a minute or two. The reason is that it is very easy to introduce unwanted tension – I have noticed that even under guidance, in the first few weeks, people will want to bring their hands up to their mouths as if they were lifting a great weight, or jut the head and neck forward and down to reach the hands. You are not lifting or straining anything – just *float your fingers up* into your mouth.

- Notice how your mouth feels now. It will hopefully feel very big, soft, marshmallowy, spacious and free. All good sensations, you can see and feel how that is now going to allow sound out into the space much more easily (and it lets breath in far more easily too, because you are creating a more open channel.*)

Clean-hands exercise (ii) – the tongue   `1.4.2`

- Stand freely and easily with even weight distribution. Notice how your tongue feels – be very clear about what it feels like.

- While your hands are still clean (albeit rather damp!) you can work on the tongue – quite simply, get hold of your tongue and give it a massage. Massage as much of it as you can – the tongue tip, the sides, the middle.

- This will feel very odd at first but persevere and just get over the 'ugh!' sensation and enjoy it.

- As with the mouth and cheeks massage, rest and repeat. Then repeat it all again.

- Notice how your tongue feels now. Probably larger, certainly freer, and you are far more aware of it.

Alternative tongue massage

You can also free up and massage your tongue by gently biting it. Begin with the tongue tip, and gradually go over the whole of your tongue, or as much as you can, with your teeth gently but firmly biting into it. Do it once, relax and then repeat the whole thing. This really wakes it up, and it will feel much more alive, responsive and much bigger. It also produces quite a bit of saliva, which is very important for good speech. Keep checking that the jaw is soft, and that you are breathing easily!

1.4.3   The jaw lets go

- Having done all that massage work, your jaw will feel a lot looser, hopefully, but it will still need some help in order to release* and relax. Stand free and easy, and ask the jaw to drop open – don't pull it open, just let it hang.

- Gently stroke down the jaw with your hands, so that the lower jawbone feels as if it is being eased firmly but gently down, the mouth opening as you do so.

- Check that you have not collapsed through the spine in the process – don't let the head–neck relationship be compromised. It is your jaw that is hanging loose, the rest of the body is still grounded* on the floor and at the same time is floating upwards into good alignment. The jaw hangs open.

1.4.4   The little jaw chains

- In order to encourage the jaw to keep on releasing, try this. Imagine that you have very fine little chains attached to the underside of your jawbone, one on either side. Now take hold of those chains, in your imagination, very delicately between your thumb and forefinger, or thumb and middle finger.

- You now gently pull down the chains – the jaw will slowly and smoothly ease open and down. In order to let it go back up, you delicately let go of the little chains – the sensation should be that the jaw floats back up, the lips may close but the teeth and jaw remain slightly apart.

- This should be a delicate, free and easy-feeling. Repeat a few times, and sound out on the opening – your sound will follow the direction of your hands and be gentle and forward. Nothing is pushed or pulled.

'Do the wrong thing in order to find the right thing'

Sometimes, when you are learning a new process or exercise, it is very helpful to have a go at doing it the wrong way, so that you can really get the feel of the 'right way', and here is an example. Big jaw chains. Imagine the chains are big and heavy so you have to grab onto them with all your fingers, almost in big fists, and pull down those chains – you will now be pulling the jaw down and open. You've got plenty of space but at the terrible expense of serious amounts of tension, which is complete anathema to voice and speech work. If you sound it out on an 'aahh', you probably sound constricted and forced, not nice at all. Let them go and the jaw snaps shut like a trapdoor. Not good. Do this only once!

Go back to the 'right thing' – the little chains – and notice a huge difference in feel, sensation, and above all, in the effect. Sound out with your voice and you can hear the difference. Your sound is free, easy, more forward, and much more communicative.

Use the prop for the first time ☺ 1.4.5

- Put the prop between your teeth and have a go at speaking with it – just gibberish is okay, but talk to yourself or a partner in everyday conversation, not with a written text to start with. This is very important.

- Let it be incredibly loose (this is absolutely essential) – so loose that it practically falls out of your mouth. You will gain control really quickly, but you must work with looseness and ease at the start. I think where people go wrong with bone props is that they just don't realise how easy they are to use if you get it right at the start, and that means loose, loose, loose. You will sound practically unintelligible. Good! Let it be so.

- Rest, take it out, and then try again. Speak with the prop and waggle the ribbon or string it's attached to, so that the prop 'rattles' somewhat between your teeth, and then speak again.

- Keep gently tugging on the ribbon. Keep speaking and gently pulling so that you know it's being held very loosely between your teeth. If working with a partner, you can get hold of each other's prop ribbon – it will help both of you to discover how much 'holding' is going on. If, when you gently pull, the prop remains hard and fast, it's too tightly held – it should virtually fall out on the slightest pull.

- Now begin to mobilise the lips. You may well find at the start that all this 'loosening' instruction is making you sound rather dopey and indistinct. That was important. You can now begin to use the lips more. Get them mobile and a bit muscular, keeping that gentle hold of the prop between your teeth.

- Check now the position of your prop – it should be held vertically between your front teeth. You may need to 'float' the lower jaw forward a little in order to keep it upright, and this is fine. It may feel a bit odd, but as long as you maintain a relaxed awareness, that's okay.

- By only the second time of doing this, you should have got the technique. Of course, you must practise this regularly, but you do get the hang of it really quickly – as long as you start out in the right way, by being easy. There is often no way back if you begin with dreadful tension and set unhelpful patterns. Set yourself good patterns, good practice.

- Daily conversations – Annie Morrison suggests you have five bone-prop conversations a day, and I have found this really does work. Do them for no more than half a minute to a minute at a time in the first couple of weeks, then build up to one or two minutes, five times a day. Ensure that you remove the prop when not speaking.

Now to some breath and voice work today.

Taking a baby 'f' for a walk (i)

This is a signature exercise that exemplifies for me everything about the integrated voice. It could have been a subtitle for the book, were it not quite so esoteric-sounding!

- Stand freely and easily in the space and imagine you are taking a baby 'f' for a walk. Let the breath into the centre, as usual, and then go for a walk with the baby 'f'. This simply means releasing your out-breath on a constant stream of 'f', a continuous sound, breathing anew when you need to. The idea is that you imagine you have a little 'f' on a lead, and as you walk round the space with your 'f', centring the breath and then releasing the out-breath on this sound, you will be taken around the room on a very easy breath stream.

- Take care that if your little 'f' is on a lead, that you are not leaning over, or bending down – if that is happening, imagine a longer lead. If it is in your hand, let your hand go out away from your body, so you are not hunching or holding it back towards you. Free up and open up the body.

- At first, it is helpful to stop when you need to let the breath in, and move off on your walk as you connect to the 'f'. Ensure that, when you stop for a new breath, you don't hang around for ages – simply stop at the end of your 'f' breath, let the new breath come in, and move off. Concentrate on the out-breath, that is the most important part. As you do this, you will notice that the out-breath gets easier and lasts longer. This is good.

Why does this happen and what is this doing? The breath lasts longer and the sound is much easier because you are not fixating on it. Any image helps, but the idea of the baby 'f' is to stop you releasing all the breath at once, and it also stops you from pushing out a great big 'FFF'. It is an incredibly easy, gentle sound on a relaxed and steady stream. The idea of the breath lasting longer is also establishing an important principle and technique – eventually you will need to build up stamina, including greater breath capacity, in order to achieve a free but strong sound, and to handle long or complex thoughts in text. I don't want you to think too much about all that for now, so that's just a brief taster of things to come. For now, just have a go and see how easy baby 'f' breathing enables you to breathe more freely – and hopefully lets you feel good too.

Your imagination is engaged, and what you are now doing, effectively, is walking and talking at the same time. That is an example of integration of the voice. You are also connecting breath and thought, once again without realising what you are doing. I like the idea of tricking the body and mind into doing something without the intellectual brain/body getting in the way of the sensory breath and voice. The intellect and analysis comes later.

- Take the little 'f' for another walk, and then put it down somewhere safe in the room. Make a note of where you have left it, and move away.

- Do you feel connected to it in some way? Do you feel you want to go back and find it again? It is an endearing feeling to covet your little 'f'!

- Take a baby 's' for a walk, using the other hand to lead you. Let it walk you round the space, for a good minute or so. Put it down somewhere, either next to your little 'f', or somewhere on its own.

- Next we take a baby 'sh' for a walk. This time you can let it get a bit excited, so you are moving more quickly, but just as easily. Leave the 'sh' alone somewhere in the room.

- Take a baby 'v' for a walk. You are now voicing, easily, freely, and with imagination. Your breath is engaged from your centre, you are connecting your voice to your centre, you are sounding and voicing from your centre, and connecting it to a thought or impulse. This is acting – walking and talking with a thought and with imagination. (It is not a great leap to doing this with text, but we need to get these initial stages 'bedded in' to the body first, so will repeat this for a couple of weeks.)

- As you continue to walk the little 'v', let it explore the furniture in the room. Let it run along the radiator or the windowsill, let it jump up and sound itself along the piano, or whatever is in the space.

This first stage may feel very centred and internalised, which is a great feeling. You may find that there is an external sense, because you are being led by your hands. That is fine too. After doing this for a week or so, you will move on to stage two, but don't do it just yet. Be patient, repeating the work until it is settled in you as a process, so that you 'own' your little sounds.

The tide of breath
1.4.7

- Lie in semi-supine. Repeat the tidal breath from the last session (1.3.4). Lie on the floor with a book under your head, go through the releasing sensations of the lengthening and widening spine, and then through the idea of the breath as a tide coming in and going out. Go back to your beach and feel the breath, see and feel the tide, going out on an 'f' then a 'sh' – the 'sh' will sound very like the tide does at the beach – see it, imagine it, hear it and feel it. Once established, you can take it onto sounding the 'v' tide (around or just above the middle of your pitch range), and then the 'z' tide, and then a humming tide.

- Take it from the hum into a 'mmaah'.

Touching sound from the centre on 'hah'
1.4.8

- Let in another breath into your centre and release it on an easy 'hah' (as in 'calm', 'hard').

- Repeat several times. As you release this easy 'hah' sound, try not to put too much 'h' at the start, just let it be very light, a brief touch of 'h' before the 'ah'.

- Let the breath in and sound from your centre on a light 'hah hah'.

- Do this several times, then let in a breath and go on to 'hah hah hah'.

- Keep building up, ensuring that the breath comes into and the sound goes out from your centre, each time, until you are gently laughing.

This is quite strenuous work, but is also very easy. It tells your body and imagination where the voice comes from. The breath drops into the centre, and you let a sound come from that place and connect it to your thoughts, imagination, to your voice and speech, and to the outside world. Everything in voice is like this – whether you are talking at a normal, everyday volume in a café, or speaking quietly or loudly, or eventually (in a year or two!) shouting and screaming at will, using your technique. It all has the same basis, you just learn to use more 'oomph' and employ certain extra technical skills – but it all starts here. You won't be able to do the big stuff unless you get this early stage right, so just go with it and trust it. The simple work is the best and perhaps the most satisfying. It supports you in everything; it supports your voice and your confidence.

1.4.9 Touching sound from the centre on the word

- Let another breath into your centre and release it on an easy 'hah hah hah'.

- Repeat several times.

- Let the breath in and sound from your centre on a word or phrase, starting with just one word – 'now', or 'winter', or 'hungry' – saying it over and over. Then say 'now is' or 'I am', going on to the phrase 'now is the winter of our discontent' or 'I am really hungry' or 'what a lovely day, the sky is an amazing blue'.

- Do this several times, ensuring that the breath comes into and the sound goes out from your centre, each time, until you are speaking either a whole (short) speech or simply chattering away to yourself (but it is a connected, centred chatter).

- Have a little hum to yourself, then stretch easily. Move around on the floor with your hum, and then use the words/text you've been playing with to bring yourself slowly to sitting, and eventually to standing. You are now integrating your movement with sound, words and text, and morphing effortlessly from one state (lying on the floor) to another (standing, moving round the space) – *whilst at the same time* you are speaking and sounding. This transition is important. It is perfectly possible to stop at the end of an exercise, then get up, and start again with something new – many people do this. I find the integration as well as the flow of the work is just so much better if you let it be continuous. It is also actually much easier to get up from the floor to standing if you are making some sounds – try it.

- Once up, speaking and moving, you can then take a pause and talk about the experience so far, how you felt about the last exercise, and so on. But you have brought yourself forward to the next stage very fluidly. When you pick it up again, it is easier.

Take it further onto text

1.4.10

- Your voice should now be flexible, warm and easy, and you should be able to go on to some text. Take the rhetoric speech, if you have one, and, choosing a small section, physicalise it. Walk round the space, dance with it, move with it, and physically describe the words and phrases with your whole body.

- Chew up the words – what I mean by that is to really relish the words, exaggerate if you like, and really get your mouth and speech organs involved. Don't worry if this feels odd, it *is* odd, so just go with it.

- Do a little massage of the cheeks and lips – if your hands are not clean, bite the tongue gently. Now do a little bone-prop speaking, initially just chatting about the weather or your next meal, and *then* speak your speech (or another piece of text you have chosen) using the prop.

- Speak it without the prop.

- Roll the words around in your mouth, and see what discoveries you make. Notice any new meanings that are revealed, or simply concentrate on the types of words being used. For example, in a famous speech by Martin Luther King, 'I have a dream', just saying that phrase will make you feel something very strong. It is simple, direct and strong language. Have you ever said that – 'I have a dream'? You may have said 'I had a dream last night', but that is different. What is *your* dream for humankind? What would you like to happen in the world to make it a better place? Try King's dream for size and see how it feels to actually say those words. You could try using Queen Elizabeth I's speech, 'I know I have but the body of a weak and feeble woman; but I have the heart of a king,' – don't be fooled into thinking that a modern sensibility would scorn to say a woman is weak, she is not saying that. She is saying that she is equal to any man. But in a way it doesn't matter what your viewpoint is at this stage – you have to take that text and make it your own. Try it out for size.

Session 5

Clean-hands exercise (i) – lips and mouth

Repeat these (refer to Session 4, if necessary) – you will do this every session from now on.

- Stand freely and easily with even weight distribution. Notice how your mouth feels.

- Massage the temples and then take your fingers up the scalp so that you are massaging on either side of your head. A lot of tension resides here – if you place your fingers either side of your head above the temples and clench your teeth, you will feel the muscles in this area tightening. If they are tense, then your jaw will probably be holding tension, so it is always a good idea to begin the massage from here, softening down over the temples, and then the jaw joint.

- Go through the mouth and cheeks massage with your fingers on the inside of your mouth, and your thumbs on the outside. After just a few seconds, remove your hands and rest. Shake out.

- Repeat, checking that the shoulders haven't lifted. After thirty seconds or so, stop, remove hands, shake out and rest for a couple of seconds.

- Repeat for another thirty seconds or so.

- Notice how your mouth feels now. See if you get that big, soft sense of being spacious and free. A reminder that it lets breath in far more easily too, because you are creating a more open channel.

1.5.2 Clean-hands exercise (ii) – the tongue

- Stand freely and easily with even weight distribution. Notice how your tongue feels.
- Get hold of your tongue and massage as much of it as you can – the tongue tip, the sides, the middle.
- Persevere with the 'ugh' sensation and enjoy it.
- Rest and repeat. Then repeat it all again.
- Notice how your tongue feels now.

Alternative tongue massage

- Massage your tongue by gently biting it. Keep checking that the jaw is soft, and that you are breathing.

1.5.3 The silent 'ah'

Repeat this from Session 1 (1.1.5), and try to keep coming back to it.

1.5.4 The bone prop

- Check last session's detail on using the prop and have a gentle conversation, ensuring that it is held very loosely between the front teeth. Gradually mobilise the lips more, so that they become involved but still free and easy.
- Waggle the ribbon to keep the prop loose, and at the same time begin to feel a little muscularity joining in. It starts to become much easier.
- Feel the space in the mouth from the massages, and allow the lips and tongue especially to respond to this space with the bone prop – words are now becoming clearer and more fun to say.

The jaw lets go

Repeat the easy letting go of the jaw (1.4.3), and the little chains exercise (1.4.4); then try a little more prop work.

Spinal, body work and the 'f'

- Let a breath into your centre: place a hand over your navel, and the other one on your back or kidney area, and you may notice movement both front and back. Don't force it, but be aware of the possibility of the breath coming into the whole area between your hands. Release the breath stream gently on a little 'f'.

- Allow and imagine that little 'f' to be dancing around the inside of your head and with your hands, trace it around your head, down your face, and then through and down your body. Show with your hands how it gets down from your head and mouth, down the torso, around the pelvis, down the legs through the knees, ankles and feet. You are 'tracing' your little sound from tip to toe.

- Now internalise that process – the little 'f' is being created by your breath stream as you let in the breath and release it on the 'f', and you vivdly imagine that the 'f' is taking an internal journey through your body. The first time was more external – you used your hands to literally trace its journey down your body. Your mind and thoughts now trace its journey on the inside of you, so that the 'f', which you are continuously sounding and breathing, arrives at your feet via an interior route. The breath should now be very well centred, free and easy.

- You can repeat this whole process with a 'v' sound, going on to 'sh' and then 'zh' (as in 'measure'), and then with a hum. Remember to ensure that your 'v', 'zh' and hums are around or just above the middle of your pitch range, as it's easier to warm the voice up on mid- or slightly higher notes.

- Throughout this whole process, your body is totally involved with your breath, your sound and voice, and your spine is integrating itself with the breath of voice. The sounds themselves give the spine and whole body a kind of massage too, and you should be feeling very free and easy with a strong connection to your centre.

- You can take this whole process further with more exploratory sounds – try percussive sounds like 'bbb' and 'ddd' and 'ggg', etc. Then you introduce words and do the same thing, culminating in a piece of text, either something you've learned, or something you improvise in the moment (what dinner you'd like to have later, or a favourite programme or book). Talk yourself through the body with these ideas or texts. This is integration.

1.5.7   Taking a baby 'f' for a walk (ii) ⊛

Having established the exercise, and repeated it for a week or so, try this:

- Take a baby 'f' for a walk on its lead, as before. You may find it still sitting on the shelf where you left it, or perhaps it has been with you the whole time. Now I want you to imagine that the *lead is coming from your centre*, rather than being attached to your hand. Walk with the sensation that, once the breath has dropped into your centre, you go off, walking round the space with your little 'f' as if the stream of 'f' is coming from your middle and going ahead of you around the space. Notice how that feels, and if it is different from stage (i).

You may find that the whole sensation of your breath and sound is much more internalised, which is good. If not, it doesn't matter; we all respond in different ways. If you find that this causes you to go out of alignment and you are leading too much with the tummy, so that you are getting a bit of a sway back, try this:

- Take a baby 'f' for a walk, and imagine that the *lead is coming out of your sacrum or lumbar region, instead of at the front*. Imagine the 'f' is spreading out or walking behind you whilst at the same time you walk forwards. This should help any alignment issues, and you may find an even stronger connection between your centre and the breath/sound. Put the little 'f' on a shelf.

- Repeat all this on 's', then with a 'sh'. Send the 'sh' gently to your baby 'f' on the ledge, coating the 'f' with 'sh'.

- Repeat the 'sacrum lead' idea with 'v', and a hummed 'mm'. Explore this for several minutes, or certainly long enough to get the idea – then the feel, and finally the effect – of what you are doing.

- As you establish the hum, set up two hums – one in each hand, or on two leads, so that you are moving around the space with both hands/arms leading out with the hum going through you, into and around the space. You may well find that this really opens up your body, and the sound is easier.

- Go through the whole process with a hum into 'ah' – 'mmmm-ahhh'.

The sound should be free, easy, and just pour out of you without effort.

Floor work into release, tide, and capacity

`1.5.8`

- Lie on the floor in the Alexander position (1.3.4).

- Go through your checklist of ease, lengthening and widening, and of letting go into the floor.

- Repeat the tidal-breath sequence, using 'f', 's', 'sh', then 'v', 'z', 'zh', and then a hum. As you do this, imagine the tide of sound as a colour. You will most likely find that the colour changes as the sound changes, so let that happen.

Now clear the channel – this means to use the breath and sound into and out of a very clear and open passage. It is as if your breath comes in through a clear pipe, and the sound goes out through clear and clean pathways – try the exercise and see if you can find that sensation. Let the hum fall out into a 'mm-aaah' – a long, easy, relaxed sound from a hum into an 'ah' allowing the lips to just fall open. The vowel sound may be fairly indistinct at this stage. That is fine. We will shape it more clearly later on.

We start to become more aware of capacity. You have already been working on breath capacity for a few weeks without realising it. Now your attention is being brought to it very specifically.

- Let the breath in and release again on 'f' and see how long it lasts – but don't strain.

- Do the same with 'v' and those other sounds.

- Just for one or two sessions, we are going to quantify this breath – by literally counting out. So let in a breath and speak aloud from one to ten.

- Do this several times.

- Count from one to twelve.

- And from one to fifteen.

Notice how you feel. If you don't get to fifteen or even twelve it doesn't matter. Just wait for the breath to come around and try again. If it's easy, you can go to twenty. In just a few weeks it will be far, far easier, but I prefer not to just count for capacity, because a) it's boring, and b) it doesn't always help you integrate the reason for doing it. Here's a way to make it more integrated, and hopefully more interesting because it engages your imagination:

- Let the breath in and count to three in French, if you can ('un, deux, trois') or in Spanish ('uno, dos, tres') or in German ('ein, zwei, drei'), or any language you may know. Ask others for ideas. You may find yourself counting to three in Mandarin or Swahili!

- Now count something else – count ten oranges, then count ten kittens, ten elephants, and so on. You may find that your voice responds automatically to the image, and changes quality accordingly. If, when you are counting ten or fifteen kittens, for example, and your voice seems loud and brash, imagine that they are tiny kittens, a week old, and see if this changes the sound.

- Play with your own ideas.

- Roll over and come to sitting, whilst counting or sounding out. Then try it all standing, and imagine those cats or elephants in the room. Really see them as you count them.

As you progress, we will continually work on capacity, and hopefully it will become more and more apparent as to the point of it all. I do want to say here, though, that increasing breath capacity is not for its own sake, and it's not a competition. Also, just because we always have enough breath for a thought in 'real life', does not mean that we can automatically breathe another person's (or a character's) thoughts. Over time, this concept will become clearer; the more you integrate this into the everyday, and the more you work on acquiring basic techniques, the easier it will be to make sense of all this and use it in the most creative way possible.

Support   1.5.9

Here's another concept – supporting the voice. It is highly likely that you have already been doing this for a week or two without realising it. You breathe, or *let* a breath, into your centre. You then connect that breath to a thought and make a sound, whether it be an 'f' or a 'v' (or 'potato' or 'I have a dream'). Because it has come into your centre, and has sounded out from your centre, you have probably been supporting that sound. The breath stream is supported by the musculature of the abdomen, and to an extent the intercostals (inter-rib) muscles. Other more muscular work will kick in later on, but let's leave it simply at that for now, and become consciously aware of support.

- Lie on your back in semi-supine and go through a bit of sounding on 'v' around the middle of your range, and the hum – then taking it into 'maaah'. Notice that, as you let the breath into your centre, with your hands on your navel area, the tummy rises, and as you sound out, your tummy lowers. This is the body doing its job naturally to support the voice. Now get more active.

- Roll to one side, and then take yourself onto your front, with your knees bent beneath you in the prayer position (also called the 'pose of humility' or 'child pose'). Breathe and sigh in this position and keep letting go, using the breath and sound to help you ease further into it.

- Come up for a moment, and place your hands at the crease of your groin, with your palms facing upwards. Your little fingers are at your hip bone and the backs of the hands are resting against the upper thigh.

- Bend forwards into the prayer position so that your hands are now gently trapped between your upper thighs and your tummy. Let in a good breath and 'rev up' like a motorbike on a 'v' sound. 'V-vv-v-v-v', etc.

- You should notice a really strong movement in your tummy – that's the abdominals working to support the voice. It's a fun and effective way of really feeling what is happening, and you get a good strong sound from it.

- Repeat several times, then bring yourself slowly to standing.

- Now try to get the same sensation standing up, with your palms against your tummy. Get the same strong movement and the same strong sound.

1.5.10 Standing capacity and support

- Standing, you can go through the counts again, repeat several times.

- Count animals and other images.

- Let in the breath and release at length on 's' and 'z' and 'v' and hums, and colour it all while you do it.

- Chant or intone the numbers from one to five (chanting is like singing on a monotone). Do this a few times.

- Speak the numbers six to ten.

- Now you make an easy transition – chant one to five then speak six to ten, and ensure that the transition from singing/chanting into speaking is as smooth and natural as possible.

- Repeat this exercise with a bit of text.

Wall and other support

You will find a lot of variations on this exercise – many voice practitioners use the idea of a fixed object or person to give you the sensation of strong support in one way or another. Pushing against a wall, or a heavy object, lifting a chair above your head as you breathe and speak, or using a partner to push against, are all tried-and-tested methods of accessing better voice support. (Actor Yul Brynner was observed using this technique in 1951 to conquer nerves by grounding his support system before going on stage.)

- Now standing, push with your hands against a wall, or hang onto a door, or use a friend to push against. At the same time, let in a breath and release on a 'v'. Repeat this many times, taking it onto humming and eventually into 'mah' and 'ah', and then words and speaking.

- It is important that you are firm in your intention, but at the same time are relaxed and free. This applies especially to the amount of effort you put through your arms and shoulders. Check that they firmly engage but are not locked or held in excessive tension.

- As you push, keep the back of the neck long – don't throw the head back, because shortening in the back of the neck can constrict the larynx and compromise your sound.

- Each time you do this, you need to just let in the new breath easily and freely, and then commit on the out-breath to the engaged, strong, supported sound.

I also use the floor a great deal for supporting the voice, and we will play with that idea in the coming weeks. It won't entail just lying down, it will be very active, but it's good to start with a slightly more static approach like pushing the wall, object or person. Again, just make sure when you do this, that you are breathing easily and that all the musculature involved – from your abdominals, through your arms and hands, in your shoulders, in your legs and feet – are all engaged, but in an easy and released manner. You combine ease with strength, release with muscularity, and the two notions must always go hand in hand. Your voice will soon tell you if they are out of balance. If too weak in your muscles, the voice sounds weedy. If you are too strong or tense, the voice will sound strident or pushed. The voice helps your body and the body helps the voice. Let them listen to each other.

1.5.12 Text

Apply all this to text – either your piece of rhetoric or a different speech or poem.

- Give your facial muscles a quick massage, and move them around a bit, chewing and manipulating the cheeks, lips and tongue in muscular but easy motions. Let it all be quite generalised. We will get specific later.

- Speak the speech. Then speak it gently with the bone prop, then without.

- Look at how the speech is structured. A very good way into this is to look at the journey of the speech, which means literally starting the speech in one spot in the room and then moving off when the speech moves. If you begin with 'I have a dream', note where you are in the space, and on the next line you move forwards. Keep moving every time a new idea comes in.

- The important bit is to note any side issues or tangents – you go off, but then return to your last stopping point, before moving off again.

- Equally essential is to note any repetitions. If the speaker repeats something, you have to walk back to the spot you originally spoke it on, say that line or phrase again, *then* you return to where you'd left off, and pick it up again. The amazing thing about Martin Luther King's famous speech is how many times he says that famous line. You will find yourself going over and over the same route. But the intention will keep you moving forwards.

By doing this, you not only understand how the speech has been structured, you also imprint it into your body. This means that the voice will automatically do more with it, do what is required by the speech, not by what you think it should be. Honour the text and the speaker or writer. You make far more discoveries that way.

Interval

Applying Breath and Voice to Movement

Occasionally, students/actors come to a voice session or early-morning warm-up in a state of aching muscles, perhaps a day after a particularly demanding movement session, or after playing football at the weekend. It is perfectly normal, especially when the body is unused to exercise, to ache. I get them to show me the exercise or movement that they feel led to the aches, and we then apply voice to the area, rather like a massage or hot compress!

Example 1:

- A great stretch is to get into the prayer position/child pose (kneel down, lower your haunches and your head towards the floor with your arms out in front of you) and then stretch out one leg behind you. This is a wonderful sensation in the body, if a bit challenging at first, and quite demanding on an inflexible body. Go with it.

- Go into the stretch, let the breath into your centre, and release the breath easily through a 'sh' sound, visualising the 'sh' going right through the body.

- Repeat a few times, and now take it onto a continuous 'v' and then into a hum. Let these voiced sounds go into the areas with the strongest stretch.

- Release a little, and then repeat.

- Really feel the vibration of your hum, feel it coursing and easing its way through your body. Let it (imagine it) vibrate particularly into any part that is aching or feels stiff. You will find this really helps any aches and pains, and it also improves the quality of the stretch. Bring the extended leg back into the prayer/kneeling position.

- Repeat on the other side (the other leg extended behind you).

This works severally – a) you are taking your mind off what hurts, for a start! b) the vibration of the voice is actually healing – it's like getting a massage from the inside (it could be said that it isn't *like* getting a massage, it actually *is* a massage), and c) it is aided by increasing the blood flow and getting more oxygen into the system.

Example 2:

A student was missing her ballet classes and was going through a few ballet positions, but felt rather tight and constricted. She noted that her abdominal area was very held, so I suggested that, as she lifted into the various positions, she release her breath on a gentle, steady stream of 'f', and then on a 'sh'. Her big smile said it all and her body eased into the work with much greater ease and fluidity. Try this – always start with a baby 'f' to get the breath centred, easy and unforced, take it onto 'sh' and then bring in the voiced sounds like 'vvvvvvvv' and 'zzzzzzz' and onto easy humming.

It's a great way of rehearsing something very physical, adds to and aids the experience, and it can also help you to connect imaginatively to what you are doing. The breath, the sound, are your thoughts, your text.

How to Stretch Without 'Stretching' – Blowing Bubbles

At the start of a session, you often want to stretch out the whole body to get it warm and moving and 'alive', but sometimes a series of stretches is done without regard to release through the body. This can actually cause unnecessary tension and tightness, which will be unhelpful to the ensuing voice/body work. It is a good idea to do the following 'exercise' in a group, so that you can observe the effects. First of all:

- Stand easily in a centred position, with your weight evenly distributed.

- Let the breath into your centre.

- Release the breath on a gentle 'f'.

- Repeat several times, and then release it on a 'sh', and, as always, let it come from your centre, around the navel.

- Begin to 'blow bubbles' of 'f' using your hands to direct the bubble out of your mouth, from the lips out into the air space around you.

- Extend these bubbles, and as you do so, make bubbles with your arms extended, so that these bubbles of 'f' get bigger and start to take on different shapes. The 'f' changes to a 'sh', but the release of the breath onto this (voiceless) sound is still gentle but clear and committed – you can feel a constant breath-stream coming from your centre.

- Extend even further so that you begin to step into your bubbles ahead, to the sides, and behind you – create bubbles of 'f' that are all around you, above and low down as well.

- Occasionally go back to making a little bubble.

- Take the breath onto an extended 'v' sound, then onto 'z' and eventually into a hum.

- The room is beginning to fill up with bubbles of sound, or bubbles of hum.

- It can now go into 'mmmaaaahh' (humming on an 'm' into an 'aaahhh').

Notice how you feel in the body, how your breath feels, and how the voice feels and sounds. If you are working in a group, you can try getting one half of the group to do some stretches whilst the others observe them. It's fun to watch each other sometimes, and really instructive too.

- Watch some of your colleagues doing a variety of sport-based or 'gym' stretches.

- Then ask the same group to create their bubbles of sound.

You will see that they are stretching quite extensively and their bodies are getting a real workout, but the breath and sound coupled with the imaginative process will integrate the body and voice. You can see that the movements are imbued with a great sense of ease through the extensions of the bubbles. They – and you – will be integrating the work into the creative process. I am not suggesting that every time you do body work/dance/movement, you have to incorporate voice, but if you try it out as often as you can, you may be surprised by the results.

If you then take this onto text at a later stage (for instance, later on in the first year, or beyond), you may make further exciting discoveries. Try it and see what happens.

Part 1b
Session 6

1.6.1 **Clean-hands exercise (i) – lips and mouth**

Repeat these (1.4.1) – yet again, you begin the session with the clean-hands exercises, loosening lips, cheeks, oral space, softening the jaw, and the tongue.

- Repeat the little chains exercise (1.4.4), to further encourage a soft released jaw.

By now you will notice this is all becoming much easier, the oral space is increasing, and so the tongue has more room to move and is itself much more mobile and ready to work.

1.6.2 **Big cheeks and blowing raspberries**

- Massage the cheeks again, and now blow them out big, relax and repeat.

- Blow them out again and 'pop' them with your fingers, so that you get a really pleasing 'raspberry' sound.

- Do this a few times. You will find that both the cheeks and the lips feel quite muscular.

All the massage and softening you have done prepares the cheeks and lips so they are loose and flexible, and now the raspberry-blowing and cheek-popping is strong and muscular. It is the same principle as when we work on breath, voice, body, everything – you need to be very soft and released, and at the same time muscular and firm; a constant dichotomy of two states that are not opposite but perfectly complementary. Cheek tone is very important for voice – if your cheeks are very floppy you lose good tone, but if they are tense, you only gain stridency. The cheek-popping exercise is also just funny, especially when lots of people do it together, and it is really important to find things that make you smile!

- Try it out – speak aloud some text or just chat about the weather, and let your cheeks be really floppy. You may sound very indistinct or 'mumbly'. Now speak again, tensing up your cheeks (which will probably mean you are also tensing your jaw and tongue), and you most likely sound very harsh and quite odd. Speak again with those soft but firm raspberry cheeks, and the tone should be firm and strong, but not in any way tense.

Use the bone prop ☺   1.6.3

After your cheeks, tongue and lips are massaged and loose, chat with your bone prop. Notice how much easier it is now becoming to speak clearly and easily with it between your teeth. Revise its very gentle use by revisiting the DVD exercise.

It is also important to ensure that your lips are very engaged and mobile – get a partner to check and watch you, or you can have a look in the mirror as you do this. It may still feel odd to use the lips so much, but it really brings your voice forward (off your throat) and forward into the space, at the same time you are getting more oral space and therefore more tone into the voice. The prop should by now be giving you slightly clearer diction, but it is also improving the placement and tone of your voice. However small and subtle the changes are, they are definitely happening.

Taking a baby 'f' for a walk (i and ii)   1.6.4

- Take your baby 'f' for a walk. Repeat the first basic exercise (1.4.6) and then go on to the lead at the centre (1.5.7).

- Now walk the baby 's', 'sh', 'v' and 'z', remembering to let them play with the space, running around chairs, up on ledges. Really engage your imagination, be constantly aware that this is all coming into your centre (the in-breath) and emanating out from your centre (the out-breath, the thought, the sound).

1.6.5 Parallel technique – abdominal engagement and the rib swing

A. Discover the rib swing 1 – with a partner

Technically, it's helpful to know that when the diaphragm contracts, it moves down, causing the lower ribs to move outward, stretching and enlarging the tissue of the lungs. The ribs swing out in order to let the breath in, and before too long you will learn to resist too quick a deflation of the ribs when sounding on the out-breath. Think of the ribcage as a concertina, or an old-fashioned pair of bellows used to put more air underneath a fire. As the ribs swing out, the breath then comes into the body. When you sound, for example, on a continuous 'f' or 'v', the ribs can collapse back very quickly, or you can control them with an easy resistance using the abdominal and intercostal ('between the ribs') muscles. First of all, discover the swing.

If possible do this with a partner – stand behind your partner and put your hands on the sides of their ribcage at the widest point. As s/he breathes in, you will notice some movement outwards. As she breathes out, the ribs will relax back to their starting point. Your hands help guide their ribs, and you also get the experience by observing someone else's body. They then let the breath out on a gentle 'f' then 'sh' and then on a continuous 'v' sound. If you sound as well, even on an 'f', then not only will you feel the experience, this will also help prevent you putting any tension into your partner's body.

It is very helpful if you are working with a group, to go round feeling other people's ribcages. We are all different, and some people have naturally far more rib swing than others – but we can all encourage our own bodies to shift, and if you feel that swing in other people, it helps your body find new experiences. Don't force it, but practise this and you will find your ribs respond very quickly. Within a few weeks you will have transformed your ability to move them. This gives you more breath-capacity possibilities, and, later on, more capacity and strength for supporting the voice itself.

Work with both abdominal and ribcage awareness:

- Put one hand on your tummy, over your navel area, and the other hand on the side of your ribcage. Check that you are not tensing or hunching the shoulders.

- Go through all this by allowing the breath to drop into your centre, and then releasing it in an easy, controlled way on those sounds of 'f', 'sh', 'v', 'z' and a hum. Feel that, when your breath drops in, your tummy rises or releases outwards (the rise and fall you feel when doing this in semi-supine on the floor), and when you let the sound out, the tummy draws gently in (or down, in a horizontal lying position). At the same time, feel the ribcage swing out beneath your hand on the in-breath, and gradually recoil and return on the out-breath, on the sound. If you are unsure about the rib swing, take a moment to place both hands on the sides of the ribcage and go through a few breaths, releasing on 'v' or a hum, and feel that big, easy movement out and gradually back in; then go on to one hand at your centre and the other on one side of the ribcage.

Apply this to the baby f:

- Take the baby 'f' and 'v' for their daily walk, whilst at the same time feeling the abs and ribcage move. You will become very aware of what is happening physiologically, so note the effect.

B. Discover the rib swing 2 – for yourself

If you are working alone, you can try holding a scarf or towel around your ribcage and noticing how it moves with the breath, or put your hands onto the sides of your ribcage for the same effect. Try it with your palms on your sides and the fingers coming round towards the front, or you can also try this with the backs of the fingers/hands on your ribs at the sides – whichever is easiest. Check that you are not tensing or hunching the shoulders. It is also helpful to try and feel movement, particularly into the back of the ribs rather than just at the sides – it is more efficient and you get greater swing. It will also become important to feel the back moving at a later stage in training when we come to stamina, and then on to resonance, so it's good to get it going gently now.

Go through all this by allowing the breath to drop into your centre, as well as into the lower ribs, and then releasing it in an easy controlled way on those sounds of 'f', 'sh', 'v', 'z' and a hum.

As you sound out, it is important that the ribcage returns slowly, with some resistance, to its natural recoil (so that it doesn't collapse straight away), but without tension or holding. It is quite strenuous work but not effortful.

C. Discover the rib swing 3 – move on

- Now you walk around the space. You have somewhere to go and it's a pressing appointment. You need to walk very quickly or you'll be late. You stop, you arrive.

- Place your hands at the sides of your ribs again. Notice if you feel any difference, notice how *you* feel.

- Repeat with sounds as before. Arrive, and feel/notice the difference.

- Repeat with a few easy words and phrases. Arrive, notice the difference, how you feel, and see how easy it is to speak and move the ribs.

- Repeat with sounds as before, and then with a bit of learned or improvised text. Arrive, and notice the difference.

Feel the effect of the diaphragm – the anti-vanity exercise! `1.6.6`

I call this the anti-vanity exercise because you have to get over any worries about having a nice flat tummy. You are not going to get fat or lazy or untoned. Quite the opposite. Let it be an innocent acceptance of you.

You may have come across this exercise elsewhere, again it's quite commonly used to help you become really aware of what's happening when you breathe.

- Working with a partner, one person kneels on all fours and breathes easily, releasing out on a 'v'. Your partner places a hand on your tummy. When you breathe in you let your tummy flop down into their hand. You just let it all go. When you sound the 'v' on the out-breath, your partner's hand will rise with it; as you next breathe in, your tummy flops down into their hand and they feel it.

- Repeat it all with a hum, then with text. Then swap over so you both get both parts of the experience, doing and feeling.

By doing this, you will not only get the right idea of releasing the abdomen on the in-breath easily and efficiently, and then engaging (not tensing) those muscles to control the outgoing breath and sound, but you will also integrate your process into thinking and speaking.

Floor work and released tide of breath `1.6.7`

- Repeat the breath tide on the sequence of sounds. For a reminder, see Sessions 3 and 4.

- As you do this, add in coloured tides, or see it in your mind's eye as a stream of light or warmth. Let a breath into your centre, feeling that tide coming up the beach and on the expiration, on an 'f', 'sh' or 'v', etc. See the tide going out and notice what colour it is. The tide of your breath may become a tide of pale-blue 'f' or a stream of golden 'sh'. Don't decide in advance, just notice. As you change sounds, notice if the colour changes.

- Keep thinking of a sense of ease and great space, so that when the breath drops in and goes out, it is going through a great, wide-open channel. (I explained this notion in 1.5.8.) We will look at this when standing, too.

1.6.8 Capacity – technical and counting

- Repeat the counting from Session 5 (1.5.8) – let in a breath and count aloud to ten, twelve, fifteen, and so on. Build easily up to twenty-five. Don't force it, and if you don't get there *it doesn't matter*. What is really important is the sense of ease. The more gentle and easily focused you are, the sooner you will progress. Work, but with ease.

- Repeat the counts with imagination, integrating the count, the capacity, into something meaningful. Work with images.

We may only occasionally do this counting again, just to check in on progress. I prefer capacity and support to come through the imagination, and be directly applied to image and text (and there-fore to thought), because if people spend too much time on these very literal exercises in only a technical way, they can become an end in themselves, and not much use. We will work the muscles very strongly, but are going to use text to do it.*

1.6.9 The open channel *

In order to ensure that your breath channel is free and open (and so prevent you constricting the breath and/or speaking on your throat and not from the centre), here is an exercise to help you get everything open. It will enable you to let the breath in with-out any interference.

- In semi-supine position, place your hands at the sides of your neck, gently cupping it at either side.

- Breathe in (through the nose or mouth, whichever you like right now) and as you do so, float the hands and arms right out to the side, away from your body.

- Repeat, this time breathing in through the mouth, and bringing your hands away with the sense of opening-up your throat into a huge, wide-open pipe or funnel. Any image works, as long as it is like a big, wide-open vessel. An open throat means that you are not tight or constricted in your neck and throat, and is important for ease of breath, a free sound that is not tense, and gives you a greater connection to your physical and emotional centre. It really is about a lack of inhibition.

- As you do this, feel the air pouring into your lungs and down deep into your body, the wide, open channel going all the way down.

- If you now release that breath on an 'f', 'v' or hum, you will feel it coursing back up your body through the same wide channel, supported by the abdominals and intercostal muscles, warm and wide and free.

Now do it all again, this time with some words about how you feel, then about that dinner again, or what you watched on television – hands on neck, breathe in silently as you remember the film you saw; speak those thoughts on the out-breath. This sound should be very free – let yourself be taken by surprise and really relish this big, easy sound.

- Now, whilst humming or sounding something, anything, roll over, come gradually to sitting and then to standing.

Repeat the open-channel exercise standing up

1.6.10

Do it all standing. You will find that this works even better, because your hands and arms will really open out the body, increasing even further the sense of openness in the larynx and through the whole channel of breath.

Support and strength

1.6.11

- Repeat all the support exercises: push a wall or heavy object, do some 'revs' (see 1.5.9).

- Do the revs lying down, then try it sitting on a chair and leaning over – this is a very useful alternative if you are injured, or just find the prayer position difficult for any reason. There is always a way to do the work, whatever your physical capability. If someone has a broken ankle, that doesn't mean they can't breathe and hum! Besides, breathing and humming may help the healing process into the bargain.

1.6.12   Walking and talking – walk the line

- Think of a line of text. It could be from a poem, a play or nursery rhyme – anything that you can recall or use easily.

- Stand with your feet just touching a line or mark on the floor, and fall into it and over the line as you speak. Repeat several times.

- Stand with your feet just touching the line or mark on the floor, and step back slightly as you speak. Do it again and be bolder, falling back away from the line as you speak. Repeat several times.

- Finally stand and speak on the line.

- Repeat the whole sequence a few times, so you really feel the exercise.

- Do the whole sequence again with a thought from the everyday, such as: 'I'm dying for a cup of tea/bar of chocolate' – always integrate your work into the everyday voice so that the whole process becomes habitual.

This simple exercise will hopefully show you first, when you are late on the line or thought, secondly when you are ahead of the thought, and finally when you are thinking, breathing and speaking *with* and *on* the thought.

- Do this while physically moving.

- While still, but thinking before/after/on, etc.

- Then walk along the line and talk!

- Then stop at the end of a line (of text), and change direction very smartly and precisely when you have a new thought, a new line of text.

In other words, you are now walking and talking. If you watch each other doing this, observe one person at a time very carefully. You will see instantly if they are the type of person who is always rushing when they speak text, because the gabblers won't be able to change direction without rushing ahead either physically (the body is ahead) or vocally (the mouth is ahead). Equally, it shows up people who have trouble being ready for the thought, because either the body or the mouth will lag behind. It's a lot of fun to do this in pairs, because when you properly observe someone else's habits, you learn a lot about your own, and both of you gain from the process.

Walking and talking – formalise with text

`1.6.13`

- Take your piece of rhetoric or other text, and try it out with the line-walking exercise.

- Now go through the journey of the speech again. It will start to become very familiar and, most importantly, much more precise.

- Get even more specific with your speech's journey. As you move round the space, locate each concept, idea or concrete thing mentioned, by placing it at a very specific point in the room. For example, 'I have a dream' is a spot on the floor in the middle of the room. You move forwards to 'one day on the red hills of Georgia' (these might be pointed out beyond the window in the room); 'the sons of former slaves' (point to a few of your colleagues in the room); 'and the sons of former slave-owners' (a different group in the room); 'will be able to sit down together at the table of brotherhood' (take them to a table in the room).

- You then have to walk all the way back to 'I have a dream', and then walk forwards again to the last place in your speech, literally to the table, to then move off again, to 'even the state of Mississippi, a state sweltering with' (if Georgia was outside the window, maybe Mississippi is beyond the door); 'the heat of injustice' (this may be a spot on the wall); 'sweltering with the heat of oppression' (a different mark on the wall); and so on.

You will then have an absolutely precise map of how the speech is structured, but also a very clear and personal attachment to each idea, place or person mentioned. If you then apply this technique to dramatic speeches, you will not generalise your work. It is incredibly useful if you are stuck on a difficult speech. It instantly clarifies exactly what is going on.

Session 7

A Word About Vocal Health

Before starting this next session, it is useful to pause for thought about your vocal health. All the work we are doing is going to help you find a naturally healthy voice, through safe and effective usage. But you can help it further by ensuring that your body, and therefore your voice, is well hydrated. You don't have to drink gallons of water, but taking sips of water little and often will help the whole mechanism stay healthy. And the act of swallowing relaxes the larynx too, so that in itself is helpful. So get into the habit of taking in regular water. If your throat is sore, see the section on steaming at the end of Part 4.

Clean-hands exercise; alignment and breath centring   1.7.1

- Go through the whole clean-hands exercise (1.4.1), and take it onto bone-prop chatting.

- Repeat the little chains (1.4.4) and soft, open-jaw exercise.

- Repeat easy alignment work, for example the bubble walk with 'f' and 'v', etc. (Sessions 2 and 3).

- Have some short conversations using the bone prop. Get someone to check that it is still being used very lightly but clearly with full mobility in the lips and tongue. It is getting much easier and more like second nature already. Remind yourself to do this every day.

- Remember not to sit around with it in your mouth when you are not speaking.

1.7.2 Open the larynx

- Place your hands at the sides of your neck, then bring them away, as we did in the last session, for the open-channel exercise. As you take your hands from the neck and away to the sides, smile and let everything open up, to let in a silent breath. Take this onto working with the out-breath on 'f', 'v' and humming.

1.7.3 Further release constrictions or blockages

- Gently massage the throat and back of neck.

- Bunch up your face and release (don't control the release, just let it happen). Repeat. The face is invigorated and open.

- Pucker then stretch back the lips (bare teeth) a few times.

- Big smile then let the jaw open – really just drop open. This opens the face and back of throat.

- Do this, concentrate on the breath, and you should feel a sense of the air coming from the abdominals and passing through the body and throat without interference. Try it with one of your bad habits (tense shoulder/jaw, etc.) – you'll immediately feel the blockage you are working to free.

Open throat with a yawn

- Yawn. With plenty of breath, count to ten on a yawn. Feel the throat open and stretch.

- Now count or speak with the thought or feel of a yawn (in other words, you just think the yawn, but don't do it). Because you imagine it's still there, your throat is still very open.

Baby 'f', 'v', 'sh', 'zh', 'hum' and 'mah'   `1.7.4`

- Use different levels in the room, and different ways of engaging (excited, dull, etc.), and use the whole space.

Semi-supine – tidal breath   `1.7.5`

- With 'f', 's', 'sh', 'v', 'z', 'zh', 'm', 'mah', with colour again this session.

- Using sound (abstract sounds like 'v' or 'zh' or a hum, or gently burbling to yourself with words), roll over and come to sitting then standing. Keep playing at doing this, because it continues to aid integration, and move from one physical state to another with thought, breath and intention, all of which are a part of the actor's essential needs.

Here are two more 'games' to get you sounding out from your centre.

The colander (constantly self-refilling)   `1.7.6`

- Stand freely, centred and easy. As you let your breath in, guide it with your hands down to your centre. The hands go to the mouth, it breathes in, and the hands travel from your lips down your body until they arrive at your navel. As this is all on a quick and easy in-breath it won't take long! Let the breath out of an 'f' and, as you do so, the hands/fingers release and fan out from your tummy into the space.

- Repeat this several times. The hands bring the breath from your mouth to your centre, and take the little 'f' out from your centre into the space.

- Now do this with a long continuous and very easy 'v', and start to use your hands to let this sound really spring out of you, as if the middle of your body were a colander or sieve. The hands now begin to make the sound come out of your sides, and out of your back, still at the centre. Imagine you have sprung a leak, then lots and lots of leaks all round the centre of your body, and these leaks come pouring out of you. They just happen to be leaks of sound, leaking 'v' and 'z' and hums. The 'z' is really good for this because it is such a strong, buzzy sound and is lots of fun. And because you keep breathing into and sounding out of your centre, there is an inexhaustible supply of sound, hence the idea that this is a colander that constantly refills itself.

- You then do it without the hands – you simply play with the idea, and you move from your centre. You will find this gets incredibly physical, the spine is undulating and your waist and hips are very involved. In fact, this gets the whole body involved, because you simply can't stand still. You will look bizarre but sound great! It is a very direct way of sounding and supporting the sound from your centre.

- You can then, of course, take this onto words. And because you have been working with the whole body, the oral space is huge without you realising it – your lips and tongue are highly mobile, and so you are most likely fully articulating 'for free'.

The body moves in all directions and the sounds ('zzzzzz', 'mmmmm', etc.) are coming out from your centre and from everywhere!

1.7.7 Horizontal abseiling and bungee jumping your voice

This is also a bit surreal but it works, partly because it's funny, and partly because it really makes you connect to your centre, integrating your thought, breath and text in another way.

- Stand freely as before, this time in front of a wall, a foot or so away from it. When the breath has dropped in, use your hands to attach from your centre an 'f', as if it were an elastic string, like a bungee. Attach the bungee of 'f' to the wall, sounding the 'f' as you do so.

- Gently but firmly push off from the wall as if you were abseiling, so that you step or lightly jump backwards from the wall, but with the idea that you are attached to it, still, by your string or elastic of 'f'. You then bounce back in to get another impetus to abseil away. It's horizontal for obvious reasons!

- Keep the neck long, so it doesn't collapse as you move back.

- Repeat this with 'v' and then play around with lots of other sounds. Experiment.

- Now 'bungee jump' around the room. Create another elastic 'v' from your centre or from your waist at the side, and using your hands to take it out from your body, sound out on 'v', then guide the 'v' sound and attach it to the other wall in the room. Now you can create and attach several more strings of sound, but you don't have to go right over to the wall, you can just send them, simply using your thoughts and imagination to attach them.

- You are now attached in your mind to all four walls in the room and you start jumping around, the impetus being your sound and those elastics. Your voice will spring out and be very supported, strong and very free. Create lots of 'hums of elastic'. You can then play with words.

As with other work, don't be surprised or disappointed if, the next time you speak a text in an acting class or in the green room, you can't be clearly heard. This all takes time. Just keep practising and working on it, be patient, and it will eventually become second nature. It is all about repetition.

Parallel technique (i) – forward placement of the voice 1.7.8

In order for your voice to reach out to an audience, it needs to be 'placed forwards'. This means that it is not pulled back into your throat, is not created by tension in the throat area, and it sounds full and forward. This is *not* a pushed sound, quite the opposite. By 'thinking' your voice forwards and out, you communicate more easily through an open space and with clear intention. This helps particularly with getting the voice out there, not necessarily with volume, but certainly with warmth and clarity.

Sometimes people refer to the outgoing voice as 'projection'. It is an old-fashioned expression that certainly has its uses, but I agree with Cicely Berry[4] – she talks about projection as being a term that suggests your voice is outside of you, when of course this isn't the case, as it is created inside your body. It is the vibration and resonance of the vocal sound, and the sounds created by the organs of speech, that are *heard* outside of you. A much better way to think of it is to *share* your voice with the audience (whether they be in a theatre, or indeed just some people you happen to be talking to. You just need more 'oomph' in a bigger space, and we'll get to this in time). For now, learn to place the voice.

- Stand in a centred, easy stance and look ahead of you to a point on the wall or an object ahead of you in the room.

- Breathe to this point. Ensure that your breath is silent, so that there is no constriction in the channel of breath and therefore the channel of thought.

- Release that breath on a baby 'f', so that it floats firmly but easily to that place in front of you. Repeat several times on full breath, taking your time. Simultaneously, let your hands move forwards and up a little to gently guide your sound.

- Repeat this with a little, constant, firm and easy 'v'.

- Repeat with a hum and then a 'mmaah' and really connect to the point on the wall, so that it becomes very familiar and easy.

- Try all this on other sounds, going from a consonant, like 'v', 'z' or 'm', into open-vowel sounds. Extend it, lengthen the sound, whilst maintaining a very clear sense of support coming from the abdomen, aided by the intercostal muscles.

- Play with this sound and then take it round the room, looking for other places to send it.

- Share this sound with another part of the room, perhaps higher up towards the ceiling – but check that you don't collapse through the back of the neck. Keep the neck long and floating upwards (you may need someone to check your positioning here). Having done the abseiling of sound, this should be very easy.

- Share the sound with someone else in the room, just across the space from each other.

- In pairs or in a group, stand and hum, and gently 'mah' your sound to the opposite wall, keeping it easy, unpushed, unforced.

It is your *intention to share* that is critical here. If you want to share your sound, you will find you have absolutely no need to push.

- Now try it with some text. 'O for a Muse of fire' will do, but so will 'I had a great journey here today' or 'D'you want a coffee or tea?' What matters is connection and intention. If you are doing this with a group of people, you will immediately hear if they are competing and pushing. Remind yourselves that this is easy, easy, easy, and you will be delighted at how well your sound carries. It is a wonderful feeling to reach out with your voice and find it's there for you, even at this early stage in training.

Forward placement of the voice (ii) 1.7.9

- Do the whole lot again, starting by sending your sound to the wall/object opposite you, but this time open up and step back into the hum whilst looking at the wall ahead. Feel your voice coming forward and at same time going into your back.

1.7.10   **Sustain and extend the voice**

- Play now with all of this by allowing your sound to extend for as long as is easy and comfortable. Again, be prepared to be taken by surprise, don't try to compete with yourself or anyone else, but just allow your breath and support system to extend that sound over time.

- If you want to, you can do this with counting those kittens and apples, or just numbers, but perhaps with an added image of how those numbers look.

- You can then use some text (it doesn't have to be memorised) – and share it with your real or imaginary audience.

Think of the sound coming from the centre of your body, from that navel 'lead' or elastic, or the leaking colander.

It is very important to keep your jaw, neck and shoulders very free and easy during this work. Don't worry if you notice they have tensed up, simply remind yourself to let go.

1.7.11   **Check the jaw and tongue – 'do the wrong thing to find the right thing'**

By now you have developed quite a sensitivity to what is going on with your breath, voice and body. When doing jaw- or tongue-release exercises, you will automatically be aware of what happens when you go through some simple sequences, so it is now safe, and a good idea, to occasionally 'do the wrong thing to find the right thing'. By doing so, you reinforce good practice by realising physically what bad or unhelpful practice is. Here is an example:

The jaw

- Stroke down the jawline with your hands, so that as you gently pull down the face, your jaw opens and your mouth gently widens into a 'duh' position.

- If you want to gain more space, and more opening, you can draw your hands down even further.

- Release the jaw back slowly – let it float back up.

Now do the wrong thing:

- Stroke the jaw down, guiding it with your hands, then pull your hands back up quickly and let the jaw follow that action, so that it snaps back up like a trapdoor. That is clearly not what we want.

- If you go back to the 'right thing' – stroking down, then gently float your hands back up, the jaw will follow that soft instruction, and be far more at ease.

What this means is that you don't undo the good work. It's like doing lots of alignment or postural work, only to then slump horribly when you are listening to the next instruction, or are speaking text. Or you fidget like crazy, pulling down your top or fiddling with your hair immediately after a spinal roll, for example. It takes away your focus and can interfere with the process you have just gone through. Don't undo what you've just done.

- You can also repeat the little chains exercise from Session 4.

Do the same 'wrong/right thing' with:

The tongue

- Stroke the jaw open and stretch the tongue out over your lower lip, using your hands to guide you.

- Let the tongue float back into your mouth of its own accord.

Now do the wrong thing:

- Stroke the jaw open again and stretch the tongue out over your lower lip, using your hands to guide you.

- Pull your hands back up quickly and the tongue will follow, snapping back into your mouth. This creates a lot of tension and, of course, undoes the good work.

- Go back to the 'right' thing – letting the tongue gently stretch out and down, and then floating it back in at the end. As always, let the hands guide it.

1.7.12 Text

- Release the mouth and jaw again. Now go through your rhetoric or other speech with the prop, once.

- Then without the prop, really connecting to your journey and what you are trying to say. *Do this quietly and gently without pushing. Let it be internal.*

- Choose three words in the speech which you like, are juicy, perhaps – either how they sound, or what they mean. Try them, break them down (e.g. 'dream' – 'ddd dr dr dr eeee mmm', etc.)

- You might then listen to all the speeches.

- You can discuss what you have learned from rhetoric – the journey, the need to say this, what the speaker was getting at and what you felt about those thoughts. Then ask yourself how might this apply to dramatic text – have a think about this over the next couple of weeks.

Session 8

As a way of making the transition from your first term or semester when you have perhaps looked at rhetoric speeches taken from 'real life' (as opposed to written drama), we now look at a piece of Shakespeare which tells a story. Storytelling is at the heart of the actor's art, and this particular piece is pretty accessible. You needn't worry about understanding it all, because next term we look at how to get at a piece of complex text through a process of 'demystification'. But we'll use this to get started because it fires the imagination and has a great opening thought – which is lovely for putting all this capacity and support work into practice. So either create a copy of this speech for yourself, before starting this session, and/or get a willing tutor or friend to read it a bit at a time, as I'll explain when we get to it. The speech begins 'Now entertain conjecture of a time' and it is the chorus just before Act Four in *Henry V.*

Preparation 1.8.1

- Go through the whole clean-hands exercise, and take it on to bone-prop chatting.

- Repeat little chains and open soft jaw.

- Blow some raspberries, popping the cheeks with 'p' and 'b'.

- Repeat easy alignment work, for example the bubble walk with 'f' and 'v', etc.

- Have some short conversations using the bone prop. Check that it is still being used very lightly but clearly with full mobility in the lips and tongue.

1.8.2 Open the larynx

- Repeat the 'hands on throat' exercise (1.6.9 and 1.6.10), allowing the breath to drop into a wide-open throat, and take this onto working with the out-breath on 'f', 'v' and humming.

1.8.3 Warm and place the sound; check against forced sounds

- Use either the baby 'v' or other warming and placement work.

- Let the baby 'v' take *you* now. Let it lead you very strongly round the room, as if it's pulling you along. You may get a nice strong sound, or you may find that it is forced and pushed.

- Let the baby 'v' drag behind you, like a little dog that doesn't want to budge. The sound may be pulled back or weedy.

- Now walk along together in harmony, in sync. The sound is connected and in harmony with you, your body and your thoughts.

This is a good way to check, as with the 'walking the line' exercise (Session 6), that you are not running ahead of the thought, are not dragging back from it or some way behind it, but are *on the thought*. This may make total sense by now. If it doesn't, don't worry, it will become clear over time. Trust the work and the process, and above all trust yourself. Your mind, body and voice know a lot more than you think. But imagining you know nothing is very liberating and very healthy. Another of those curious dichotomies. Just go with it.

Open throat with a yawn

- Yawn. With easy breaths, count to ten on a yawn. Feel the throat open and stretch.

- Now count or speak with the thought or feel of a yawn. The throat is still open.

Clean vocal onset – technique and imagination

This simply means that you have a clean sound, without tension or constriction in the throat and larynx. If when you say a word like 'apple' or 'only' and your sound at the start sounds harsh and pushed, this is known as glottal onset, or glottal attack if it's particularly hard and strident. If your sound is rather breathy or raspy, then this is also often a sign of constriction. You may not be doing this, as much of the work so far has been about release and ease. But just to check, go through the following work to establish good and clean onset of sound.

- Lie in semi-supine with a book under your head to ensure good alignment.

- Bring your hands together with the palms pressing lightly but firmly together.

- Open the hands and bring them out to your sides so there is a wide gap between them.

- Imagine this gap as the gap between your vocal folds (vocal cords). I want you to keep the hands far apart so that you get the idea (and, more importantly, the feeling) that the gap is wide and very open (like the open channel we've worked on. It's the same thing, now looked at in more detail).

- When the vocal folds are apart and you breathe in and out, *there is no sound*.

- If you can hear your breath rasping, you are constricted. Try to breathe out on a silent 'ah'. All you have to do is tell yourself it is silent and you will magically cut out that breathy sound.

- Bring your hands towards each other but not touching. Let them oscillate, wave gently back and forth an inch or two, towards and away from each other, microscopically moving. This is like a whisper, and you can let your breath gently sound on a whisper as you do this.

- Bring your palms together. Then, placing the heels of the hands together, gently but firmly bring the hands and fingers together, and open and close the hands with this motion, like a wave. You are now sounding as you do it, on an 'ah' or 'mah'.

- Release the hands and open them out to the sides – this is your in-breath.

- Find out what a glottal attack is: let the breath in on open hands, then slam them together. This is your pushed, glottic sound. Not pleasant, and if you kept doing it, you would hurt your hands and therefore you would be hurting your voice.

- Go back to the easy onset, the easy wave of the palms and fingers, firmly connecting and sounding at the same time. You are using your hands to simulate the vocal folds approaching each other, and vibrating together to create sound.

- Find out what happens if your hands waving together are only feather-light in touch and rather 'weedy' – the opposite of the slamming. Now you sound a bit woolly and a bit weak. So that gentle, firm undulation is what is required, and it goes directly into the voice. Try it and believe it!

- Now use text – try it with an 'h' at the beginning of the words first, like this:

  '(h)only (h)old (h)ants (h)eat (h)apples (h)in (h)Amsterdam.'

- Then repeat it all without the h:
  'Only old ants eat apples in Amsterdam.'

- Aim for a clean, free and easy sound. If the 'h' doesn't quite do it for you, try putting an 'm' at the start of the words.

- Sounding out with your voice, come over onto your side, then to sitting and standing.

- Repeat all of the above standing up.

Capacity work taken on to text   1.8.6

Find the text and get someone to read it for you, as below. First of all:

- Lie in semi-supine and go through the tide of breath to ease you into this.

- Repeat the counting – let in a breath and count aloud to ten, then twelve, fifteen, and so on. Build easily up to twenty-five.

- Now with text. Let in a little breath and say 'Now'.

- Let in a little breath and say 'Now entertain'.

- Let in a little breath and say 'Now entertain conjecture' (don't worry about the meanings just yet).

- Let in a tiny bit more breath and say 'Now entertain conjecture of a'.

- And a new breath for 'Now entertain conjecture of a time'.

- So you go through the whole of this thought, adding one word at a time on each new breath. You will eventually be saying:
  'Now entertain conjecture of a time
  When creeping murmur and the poring dark
  Fills the wide vessel of the universe.'

It will also really help, of course, if the person reading can invest meaning as they read each bit at a time – so that you will eventually realise you just said something along the lines of 'Imagine a time when the murmurs of people (soldiers) creep through the dark night, so that all this dark and all these murmurs are pouring down and around you, filling every part of the night and the world with their mysterious, dark, secretive sounds.' Get the sensation of the night, the quiet and the suspense.

If they read the words with good length to the long vowels ('muurmuuur', 'poooring', 'daaark'), and invest in the long, dark consonants ('ennntertainnnn', 'tie-mmme', 'mmmmurmmmur', 'ffilllllzzzzzzz'), this will enable you to really shape and articulate the thoughts, and give you the atmosphere of the text as well. This is further integration – you are doing a lot of things at once, without quite realising it.

You will find this relatively easy by now and can be suitably pleased with yourself that you just spoke three lines of iambic pentameter on one breath. (If you didn't get to the end on one breath, try it every day and very soon it will become easier.)

1.8.7   Forward placement of the voice

Repeat the placement work from Session 7 (1.7.8 and 1.7.9).

1.8.8   Sustaining the voice

Repeat either the sustain work from Session 7, or use the 'colander' and 'horizontal abseiling' to extensively sound and sustain your voice.

This is quite strong and athletic work, but you should not feel any tension or strain. If you feel as if you've had a workout, that's a good sign, as long as it is 'good' work.

1.8.9   Support and strength

From all the above exercises and work, you should be easily supporting your voice, but if you want to try out a more technical exercise to check-in, repeat the support exercises: push a wall or heavy object and the revs (Session 5).

Text

This session has been very extensive, so I am not going to pre-scribe detailed text work at this stage – but you might want to read through a few lines of either the Shakespeare without wor-rying about meanings, or rhythm or indeed anything. Just try out the words and see how they feel. Or you can read from a novel, poem or newspaper – see how words feel and sound in your mouth and in your body.

If you choose to play with the 'Now entertain' speech, remember what I said at the start of this session – look at it just as a speech that tells a story. Don't worry about understanding it all, just try it out for size and see what information is revealed. Next session we'll play with it a bit more, and in the next block of sessions we get to find out how to access complex texts without a care in the world!

Session 9

Revision and a Little New Work to Whet Your Appetite for Next 'Term'

This is about revising everything so far, going through further repetition so that the work is embodied, understood (physically as well as mentally) and applied.

1.9.1 Clean-hands exercise; alignment and breath centring

As last time.

1.9.2 Physical warm-up

Find alignment, walk with it, find the head/neck relationship with bubbles, shakes, stretches, etc., using a lot of movement on 'm', 'n', 'ng'.

1.9.3 Centring and freeing the breath

- Do the tapping exercise, and add in humming and rubbing limbs.

- Place your hands on the tummy, let the breath into this place, and release sounds out from there.

- Check your ribs are swinging strongly and easily, and that the breath and sound is centring into your abdomen, dropping in freely through the open channel and being supported on the out- and upward-breath stream by clearly engaged abdominal and intercostal support.

Clean vocal onset 1.9.4

In semi-supine and then standing:

- Release, lengthen and widen, and work your capacity on 'f', 'v', 's', 'z', 'm', 'mah'.
- Use image work – light, colour pool, radiation.
- Breathe a text – let your body breathe you and the text.
- Repeat standing.

Forward placement of the voice and being on the thought 1.9.5

Use the exercises of humming, abseiling, and walking and talking the line.

Introduction to the tongue and formalised articulation 1.9.6

I say 'formalised' because you have already been articulating for some time, by all that massaging, releasing of the mouth and tongue, and then chewing words and using the bone prop. But before the next term or semester, I want to introduce some formal and quite technical tongue exercises. We need the tongue to be very flexible and released (not tensed or constricted), and *at the same time* it needs to gain muscularity and strength. It is that dual world again of release and freedom/strength and muscle.

- Go through the jaw and tongue releases, especially repeating the 'wrong thing, right thing' from the last session. And then have a look at formal exercises.

There is a series of worksheets printed in the Appendix, which you can copy for ease of use when working. I will quote the principles here, then you can turn to the pages at the end of the book for the whole sequence of exercises referred to as TIV1 and 2. With 'TIV3a–d' in the first year we will only use a and b. Before we get to that, let's do some specific tongue exercises.

- As always, you need to warm up. Massage the tongue either with your fingers or the gentle biting. Notice the difference. Repeat.

- Allow your tongue tip to *flop* onto your lower lip. Flap lazily up and down between the lips.

- Allow to *roll* out over lower lip, and gently retract (not pull back).

- Massage the tongue root (rub the fleshy bit underneath your jaw).

- Shake head gently forward and loll the tongue.

- Go through the rest of the exercises in Appendix TIV2a.

I then go on to separate the tongue exercises into *aerobics*, which include 'tongue press-ups' and so on, and *ballet*, which are more fluid and flowing exercises. You therefore get both strength/muscularity, *and* released, easy and free work. Both are essential for clear, mobile and fluent articulation. Have a look at them all.

As often as possible, you should be making sounds to accompany these exercises. For example, if doing the big tongue stretches, vocalise some really luxurious long sounds. When you do the 'precise' stretches to the corners of the mouth, the sounds are suitably much shorter, more staccato and more 'precise'. You can see and hear this on the DVD ☉. These sounds help you to integrate both voice and speech work much more easily, and, very importantly, your voice will tell you if you start to tense up. It helps you massage the articulators by remembering to breathe and by vocalising every single aspect of the work.

A vowel and consonant workout

Refer to Appendix TIV4. This will be helpful to you if you are in formal training and have had an introduction to phonetics and RP or Standard English. I don't propose to go into this in detail, as that would be a whole other book, but would point out that in the first term, I parallel the practical voice classes with an introduction to rhythm in text, elementary 'ear training' (which involves listening to each other and other voices for stress patterns, intonation and tune, and rhythmic patterns), and the beginnings of learning about phonetics and accents. All this complements articulation, tongue and lip work, and voice work itself.

Appendix TIV4 consolidates all the sounds used. If you don't know phonetics, it doesn't matter, as each sound is expressed in words. For example, the sound written down as [a:] has the word 'hah' as in 'car' below it. The sound written down as [θ] is 'th' as in 'three' or 'thirsty', which immediately follows. If you are studying phonetics, however, this sheet also acts as a handy reminder of all the basic symbols.

Text: *Henry V*, Chorus IV

It will be very helpful if you can get someone to lead a group in this work, but if you can't, have a go anyway. Find your text 'Now entertain conjecture of a time...' and get into a circle.

- It is very important that you go straight into the physical work first. Don't sit and analyse or even read through the text first. Try and go with this, trust it. Just get up and have a go.

- Read it aloud, and at the same time physicalise every part of it. Leap around the room, stretch, shape and generally play around with it, as madly as you like.

- Do it all again, this time in unison as a group, but with each person doing their own gestures or movements to express the text.

- If you don't understand something, make it up! It is very important to just play around at this stage.

- Read it all again, in a circle, still in unison, but with less movement.

- Sit down in a circle. Get close to each other, and read it again, perhaps taking a thought, a small chunk each. As much as possible, look at each other as you say the words.

- When someone else is speaking, look at them to give them encouragement, and also to ensure that you are 'being an audience'. When your turn comes, you can easily find your place if you glance down occasionally. If you get lost on the page, someone next to you will help you. This is being part of a company of actors.

- Do it again, and this time be much more 'conspiratorial' in tone, and imagine the fear of the night-time, the various sounds that come through the night air. Get someone to guide you through the incredible sense of this story.

Have a chat about what you got from the text, first in terms of what atmospheres you picked up on, and any feelings or sensations you got, and how much of the story you understood. A little or a lot, it doesn't matter. Just go for the feel. There will be much greater detail next term.

How does your mouth feel? How does your body feel? And how did your voice and speech sound? Don't judge, simply notice how much more alive it all is, and how much you can now do.

Additional Sessions

If you have time in your schedule to do a week or two more of formalised sessions, go right back to doing Session 1 again, and then Session 9.

Own Study and Practice – Vacation Work

Hopefully, by now, it is absolutely part of your daily routine to do a bit of voice and body work. If not, get into the habit – because the voice is a physical thing, it will only improve with practice. If you leave it and do nothing for a few weeks, or even less, the work will all but disappear. Imagine an athlete or a musician at the start of their training, doing absolutely nothing. You would have to go back and begin again. When it is all in your body and you have put in the years of training, you might afford a longer break. But just now that is not the case – use it or lose it.

Devise your own daily routines. If you have just completed the first term or semester of actor training, then doing about twenty minutes per day during 'vacation' time is probably about right. Aim to do half an hour sometimes, not much more. If articulation and clear speech are particularly problematic for you, then do a bit extra, but in short bursts. It is much better to do ten minutes articulation twice a day, than one session of twenty minutes, because it is very tiring and can be counterproductive. This is in addition to the other voice work (breathing, placement, resonance). You should be able to come up with a few different workouts, based on the work we have covered so far, and also using work you have been doing with other tutors or that you have started to practise from your own research. Mix and match, because different styles and techniques are nearly always going to be complementary.

Vary the routines so you don't get bored, and also so that the voice and body don't get too used to one way of doing things.

Read aloud a little every day too, especially if this is not one of your strengths. Sight-reading is an essential skill for actors, and you will almost certainly be taught this formally, but you can make an enormous difference to your own ability in this area just by practising. If you are not an actor or in training, but doing voice work for your own interest or as a help to you personally, reading aloud every day can still be incredibly useful to boost your confidence. So next time you are reading a book, or a newspaper, or a comic, read a bit aloud. You can also read (aloud!) the label on the coffee jar, or the instructions on your conditioner bottle as you take a shower or bath. You can sight-read aloud someone's T-shirt slogans. Anything and everything, in other words. You will gain a bit more confidence, get used to an important skill, and, of course, you are practising your vocal and speech skills. If you are already good at reading aloud, you can only get better the more you do it.

Enjoy a break as well! Look forward to consolidating and progressing in the next phase of your vocal development.

Part 1c
Session 10

Keywords: *Revision; introduction to demystifying Shakespeare*

This part is roughly equivalent to a second term of training. It involves further repetition so that the work is embodied and understood.

First of all, ask yourself what you discovered in that first block of work, both physically (what did you notice physically, what did you become aware of, what has changed?) and intellectually (do you have some knowledge of vocal anatomy and physiology, for example). What do you understand by 'breath support'? What is breath capacity and why does it matter?

What is your understanding of the nature and importance of the head/neck relationship and alignment; the importance of feet, through release and grounding; the diaphragmatic and intercostal breath, forward placement, the need for 'soft' and not pushed work? When you look at that list of questions, you realise how much has been discovered and worked on in only a couple of months. Your knowledge may be a little hazy in places, but you will have worked on all these areas, and just asking the questions will bring you to an understanding, simply through sensation.

We will work further, very physically on voice *and* text, but with effortlessness. Less equals more. Not through tension or effort but released engagement.

1.10.1   Clean-hands exercise; alignment and breath centring

- With clean hands, stand or sit, but freely and as aligned as you are easily able to do. Lick your lips and get those fingers working the inside of the mouth, and then the tongue. Yawn, close the lips gently over the space and yawn again.

- Let a nice, easy breath into the body through the open breath channel.

- Place your hands at your navel area, or one on the front and one at the back, and let the breath into the body, and release on a gentle 'f' or 'sh', swaying and moving gently as you do this.

1.10.2–1.10.4

Repeat 1.9.2–1.9.4.

1.10.5   Forward placement of the voice and being on the thought

Use the exercise of humming ahead of you, but also find your forward-placed voice by abseiling and walking and talking the line.

1.10.6   Articulation

Repeat the tongue and formalised articulation exercises (1.9.6). Remember to make sounds to accompany these exercises.

As explained at the end of the first block of work, we need the tongue to be very flexible and released, and *at the same time* it needs to gain muscularity and strength. This duality of release and strength also applies to the lips.

1.10.7   A vowel and consonant workout

Refer to Appendix TIV4.

Text: *Henry V*, Prologue

If you are very new to Shakespeare, or have had anything less than a positive experience with his work, it is a good idea to talk about him, his work, and your various loves, hates, likes and dislikes – in other words, discuss any preconceptions you may have. If in a group of people, you might take a 'straw poll' of the varying degrees to which people respond on a positive–negative scale. You can then go further and find out why you feel like that. There will nearly always be an extreme of reactions, so whatever yours is, accept it. If you already enjoy Shakespeare, the following 'ways in' should serve only to make you more enthusiastic, or at least more ready to respond openly and hopefully make new discoveries. If you are in the 'I don't get him/can't stand it' camp, then just be open to any possibilities. Shakespeare seems to divide people more than other writers. It may be down to bad experiences at school, or at the theatre, or just that people much prefer modern writing. There's nothing wrong with any of those, but for a trainee actor, or indeed a professional actor, with little classical experience (and it is so much harder to get that these days), working with these texts can open up huge potential in your voice, speech, and your connection with all kinds of texts.

Having had a chat or a good think about all this, let's begin to look at a speech – this is the prologue to *Henry V*, and we are going to start physically. Get someone to lead the group in this work. Find your text 'O for a Muse of fire...' (it is printed in Part 3 of this book).

When someone else is speaking, look at them to give them encouragement. When your turn comes, you can easily find your place if you glance down occasionally. Keep a thumb in the margin and move it down as you read down the text.

- Go straight into the physical work first. Don't sit and analyse or even read through the text first. Go with this, trust it. Just get up and have a go.

- Read it aloud and at the same time physicalise every part of it. Jump around the room, stretch, shape and generally play around with it, as madly as you like.

- Do it all again, this time in unison as a group, but with each person doing their own gestures or movements to express the text.

- If you don't understand something, make it up!

- Repeat either the whole lot again, or bits and pieces.

- What do you understand so far? Notice what, if any, elements you have grasped – just the basics will do. What is it about? If you feel you don't know, think about key words – it's about a king, war is mentioned, the theatre and the world of the play may be apparent to you, perhaps?

- Read it all again, in a circle, still in unison, but with less movement.

- Sit down in a circle. Get close to each other, and read it again, perhaps taking a thought, a small chunk each. Look at each other as much as possible as you say the words.

Have another chat about what you got from the text, first in terms of any themes you picked up on, and any feelings or sensations you got, and how much of the story you understood. Just go for the feel. Then look at it all again, and start to fill in a bit of detail.

How does your mouth feel? How does your body feel? And how did your voice and speech sound?

That may be all there is time for this week. Next week we repeat all the physicalisation, and then get down to a bit of analysis.

Session 11

Keywords: *Core skills*; *introduction to resonance and image work; demystifying Shakespeare*

Clean-hands exercise

1.11.1

Remember still to do a series of mouth/cheeks/lips/tongue massages, with little rests and shakes in between. Stroke the jaw down a few times to ensure that space if free and open. Massage the cheeks externally, fairly vigorously but very softly (so that no tension creeps in.) If you are using a bone prop, have a few prop conversations.

At this point in actor training, it is useful to look at individual speech issues, any 'faults' or problems, if they haven't been addressed yet, which should be dealt with in separate classes or tutorials. If you are working alone and know that you have a speech issue that you'd like to solve (such as a lisp), then seek out a specialist voice/speech tutor. The relevant bit here is that it is something *you* would like to work on, it's a choice.

1.11.2   Physical warm-up

- Beginning with feet massage and legs – sit easily on the floor, using your sitting bones to ground you and simultaneously float up through the spine to gain good alignment.

- Massage each foot in turn, then each leg, whilst at the same time adding in a release of breath on your little 'f', 's', 'sh' sounds. These add to the massage, and encourage the breath centring and breath support that is part of a vocal workout – you are doing lots of things at once.

- If you feel centred and easy, you can add in voiced sounds – 'vvvv', 'zzz', 'zh zh zh', etc.

1.11.3   Beach-ball sequence for capacity, support, release – a three-part sequence

This is a variation on a well-used sequence that has its origins in t'ai chi.

- Prepare by standing freely and easily, with feet parallel or slightly turned out, just slightly wider than hip width apart. Let the arms hang freely, roll the shoulders a little to release, and check the knees are soft (very slightly bent). Align the pelvis so that it is neither pushed forwards nor tucked under too far. Ask for help if you are not sure.

- Bring the arms up as if cradling a beach ball in front of you, whilst at the same time letting a breath drop in. The elbows are up and out towards the wall on either side of you. Ensure that the shoulders don't hunch up.

- Release the out-breath as you bring your hands in towards your chest. Keep the elbows up (they shouldn't collapse down to your sides – maintain space, and imagine you have a little beach ball or mini hot-air balloon in your armpits, holding your arms up – this will hopefully prevent tension *and* keep space in the body.

- Let the breath in as you send your hands back out in front, cradling the ball again. Release the out-breath as you link fingers and send the hands, palms down, towards the floor, so that your arms are long and extended right down.

- Let the next breath in, turn your palms up and outwards, and on this in-breath bring your arms up and above your head. Then release the out-breath as the fingers let go and the arms reach out to the sides and back down to the starting position.

When you bring your hands above your head, make sure that they don't go too far back, and do release very easily – as the arms come down, you must be able to see your fingers in your peripheral vision. If your hands go too far back, you will overextend and cut off or significantly reduce the air supply, and/or create a lot of tension in the body.

- Repeat the whole three-part sequence, releasing your out-breath on a little 'f' for all three parts, then on an easy 's', then on a 'sh'. Ensure that you do not release too much of the sound at the start – think of the released sound as a very slow puncture, not a sudden burst. As you do each part, let the in-breath be fairly quick and very easy, and concentrate on letting the out-breath, the sounds, be gentle but clear, slowing down and therefore getting a bit longer each time. Within a few weeks, possibly sooner, you will find it very easy to extend these sounds, thereby increasing your capacity and stamina.

Note: Keep gently reminding yourself to soften in the knees, ankles, feet, shoulders, and indeed anywhere that you find tension creeping in. As with all physical work, this becomes easier fairly quickly, if you repeat the exercise often and work with ease.

- Then do the whole sequence again, this time with 'vvv', 'zzz' and 'zh'.

- Do the whole lot again on an easy hum.

- Then you can repeat it all yet again, humming into an easy 'mah' (or 'moo' if that feels nicer). In just a couple of weeks this will all be brought on to text, so again you are going to integrate body, breath, thought, voice, speech and text in an ongoing process.

This sequence is a fantastic way to get the whole body, breath and voice mechanism going – it works on release, breath centring, capacity, support, placement and even the beginnings of resonance. If you notice tension, let go, shake a bit, and start again. The voice and sounding will help you release tension and work the body; the exercise itself will work the voice – mutually beneficial, integrated work. Text can be applied at a later stage for fuller integration.

1.11.4 Take a baby 'f', 's', 'v', etc., for a walk

Go through this, and notice if it is easier now, and also notice the effect this abstract, image-based exercise is now having. If you have time to repeat the work this session, try the baby 'f' work first, then the beach-ball sequence, and see if there's a difference.

1.11.5 'f', 's', 'v', etc., down through the whole leg

This is another way to centre your breath and warm the voice without worrying about it (see 1.2.5 for a reminder).

Sound some 'v', 'z', 'zh' down through your legs

- Go into the floor and get 'sticky' with the sound – imagine that your feet are getting sticky with 'v' or 'z' and that, as you pick up each foot whilst making the sounds, those sounds are oozing out of your foot and sticking to it and the floor. If you do this for a while, you should hopefully start to feel very 'grounded' and the sound will deepen into your body and sound strong without effort.

Walk that sticky sound

- This connects sound from the centre down into a grounded, warm sound.

- Coat the floor with 'v' then bring 'z' up through the body, up through your centre and out of the top of your head.

- Takes onto open vowel then onto text, sticky sounds – use a line from the Prologue.

- Hum to the floor and up, then play with humming and play with the floor.

Strong muscular support – walking the sit bones

Take care with this exercise as it is very rigorous. If you have back problems, yet feel able to try it, ensure that you really engage your abdominal muscles and pelvic floor. (That is what the exercise actually works on, so it can be very beneficial. If in doubt, ask a movement or other appropriate practitioner for advice.)

- Sit in an aligned (not slumped) position, then 'walk' forwards and back on your sit bones/bottom, and as you go forwards, sound out with 'vvvvv' and as you return try it on 'zzzz'.

- Your knees should soften, and the arms/hands reach forwards (as if trying to grab a partner sitting and moving opposite you), and on the return, can 'push' back with the palms facing away. This will help maintain your core.

- You could try this with one 'v' for one step – and go eight steps/eight 'v's' forward and eight back, for example.

You have to really engage your abdominals, which is good for them. The support cannot do anything but kick in, and engage. The sound should speak for itself.

- Repeat with consonant sounds – 'bbb', 'ddd', 'ggg'.

1.11.10

- Lie in semi-supine, release and lengthen and widen; centre breath, hand on tummy.

- Go through the tidal breath with 'f', 's', 'sh', 'v', 'z', 'zh'.

- Clear the channel, place your hands on the ribcage, feel rib swing, onto 'mmm', 'mah'.

- Apply to some bits of text.

- Check and do clean vocal onset (1.8.5), using hands to mimic the vocal folds. Do silent 'ah', then 'ha', then 'ah'.

- Also, sound 'v' into 'ah' ('vvvvv-aaahh'), then 'ah'; hum into 'ah' ('mmmmm-aaahh'), then 'ah', etc. Think of images to aid the easy onset of sound.

- Repeat standing.

1.11.11 Forward placement

- Stand freely and centred, with equal weight distribution. Feel the feet grounding and at the same time, the spine is floating upwards, shoulders are relaxed and easy. Look across the space and massage your jaw joints and cheeks. Stroke the jaw down and let it hang open a little. Now through that open jaw, breathe to a point ahead of you (don't look down) – there should be no sound, not even a whisper.

- Very gently close your lips over the open space and hum gently, feeling vibration on your lips. The throat stays free. Now 'oo' or 'aw' or 'ah' – whichever is the easiest, to a place ahead of you.

- Elongate the sound, but stop if you feel the sound disappearing.

- If you feel that the sound is pulling back, go back to a hum, then go into 'moo' and 'mah' again.

Introducing resonance

Resonance is vibration, that is the simplest way of describing it, and it is a sound that can only resonate, or vibrate, in a space or cavity. If you strum a guitar, the sound resonates, or bounces around, in the body of the guitar; if you play a violin, the sound vibrates in a smaller box and sounds higher; if you play a double bass, the sound vibrates in a much, much larger space and sounds lower. Other factors include the density of the wood and the strings (short and thin, increasing to long and thick). These things combined are what give the distinctive sounds to the instruments. In the human voice, we can only vibrate or resonate in the spaces of the pharynx, larynx, nose, mouth, and some say the sinuses too. There is technically no such thing as a 'chest voice' or a 'head voice', we just perceive it that way, and it has become a kind of shorthand because people generally understand what is meant by those terms. The larger the cavity, and the thicker the mass of the strings (vocal folds), the deeper the sound. There is then a *sympathetic* resonance which is produced throughout the body, though principally in the chest and skull, but you can feel or at least imagine resonance in many parts of the body (note that jaw and tongue release are crucial for resonance).

Last session and today you have been resonating some of the areas, very simply – that 'v' sounding through the legs, 'z' coming up through the body – try it again, and 'zh' to the sides, front and back. Play with sound and feel the effect on your body and your voice. How does it sound, how does it feel?

Text: *Henry V*, Prologue ☺

First of all, have a bit of a 'chew', massage the lips and tongue (gently biting) and do a few articulation sounds – 'bdg' ('bahdah-gah'), 'ptk' ('pahtahkah'), just to get a little more feel into the articulators.

Now physicalise the text again, as we did last session. This does not mean 'demonstrate' – but redirect your gesture and its physicality into the words (see this now on the DVD).

Start to analyse and break it down:

- Having established what the text is about (you can try these exercises with any piece of text), let's look at some detailed meanings.

- Textual clues – the first one is the title – *Henry V*. This tells you it is about a king, a specific king, and places it in a particular place in history. So it's a history play. It's sometimes easy to forget or ignore the obvious!

- Look at the next word – it says 'Prologue' – a beginning, an introduction to the play.

Then it gives the first character's name – Chorus – a narrator.

This is a lot of information already. We are going to be introduced to the world of the play.

Look now at the subject matter of the speech, what it is about – by checking through the nouns (for the detail on how to do this, refer to Part 3.2). We now know it is about Henry V of England going to war against the French, and it is about the theatre and actors.

Next session we will look at the action.

Session 12

Keywords: *Core skills*; introduction to resonance and image work; demystifying Shakespeare*

Clean-hands exercise

1.12.1

Massage the scalp/temples/jaw joint/mouth/cheeks/lips/tongue and then have some conversations with the bone prop, keeping everything light, free and easy. More muscularity can be introduced as you become used to this.

Beach-ball sequence

1.12.2

Repeat 1.11.3. Notice how this sequence works on your breath capacity, support system, and releases right through the body. Integrate the body, movement, breath, thought, voice.

- Go through the whole three-part sequence with a baby 'f', then onto a 'sh', then bring it onto 'v', 'z', and humming.

- Ensure that the in-breath drops in very easily and quickly with minimum fuss, and so you can concentrate on the outgoing breath, the outgoing sound. As you do this, slow down the out-stream and the sounds, each time getting slower, with the concomitant movement sequence going slower each time, so that your sound goes on for longer. Let this process take its time – it will soon become apparent that your breath can last much longer than at the start.

1.12.3   Massage the body with sound

- Rub arms, legs, and body, whilst at the same time sounding with 'vvvv', 'zzzz', humming, etc. Feel the sound coursing through the body and centring and grounding itself. Resonance develops simultaneously.

1.12.4   Take a baby 'f', 's', 'v', etc., for a walk

This can be done quite quickly now, as a reminder to keep working the breath with ease, further extending your capacity and support with image work.

1.12.5   Pouring

You are now going to learn a physical warm-up which is great for release:

- Lie down on the floor, resting on your back, and allow the body to soften. Now begin to imagine that your head could pour over to one side – look first with your eyes towards one side, then gradually 'pour' your head until you are looking over to the left or right side of the room. Try out the image of water pouring out of your ear onto the floor. You could try pouring sand, or colour, or light, anything that appeals to your sense of ease and relaxation. Slowly return your head to centre. Pour your head slowly over to the other side.

- Repeat this pouring of water/honey/light/your own image, taking your time, going from side to side.

- Let your arms move out slowly, away from your sides, and begin to let the body follow. Don't lift the arms or legs but, if it helps, you can stroke one hand across your chest area until it pours along the other arm over to the side, and the rest of the body follows. This should be very easy, luxurious, indulgent and soft.

- Repeat a few times, slowly, then return to centre and notice how you feel.

Pouring with breath and sound

1.12.6a

- Repeat the whole process, and this time as you pour to one side, imagine you are pouring 'fff' out of one ear and then out of the sides of the body.

- Return gently to centre, and pour 'fff' out of the other ear as you go over to the other side. The sound is released gently and consistently (so it doesn't all rush out at once.)

Bring the whole body into pouring with sounds ⊙

1.12.6b

- Pour now with 's', 'sh', and then with 'vvv' and 'zzz', and then humming. Hopefully you will feel incredibly relaxed and energised all at the same time, and your sound should be very grounded and released.

- If that is all going well, hum into open-vowel sounds, pouring with 'mmaaah', 'mmooo'.

- You can try this with text – try pouring a few words out of your ear, out of your body, either your own improvised words and/or the first few words of the Prologue – 'O for a Muse of fire'.

- Gently roll over, come to sitting, using soft sounds, then bring yourself to standing. From the floor work, take your sound around the space.

Pouring can be seen in the main workout on the DVD.

Check clean vocal onset

1.12.7

- Using hands to mimic the vocal folds, do a silent 'ah', then 'hah', then 'mah', then 'ah' (see 1.8.5).

Sit-bone support

1.12.8

- Walking forwards and back on your sit bones, as we did last week (1.11.9).

1.12.9 Resonance work

- Sound a 'vvv' down through the legs, 'zzz' the upper body to top of head, 'zh' (as in 'pleasure') from your centre to outward directions.

- Then 'v', 'z', 'zh' down through the legs, going into the floor – imagine your feet are getting 'sticky' with the sound.

- Walk that sticky sound down until it's grounded, warm-sounding. This will connect the sound to and from your centre more fully.

- Coat the floor with 'v' and then bring 'z' up through the body, up through your centre and out of your head.

- Move on to open vowels, then text with sticky sounds – use a line from the Prologue.

1.12.10 Forward placement

- Stand freely and centred, as we've done before, stroke down the jaw, and gently hum to a point ahead of you.

- Start to move back and forth, eventually moving around the room, feeling connected to your point on the wall.

1.12.11 Resonance, articulation and the figure of eight ⊚

We are now going to begin using a well-known and very useful sequence that was designed by W.A. Aikin[1] around 1910, into what he called the 'resonator scale'. This sequence of vowels has been used by many practitioners, notably J. Clifford Turner[2] who also presented the sequence into what has been called the 'figure of eight'. Kristin Linklater[5] also plays with this scale in her 'zoo-woe-shaw' sequence in *Freeing Shakespeare's Voice*. It takes the extreme positions of tongue and lips ('ee', with the tongue high up in the mouth, and 'oo', using the most rounded shape of the lips) and visits a sequence of vowels in between these extremes. I use this for resonance, and ultimately apply this to a whole range of consonant combinations to create a comprehensive articulation programme. The full extent of these sounds is printed in the Appendix. At this stage in training, we are simply going to learn the basic sequence, and do it very physically.

See and do the exercise on the DVD – it is much better to learn this physically first, but here it is written out:

hah	hay	hee	hay	hah	haw	hoo	haw	hah
far	may	he	say	star	for	who	saw	far

Do this in a very practical way, through the body.

Also try it out on 'pah pay pee pay pah paw pooh paw pah', and then with 't' and 'k'.

The best way to learn this is by making it entirely physical. I used to teach this from a handout, sitting and reading it through, but have discovered that it is not only quicker to learn if taught 'up on its feet', but it also seems to go in more organically – all part of the integration process. This appears to set up kinaesthetic pathways (learning through touch and feel) that have an effect on body, voice and speech organs simultaneously.

Brief articulation workout
1.12.12

- Loll your tongue, shake out, etc. Massage the lips, cheeks and tongue and have a go at the tongue exercises on the worksheet Appendix TIV2a.

Text: *Henry V*, Prologue
1.12.13

- Read through the text whilst physicalising it at the same time. This session it can be less extreme, but any action you choose, even a hand gesture or a shift of weight onto a different footing, should be clear and followed through – if you are 'wafty' or non-committed to a gesture, your voice and connection to the word will be equally weak.

- Then read through those nouns again, to remind yourself of the subject matter.

- Do a few lines with and without the bone prop.

We are going to look at the verbs. Full details are given in 3.3, so look at that now, and return back to here when you've done that.

We discover from the verbs just how this speech moves, what happens, what it is hoped will happen in the action of the play, and what the actors hope to do for the audience. We now have the action of the piece.

That's a lot of information and sensations discovered in a relatively short space of time. Let that settle.

Session 13

Keywords: *Core skills*; image and strength; demystifying Shakespeare*

Clean-hands exercise

1.13.1

Repeat 1.12.1

Beach-ball sequence

1.13.2

Repeat as before. Deepen your experience of breath capacity, the support system, and release, right through the body. Deepen the integration of body, movement, breath, thought, voice.

Remember to slow down the out-stream and sounds, with the movement sequence going slower each time, and therefore the sound lasting longer.

Massage the body with sound

1.13.3

Repeat 1.12.3

Pouring with sound

1.13.4

Repeat 1.12.5 and 1.12.6. Pour from side to side, slowly and luxuriously, and as the body releases, add in sounds to deepen the experience. Feel the sounds coming from a soft and deep core, coursing through the body, and pouring out of you effortlessly and yet strongly.

1.13.5   Release work on the floor to expand the voice – arm sweeps (i)

- Lie in semi-supine, with your head on a book if you prefer.

- On an easy in-breath, gently sweep your arms up until they are above and behind your head (they stay in contact with the floor as much as possible, all the way up).

- Then sweep your arms down in an arc, again on the floor, until they are back at your sides.

- Repeat this, releasing the out-breath on 'fff'.

In order to get the maximum benefit from this, and fully integrate body and voice work, try to get a sense of the *initiation points*. What I mean by that is – where does the movement start? Is it beginning from your hands, your fingertips, or from deep inside the spine? You can visualise where you initiate the movement. Try it as if starting from the spine, and then try it by starting it from the fingertips. This kind of movement exploration is invaluable – neither is necessarily right or wrong, but one or other will make sense to your body. Ultimately, you will get a much fuller release (I call it release rather than a stretch, so that you don't, er, 'stretch'!), and open up the back ribs in particular, much more easily. It goes back to the idea of stretching without effort and yet reaching out much further and more openly. Notice how the breath and the sounds pattern themselves through the body, and how the voice responds to this.

- Sweep again on 'fff', then 'sh', going on to continuant 'vvv' and 'zzz', and then humming the sweep.

- Check that your tongue is relaxed (if not, you may get a bottled-up or constricted sound in the throat).

- Try reversing the breathing – start with your arms behind your head, sweep down on the inhale, and sweep up with sounds on the out-breath. Try this for a couple of minutes in either direction. See which you prefer.

- Choose your favourite, and take it into an easy 'maaah'.

- Now use some text – you could try 'O for a Muse of fire that ascends the brightest heaven of invention', 'Shall I compare thee to a summer's day', any contemporary writing or your own improvisation.

Whilst doing this exercise, a couple of my students began to create their own patterns. They called it 'angels in snow', because of the soft release, opening out through the body, and especially feeling the opening out of the back ribs and shoulders across the floor beneath them. It's a lovely and gentle image.

Release work on the floor to expand the voice – arm sweeps (ii)

`1.13.6`

- Bring yourself over to one side, head last, and with easy hums and 'mahs', come gently and slowly to standing, sounding the whole time.

- When you arrive upright, move with that wide and expansive feeling in the back, around the space, sounding all the while.

- If it helps, carry on with the arm sweeping, now up and down in accordance with the breath.

- Eventually, stop the sweeping but keep sounding.

This is a great way of rooting the sound, opening up the body, and finding great placement and resonance. If a group is doing it, the sounds can be amazing, very free, released, open and, above all, full.

- Repeat and feel the sound coming out of your back. If in a group, take turns to feel each others' backs as you hum into 'ah'. Take the sound around the space.

You should feel a great sense of forward placement as well as a very warm, open sound coming out of your back, simultaneously.

Strong muscular support – walking the sit bones

`1.13.7`

Repeat as in previous sessions (1.11.9).

1.13.8 Sticky 'v'

- Stand and repeat 'v', 'z', 'zh' down through the legs, going into the floor – sticky with the sound.

- Sound 'vvv' down through the legs, etc., and 'zzz' coming up the upper body to the top of your head, and out of the top. Then try 'zh' from the centre, going in outward directions throughout.

1.13.9 The figure of eight ⊙

Repeat this work introduced in Session 12 (1.12.11), by doing it with the DVD, very physically.

Don't sit and read it through, just do it.

1.13.10 Brief articulation workout

Repeat 1.12.2.

- Try some of these with the bone prop and have brief conversations with it in between your front teeth, then take it out and speak again. Notice the effect.

- Repeat 'hah hay hee hay hah haw hoo haw hah' – do this physically, through the body.

1.13.11 Text – breath and thought

- Read through the Prologue trying to match your thoughts with the breath and vice versa.

- Go quite quickly through both the nouns (subject – what it's about) and the verbs (action – what happens).

1.13.12 Consonants and vowels

- Choose a couple of lines from the text, and try speaking one of them, but only the consonants.

- Then try the same thing, speaking only the vowels on a few lines.

- Divide up the speech. Each person in the group takes a short section and works on it individually with consonants and vowels, physicalising them. Then hear all of them, creating one piece. Chew the words so eventually you will be able to do connected articulation.

- See the detailed example of what happens, taking the line 'Can this cockpit hold the vasty fields of France' – in 3.4.

  'Kn ths kkpt hld th vst fldz v frns.'

  'A i o i oh uh aaaaah eeee eee-uh uh aaaaaaah.'

- Contrast the voiceless and stopped/short, light feel of 'k s k p t s' with the voiced (sounded) and long, earthy, visceral feel of 'n ld th [ð or 'th' as in 'the'] v ldz v n'.

Content and form match perfectly; furthermore, the difference in the body feels amazing – go through the whole exercise from Part 3.

Session 14

Keywords: *Core skills*; resonance, range, image; demystifying Shakespeare*

1.14.1 **Clean-hands exercise**

Get the mouth really soft and open, gently massaging into the lips, tongue, and work the fingers gently into the jawbone and jaw joint. Have a little bone-prop chat.

1.14.2 **Beach-ball sequence**

Repeat 1.11.3.

- Remember to slow down the out-stream and movement sequence so that the sound lasts longer – do this daily for extra benefit. Do the sequence with the usual sounds of 'f' and 'sh', then on to voicing with 'v', 'z' and humming.

- Do the whole sequence with some text – use a poem or short speech that you know well, and see how it might fit into the patterning of the body–breath cycle.

1.14.3 **Release work on the floor to expand the voice – arm sweeps (i)**

- Lie in semi-supine, with your head on a book.

- On an easy in-breath, gently sweep your arms up until they are above and behind your head on the floor. Then sweep your arms down in an arc, on the floor, until they are back at your sides (see 1.13.5 for fuller detail).

- Repeat this, releasing the out-breath on 'fff', then 'shhh', going on to 'vvv' and 'zzz', and then humming.

- Check that your tongue is relaxed.

- Reverse the process – sweep down on the inhale, and sweep up with sounds on the out-breath. See which you prefer today.

- Take it into an easy 'mah', and then on to text.

Release work to standing – expand the voice onto forward placement – arm sweeps (ii)

`1.14.4`

Repeat 1.13.6.

- Repeat again, and sweep the arms up, down, also forwards and back (don't let them go behind you, keep your fingers in your peripheral vision). Feel the sound coming out of your back, as you hum into 'aah'. Take the sound around the space.

- Play gently with pitch range.

Pool of vibrations and fountain of sound

`1.14.5`

- Standing in easy alignment, let a breath in as you bring your head to your centre, around your navel area and rub your tummy whilst sounding on a 'vvv'.

- Imagine you have a pool of sound in your tummy, and that it is a pool from which your sound begins to rise. You may find the image of a volcano helpful. Let the sound come up from your centre, finding its way like a fountain up through the body and out of your mouth or out of the top of your head.

- Use your hands to guide the sound, tracing them up your body, bypassing the neck/throat area so they glide up from the chest to the chin and lips, pausing momentarily to massage the lips. They then release the sound out into the space.

- You can also try letting the hands/fingers carry on tracing up the face to the top of the head, and then releasing up and out of your head into the space above you.

- Repeat all this with a hum, so that you imagine you have a 'pool of hums' in your middle, and this pool sends a fountain of hum up through the body and out of your lips or the top of your head.

1.14.6   Cascade the sound

- Let in a breath and, tracing this with your hands, bring the sound from the top of your head, down the face and out of the mouth, imagining it as a cascade.

The idea is to play with resonance through the body, to find an easy and forward-placed sound, and it should feel and sound very full, easy and warm. If you work from the centre, up and out, then from the top, down and out, you can imagine and release your voice through much of your body – and the voice will have a lot of 'body' itself.

Try all of this with some text. And whilst thinking about cascades of sound and pools, remember to sip some water.

1.14.7   Resonance and pitch into speaking

- Let in a breath, and play with your voice. Now speak through your range, having a little shake through the body whilst sounding, shaking your hips and pelvis and finding lower sounds; shake your ribcage and massage and gently bang your chest, and find mid-range sounds; then massage and pat your face and head and try some higher pitches. Ensure that you stay within easy distance of your whole range – experiment, extend your range, but not to the extent that it becomes too extreme.

- Try all this with some words. See what words come to mind if you are sounding way up in your head – 'ice cream!' and 'tippy toes' and 'lime green', coming down into the chest with 'bananas' and 'mañana' and 'warm hearts', coming down again through the body into the pelvic area with 'heavy' and 'bella mella' and 'velvet curtains' and anything that comes to mind, really!

'Hah hay hee hay hah haw hoo haw hah'   `1.14.8`

- Do this physically, through the body.

- Go on to 'pah pay pee pay', 'tah tay tee tay', 'kah kay kee kay', and so on.

- Repeat with 'b', 'd' and 'g'.

- Then with 'm', 'n' and 'l'.

- Then with 'th', 'f' and 's'.

- And with 'th' [as in 'the'], 'v' and 'z'.

Brief articulation workout   `1.14.9`

Repeat 1.12.12.

`1.14.10`

Working on lips, the bilabial and labiodental sounds – and tongue work. After doing that brief warm-up of the lips and tongue, go through Appendices TIV2a and 3a.

Text – breath and thought   `1.14.11`

- Speak the Prologue speech, seeing if you can identify where the thoughts begin and end, trying to match your breath pattern with those thoughts.

Consonants and vowels   `1.14.12`

- Repeat quite quickly the exercise of trying the consonants only then vowels only on a few lines. Divide up the speech and, if in a group, allocate to each person a short section to work on individually with those discrete sounds.

- Hear all of them, creating one piece.

- Relish the words, so you are working towards connected articulation.

What you may discover is that the vowels give you the emotion and the consonants give you the intellect. Put another way, vowels are the heart of a word, its feeling, and consonants give it physical structure and thought.

Finally, look at this exercise:

1.14.13   First word, last word

You will find this in Part 3 (3.5), saying the first and then the last word in each line.

By now, you will have realised that we are spending a lot of time with this one speech. Go with the repetition, and accompanying new exercises and discoveries. This is going to be revisited a couple more times. Begin to notice what you are feeling, as well as how it is sounding, each time you speak through parts of the text.

1.14.14   A further comment on the Prologue

As you start to unpick the meanings in the text, locate it in its own time by all means – understand the historical context, the social mores, the political climate in which this was written. And at the same time, look to contemporary parallels, so that it means something to you and to a modern audience. This is not just the preserve of the director who may choose to 'interpret' the text in a particular way, but it is also for the actor to make sense of the text today. Here is an example from the Prologue. It talks of Harry (Henry V) and how he should assume (take on) the port of Mars (the bearing of the god of war), and at his heels should 'famine, sword and fire Crouch for employment'. In other words, he has those elements at his disposal – this is not a climate catastrophe, this is the leader of the country inflicting famine through crop destruction or withholding food. Much as today, trade embargoes and restrictions on the food supply also cause suffering. The 'sword' is armaments, and the fire is bombing raids and setting villages and crops alight, it is napalm and depleted uranium and white phosphorus. If that is very unpalatable, perhaps that is the writer's point. Henry is portrayed as a great king, but also as a warrior-soldier. And then in the chorus preceding Act Four, we see a 'little touch of Harry in the night', where the terrified troops are comforted by his courage, his humility and his great humanity. So many sides to the man, so many ways to read the text, but it is all there, on the page.

When it comes to the gorgeous description of the Globe Theatre as this 'wooden O', imagine yourself standing in that great place, on that beautiful stage, looking around you and at the audience; picture yourself within this circle and sweep your arms and your gaze around you to include the building, the stage, the audience and yourself within this orbicular world. As you speak the lines, you can feel the history of the piece, but you are utterly, and without question, in the present.

Session 15

Keywords: *Core skills*; resonance, range, image; expansion of voice; further Shakespeare*

1.15.1 Clean-hands exercise

Repeat as before.

- Have a little chat with the bone prop.

1.15.2 Loosen joints

- Roll the shoulders around easily, using 'f' or 's', and take into gentle stretches.

- Loosen the hips, knees and ankles with gentle rotations on 'sh'.

1.15.3 Beach-ball sequence

Do the sequence with the usual sounds of 'f' and 'sh', then onto voicing with 'v' 'z' and humming; then with a little text.

- Release from this by putting your hands on your hips and do some gentle pelvic rotations one way then the other. Then gently shake out the legs, all the while using sounds.

Pour down onto the floor

1.15.4

- Pour yourself down onto the floor and ease yourself from side to side with sound.

Angel wings ☉

1.15.5

- Lying in semi-supine, bring your arms out to the sides (at a level just below your armpits) and then raise them up so that the palms are cradling your sound – using a little 'f' to get it started. Then take that on to a 'v', and a hum. Gently vary the pitch.

- The hands don't touch – keep them apart with the palms parallel, facing each other as they reach up. This opens up the back ribs more and creates more space in the back. Ensure also that as you reach up, the shoulders don't go up for the ride, but soften back into the floor. That way, you get a much better reach and a released stretch.

See if you can feel your sound as a tangible entity between your hands. Imagine this as the first part of the beach-ball sequence, only lying down. Extend right through from the spine, right along your 'wings' to their tips, as you sound out. You might find that you are holding a ball of sound between your hands – and the stronger and clearer the sound is, the more physical it will appear to be, like an energy field.

- Roll over and come slowly to standing.

1.15.6 Buzz the head, expand the voice

- 'Vvv' from the face outwards – tap the side of your head with your fingers and release them out to the sides with the sound. Repeat on 'z' and 'ah' or 'ee' from the top of your head up and out.

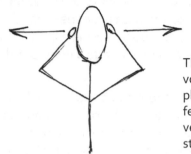

This is a great way to expand the voice to give it resonance, depth, placement and a 'surround sound' feeling. It also gets your sound very centred, supported and strong.

1.15.7 Stepping out

- Stand centred, then swing your right arm out to the right as you step out to that side. Return to centre, then step out to the left, your left arm moving out to the side simultaneously. As you return let the breath in, as you step out, release on 'f', then 'sh', then 'v', 'z', hum and finally 'mmm' into 'mah'.

1.15.8 Sumo sounding

- This time, stand centred, lift one knee and swing it out and down like a sumo wrestler. Ensure that you don't slam the foot down too hard – it should connect firmly with the floor, but through a soft ankle.

- Repeat with some voiced sounds, then consonants.

- Add in words (from any play or text you are working on).

- Stand and create a sounded fountain of water up through the body from the pool of vibrations at your centre.

Resonance and pitch

1.15.9

• Play with pitch by bringing your arms to the chest and sounding around your mid-range, and try out some words like 'amore', 'banana', 'mango'. Bring your hands to your head, trying higher sounds, and then words like 'ice cream', 'bright pink', 'ciao', etc. Finally, sound low into the body with 'bella', 'midnight blue', 'heavy heavy', etc.

• Take into speaking – everyday words or words from a speech. Play.

'Hah hay hee hay hah haw hoo haw hah' ◉

1.15.10

Speak and move this through the body, also using 'pah pey pee pay'.

Text: *Henry V*, Prologue

1.15.11

• Do a quick repeat of vowels only, then consonants only – discover the emotion and then the intellect.

• Play and physicalise these sounds and words, really relishing the words on a few chosen lines.

• Choose three or four lines to speak. Bone-prop them. Physicalise them.

• 'Perform' them.

Notice how these lines sound. See what you now understand about the meaning of the text and how it makes you feel physically and emotionally.

Session 16

Keywords: *Resonance, range, image; expansion of voice*

1.16.1–1.16.10

I suggest that the last session is repeated this week, so that you really begin to consolidate all the support work and in particular the resonance and expansion. So, after warming up as usual, go through exercises from Session 15 like angel wings, pouring, buzzing the head, and placing the sound out (1.15.1–1.15.10).

1.16.11   Now a little articulation ☉

Use the physicalised 'bbb', 'ddd', 'ggg' sequence.

1.16.12   Rhythm – introducing the iambic pentameter

Having got used to one speech from Shakespeare through playing around, let's now look at rhythm. This is dealt with in detail in 3.6, and I'd recommend that you have a read through that first – but I'll also give some basic pointers here as well.

To explain the meaning of 'iambic pentameter', here is a simple list:

Iamb: from Greek, meaning to drive forward or push.

Iambus: also Greek, means a foot of two syllables, 1 weak, 1 strong (or unstressed/stressed, or short/long). Why 'foot'?

Because rhythms originated in dance melodies, and your foot comes down on the stressed beat.

Weak/**strong**, unstressed/**stressed**, or short/**long** – 'a**like**', 'our **scene**', 're**move**', 'a**go**', 'to**day**', 'de-**dum**', 'one **two**'.

'De-**dum** de-**dum** de-**dum** de-**dum** de-**dum**' – speak these very clearly and in a really exaggerated manner, and then take them around the room.

Dance it, lightly stepping the 'de' and strongly bringing the other foot down on '**dum**'.

Pentameter: five measures of two syllables (this is also explained in Part 3), which means ten syllables in a regular line of iambic pentameter.

Make up a line, something like 'the **star**ving **dog** be**gan** to **chew** the **bone**' (you can do better than me!).

If you tap your hand on your chest as you repeat the 'te-**tum**' (or 'de-**dum**' or 'pa-**pum**') you may start to notice what it feels and sounds like. To some people, it's like horses cantering along. It is also the sound of the heartbeat, and the thing about the beat of our heart is that it speeds up and slows down – when very calm and relaxed it is slow, when anxious, excited, angry, running fast, it speeds up. And the amazing thing about the iambic is that it speeds up or slows down according to the context, and the clue is usually in the syllabic structure. For example, a monosyllabic line will nearly always be slow – 'In sooth I know not why I am so sad' – whereas a multi-syllabic line plays faster – 'Gallop apace you fiery footed steeds'. This will take time to feel, but it can be helpful to get some hints of the possibilities in this form, so that you can see the point of looking at it in this physical way.

An example of how this heartbeat rhythm works to brilliant effect is given in Part 3.

Apply to text – 'But soft! What light from yonder window breaks?'

- Look again at the Prologue. Go through it physically and 'overdo' the rhythm.
- See if you can find out why there are irregularities.

You may find this speech has some odd lines that don't quite fit the rhythm, but don't worry about it at this stage. When we come to look at the verse in more detail, you will have had a good go at starting to discover its feel. More analytical methods will come out of this.

- A basic norm is set up, and added stress is provided when the norm (or rule) is broken.

- Speak a few lines with the bone prop.

- Physicalise them, play, dance, feel them.

Session 17

Keywords: *Further expansion of voice; new text*

Clean-hands exercise   `1.17.1`

As before.

Do some tongue aerobics   `1.17.2`

Especially the ones using your fingers, whilst the hands are still clean (see Appendix TIV2a).

Warm the body   `1.17.3`

With any of the shaking, sounding, stretching exercises you feel you want or need today.

Arm sweeps   `1.17.4`

Do these on the floor, then come to standing and repeat into the space, all the while using the usual sequences of voiceless sounds – 'f', 's', 'sh', going on to some 'vvv', 'zzz', and humming – finally sounding out into easy open vowels.

Capacity   `1.17.5`

Having not looked at this formally for a while (we've been working on it throughout, but without drawing attention to it), now start to notice how it has developed.

- Lie down in semi-supine and release your sounds upwards with an image of feathers streaming up and out from your centre; or imagine you are balancing a ping pong ball on the breath stream – the sound is the ball.

- Extend this to see how your capacity and support are coming on.

1.17.6   Capacity on text

It will be easier if you can get someone to read this for you, but have a go again (1.8.6).

- Still in semi-supine, let in a little breath into your centre and say 'Now'.

- Let in another little breath and say 'Now entertain'.

- Let in another little breath and say 'Now entertain conjecture'.

- Build up a word at a time, letting in a new breath each time you repeat the phrase and add another word. Each new breath is very slightly bigger than the last one, but don't focus on this too much.

You can go through this text reasonably fast, despite the slow measure of the piece. Try it out for size.

Breath and thought, capacity, support and placement are all being brought into play, with a little extra stamina for good measure.

- Come to standing and repeat.

1.17.7   Buzz the head

Repeat 1.15.6.

1.17.8

Repeat the Sumo sounding (1.15.6) and/or Elastics of sound (1.7.7) on 'v 'or 'mah'.

Play with pitch range and resonance (1.15.9).

'Hah hay hee hay hah haw hoo haw hah' ⊚

• Working physically as usual, add in more combinations, also using 'pah pey', etc.

• Go on to 'pahtahkah paytaykay peeteekee paytaykay pahtahkah pawtawkaw pootookoo pawtawkaw pahtahkah'.

• Go around again on 'bahdahgah', 'mahnahlah', 'thahfahsah', [voiced as in 'the'] 'thahvahzah'.

Repeat the iambic dance (1.16.12).

Text: *Henry V*, Chorus IV

Read through this speech, get it on its feet physicalising it. See how quickly you can now get into a bit of Shakespeare. Use the words, enjoy them.

Session 18

Keywords: *Further expansion of voice; playing the new text*

1.18.1–1.18.4

Warm up and prepare as in Session 17 (1.17.1–1.17.4).

1.18.5   'Sprinkler' sounding

Come to standing and try out the colander of sounds springing from your centre (1.7.6). It's a while since you tried this, but notice if you 'get it' more quickly and easily now – see if it can get your sound rooted and full within just a few tries.

1.18.6   'Hula hoop' of sound

This is another image-based exercise to root and place the sound. Having done the sprinkler/colander, imagine you have a hula hoop around your waist (take care of your lower back) and play as a child does with the hoop, sounding it out at the same time. Have fun and see what happens as you bring pitch into play.

You might also try some horizontal abseiling (1.7.7) for support and placement.

1.18.7

Repeat the buzzy head (1.15.6).

Repeat the sumo sounding (1.15.8).

Stand and hum an imaginary pool of vibration from your middle (rub your tummy with your hands to help get it going), and as the hum comes up to your mouth and beyond to the top of your head, let it out into an 'aaah' or 'ooo', as if a fountain or volcano of sound were springing out of you.

Play with pitch range and resonance (see Session 15 for ideas, using words in differing placements in the body) – warm, low sounds and corresponding words in the groin, mid-pitch sounds in the chest/heart, and high sounds and words up in the top of the head.

• 'Hah hay hee hay hah haw hoo haw hah' – through the body.

• Move on, using 'pah pey', etc., then 'pahtahkah', 'bahdahgah', 'mahnahlah', 'thahfahsah', [voiced] 'thahvahzah'.

Text: *Henry V*, Chorus IV

Have a really good play with this speech, but try it very quietly, maybe just whispering some sections.

With the speech, get some atmospheres going, with some of the group making the sounds of the speech – such as the 'whispers of the watches' (the sentries on duty) – and have one or two people trying lines of text over these sounds. You are trying to create a soundscape and put the text into it, like an underscore of music.

1.18.13 New taster text – bridging the gap to the next term or block of sessions

If you have the time, you can take a look at a twentieth-century sonnet – I have placed it in Session 19 after a notional vacation, but you could also look at it here. This will depend on your schedule, but either way, it is intended to introduce the form of the sonnet with a relatively modern text in order to make the form itself more accessible to start with. As a wartime sonnet, it also links back to *Henry V*'s themes of war.

Recap, Own Study and Practice – Vacation Work

Here is a very brief recap of what we have been working on or using:

» Baby 'f', 's', 'sh', 'v', 'z', baby hum, on to vowels. Try with text.

» Breath capacity, support and sustain – beach-ball sequence.

» Ditto on arm sweeps and angel wings, on the floor and standing.

» Ditto one breath, one word; a breath and two words; a breath and three words, etc.

» Resonance – from these but also from tapping, e.g. the sides of head 'v', mouth 'z' body, etc.

» Support and resonance – abseiling, elastics of sound, etc.

» A little pitch range work too – cascading sounds.

» Resonance and articulation – 'hah hey hee hey' sequence.

» Articulation – preparation of mouth and tongue; drills, etc.

» Always apply and go on to text.

What to do over the break – using a combination of the above, do daily voice work to:

» Physically warm up the body, including release and relaxation.

» Breath centring and release through voiceless sounds.

» Warming voice onto voiced sounds, 'vzzhmmmm' into 'mah'. Slow, extensive process.

» Sounding into open vowels including forward placement and resonance.

» Warm up articulators, the lips, tongue, plus yawns, etc., for the soft palate.

» Some consonant drills and *then* phrases.

Remember that articulation is not just technique, it's about connection – to the word, to the thought, and to the situation.

» Bring the work onto text.

» Use the bone prop for both articulation drills, the text, and especially for everyday conversations.

Devise further daily routines. About twenty to thirty minutes per day is about right, for five or six days a week if you can. Always take at least one day off (so that you get a rest, and it doesn't become too big a mountain to climb). Vary the routines so you don't get bored, and also so that the voice and body don't get too used to one way of doing things. Continue to read aloud a little every day too. And have a complete break and a rest at some point.

And finally some suggestions for common difficulties:

Hints

» Downward inflection:

[*Take a breath.*] 'To' [*Take a breath.*] 'To be' [*Take a breath.*] 'To be or' [*Take a breath.*] 'To be or not' – and so on.

Think bright colours as you speak each section.

As you speak a line of text, move your hands and arms forwards and upwards to guide the sound up and ahead of you.

»   Forward placement:

Imagine the sound as a little plane taking off from the front of the tongue.

»   Weak 'r':

Lots of tongue strengthening and release. This requires individual attention, but a great tip is that singing the words helps.

»   Range:

Speak text whilst going up and downstairs.

Part 1d

This stage in the progression of the work is intended to come after about six or seven months, and if you are in formal training, the following section would roughly equate to a third term, or the latter part of a second semester.

This block of sessions will take you to the end of the first formal year of training, so that we will continue with core skills* – and develop resonance and articulation. There will be further repetition, especially on breath expansion, more muscular support work and easy placement. Physical engagement with text continues with an exploration of Shakespeare's sonnets.

Session 19

Keywords: *Revision workout; muscular capacity; sonnets*

1.19.1   **Have a gentle shake-out and spine roll** ⊘

Roll down through the spine several times, finding all-round expansion at the bottom (breathing low whilst upside down, noting the expansion particularly into the lower-back ribs) and then using the breath to come up.

1.19.2   **Spine roll and plank**

Avoid this one if you have back problems and create an alternative exercise to work the spine and core muscles. You will need to engage all your core muscles for this to be easy and released, ensuring there is no strain. It may feel like hard work, yes, but not over-constricted.

- Roll down through the spine and then out into a 'plank' position.

- Release the breath on 'f' and 'sh'. Rest the knees down and then repeat.

1.19.3   ⊘

Float up into the downward-facing-dog position, using the image of a little hot-air balloon raising your tummy up, drawing back to the spine with the soft support of the balloon, keeping soft and long in the neck and head. Release the out breath on a 'sh'.

You can see this exercise in the sun salutation sequence on the DVD.

1.19.4

On the next out-breath, float down to all fours using the 'sh'. Notice the engagement of the support system. Repeat this sequence several times.

Capacity test

1.19.5

This is similar to a Patsy Rodenburg exercise.

- Come to standing and let a breath into the centre. Release the out-breath on a long 's' sound. See how long the 's' lasts for – it is not a competition, but it is good to challenge your capacity with this simple exercise.

- Walk around the space and repeat this several times, then take it onto a 'z' sound. (If you do this daily and note the length of time you can last, you will quantify your increasing stamina.)

- If you find it makes you panic, or you can't last long, then try the image work – go back to taking a baby 'f' or 's' for a walk – it's the same thing, just expressed rather differently. See how far or for how long the baby 's' can walk, without strain.

- After taking it onto voiced sound with 'z' and a long hum, you then try it on text, building longer thoughts. We will look at this next session.

- You can also now try taking a baby 'f' for a walk up the high street, with the lightest of contact between the teeth and lower lip. No one will know you're doing it, but you are integrating your technique into the everyday.

Warming the voice and finding resonance using colour

1.19.6

- Do a series of sirens (pitch glides) on a hum, first with 'm', then 'n' and then 'ng' to get the voice warm. Do a lot of humming into the mask of the face – that is, imagine the sound going into the bones of your face. It can help to massage or just place your fingers to feel the bony structures through the flesh. If you tap as well, get that sound buzzing through the bone and out into the air.

- Try this lying down, sitting, and then standing. As you hum, imagine it is taking on a colour, and let the colours change as your pitch gradually changes.

- Take at least five to ten minutes on this humming, then open it out into 'mah' and 'nah' and 'ng-ah'; then 'moo', 'moh' and 'maw'.

1.19.7   Come on to text with intoning

Taking a few lines of text you know, or a couple of lines from the sonnet printed below, intone (chant) the words, and then speak them.

1.19.8   Articulation

- Wake up the articulators – massage the lips, rub them and get the lips and cheeks soft and mobile, and ready to work. Do some horse blows with your lips (blow out through your lips, making them vibrate together, making a sound like a horse does). Now do some exercises. Make duck lips and Elvis lip curls (see Appendix TIV1a). A mirror can help so you can see what the lips are doing and what they need to do. Repeat the horse blows and note any difference.

- Stand and let the jaw hang, massage the temples and then the jaw joint, rub the cheeks and stroke down the jaw and face, letting the jaw hang. If the jaw still feels tense, do the little chains exercise (1.4.4).

- Gently bite the tongue, then roll it out, again using a mirror to see what it is doing. Ensure that it is not tense before going on to muscular exercises. Repeat several times.

- Now do some tongue exercises – first the aerobics of pressing the tongue against your finger(s), then strong stretches (see Appendix TIV2a).

Articulation drills ⊙   1.19.9

- Go through the resonance exercise of the 'figure of eight' (1.12.11) on 'haheyheehey', and then with the sequence of 'pahtahkah peyteykey' and so on, using physical gesture and action sequences.

- We will now learn the next sequence. Take a look at Appendix TIV3b, but it works better if this is learned through movement first, so look at this on the DVD. It sounds like this:

    'Ooop-poo ohp-poh awp-paw ahp-pah ayp-pay eep-pee.'

The sequence of vowels 'oop ohp awp ahp ayp eep' was set out by Turner[2] with a number of consonant sounds, and I have developed these into a sequence that provides the basis for an entire articulation course, using also a different ordering of some of the consonant sounds and combinations.

Bone-prop conversations   1.19.10

Continue your 'five-a-day' and use the prop on all text work too.

Text: sonnets   1.19.11

First of all, ask what is a sonnet? What is the form? Think of some examples of sonnet writers. If you want more help and information, look at the short section on the history and form of the sonnet in 3.8.

This session, we will begin by looking at an example from the twentieth century. Read through the poem aloud a few times, and get the feel and general sense.

'Anthem for Doomed Youth' by Wilfred Owen (1917)

What passing-bells for these who die as cattle?
Only the monstrous anger of the guns.
Only the stuttering rifles' rapid rattle
Can patter out their hasty orisons.
No mockeries now for them; no prayers nor bells;
Nor any voice of mourning save the choirs,

> The shrill, demented choirs of wailing shells;
> And bugles calling for them from sad shires.
> What candles may be held to speed them all?
> Not in the hands of boys but in their eyes
> Shall shine the holy glimmers of goodbyes.
> The pallor of girls' brows shall be their pall;
> Their flowers the tenderness of patient minds,
> And each slow dusk a drawing-down of blinds.

- Walk through this poem and physicalise the rhythm so that you find its heartbeat – the beat of the iambic pentameter. I will leave you to discover much of it for yourself (or with guidance by a tutor), except to introduce a couple of notable moments.

- Take a look at the first line – if you find it easier, walk or tap the rhythm. It is an iambic pentameter, but of eleven syllables. The eleventh does not make you rush on because it comes at a question mark, so it makes you suspend or stop. And why – because the idea of a young generation being sent to the slaughter like cattle is so unsettling, the author wants to unsettle you and make you pause at the outset.

- Look at the eighth line – so often people will read this:

  And b**ugle**s **calli**ng for them from **sad shires.**

  In other words, they miss the iambic, and 'for them' are weak, but if you beat it out –

  And **bu**gles **call**ing **for** them **from** sad **shires**.

  Then you hear the sadness as bugles call *for* them, *from* those shires, which invoke rural England, the idyll of villages and the sadness of the people – and the shires – back home.

- Look at the rhyme scheme, and if you like, notate it (the first line ending is 'cattle', so is labelled A; the second is 'gun', so becomes B; the third is 'rattle' (to rhyme with 'cattle'), so is A again; the fourth is 'orison' (a half-rhyme

with 'gun'), to become B again. So you have ABAB).
Continue on your own, and then when you read the whole
sonnet again, you can point up those rhymed endings.
Don't be afraid to use, to really speak out the rhyme
scheme – it is there for a reason.

• Take time over the poem, put it back together when you
have understood it, and try it out.

Session 20

Keywords: *Warm-up; muscular capacity; physicalised resonance; sonnets*

A reminder here that you want to be in the habit by now of applying voice skills at *all* times when you speak.

1.20.1   Warm-up

- Start by doing the clean-hands exercise, then a very gentle shake-out, using 'f', 's', 'sh'.

- Roll down through the spine several times, finding all-round expansion at the bottom, using breath and voiceless sounds to come up.

- Roll down through the spine and out to plank. Come onto all fours, then float up into dog with an 'f' or 'sh', maintaining a soft, long neck, then 'shh' yourself up to standing.

1.20.2   Capacity test

- Repeat the extended release on 's' and see how long it lasts. And add in the baby 'f'/'s' to combine technique and creativity.

- Ask yourself why you think that capacity connected to the support system is important for the actor.

Breath capacity with text

Here is a simple nursery rhyme and a not-so-simple exercise. Take a breath for each thought (marked with /) and you will discover that the progression becomes harder as the thoughts lengthen. Try to avoid it becoming 'pat' – in other words, don't fall into a repetitive rhythmic pattern, and ensure you keep making sense of each thought and each image, using pitch range to help you. This is tiring work but it will pay off. Remind yourself to stay soft in the jaw and practise with the bone prop, so you are doing lots of things at once!

'The House That Jack Built'

/ This is the house that Jack built.
/ This is the malt
That lay in the house that Jack built.
/ This is the rat, that ate the malt,
That lay in the house that Jack built.
/ This is the cat that killed the rat,
that ate the malt,
That lay in the house that Jack built.
/ This is the dog that worried the cat,
That killed the rat, that ate the malt,
That lay in the house that Jack built.
/ This is the cow with the crumpled horn,
That tossed the dog, that worried the cat,
That killed the rat, that ate the malt,
That lay in the house that Jack built.
/ This is the maiden all forlorn,
That milked the cow with the crumpled horn,
That tossed the dog, that worried the cat,
That killed the rat, that ate the malt,
That lay in the house that Jack built.
/ This is the man all tattered and torn,
That kissed the maiden all forlorn,
That milked the cow with the crumpled horn,
That tossed the dog, that worried the cat,
That killed the rat, that ate the malt,
That lay in the house that Jack built.

/ This is the priest all shaven and shorn,
That married the man all tattered and torn,
That kissed the maiden all forlorn,
That milked the cow with the crumpled horn,
That tossed the dog, that worried the cat,
That killed the rat, that ate the malt,
That lay in the house that Jack built.
/ This is the cock that crowed in the morn,
That waked the priest all shaven and shorn,
That married the man all tattered and torn,
That kissed the maiden all forlorn,
That milked the cow with the crumpled horn,
That tossed the dog, that worried the cat,
That killed the rat, that ate the malt,
That lay in the house that Jack built.
/ This is the farmer who sowed the corn,
That kept the cock that crowed in the morn,
That waked the priest all shaven and shorn,
That married the man all tattered and torn,
That kissed the maiden all forlorn,
That milked the cow with the crumpled horn,
That tossed the dog, that worried the cat,
That killed the rat, that ate the malt,
That lay in the house that Jack built.

If you practise this regularly for a couple of months, and keep working with thought, it will become easy and you can apply the principle to every text. At the start of a 'second year' or the beginning of Part 2, we will look at capacity with breath and thought applied to complex text, and this work will have laid the foundations.

1.20.4 Warming the voice and resonance

- Using images of colour, do a lot of humming and gentle pitch glides, allowing the sound to go all over your body, and try 'm', 'n', 'ng' and see if they 'colour' differently.

Release of sound for placement and resonance – angel wings ☉

`1.20.5`

(As 1.15.5.) This can be done for several minutes, and as your voice warms, release the sound into 'mah' and 'moo', dropping the arms for the in-breath and then gently reaching up with the sound so it releases forward and out with ease. Match the length of the movement with the length of the breath, so it is a quick drop for the in, and a long slow reach for the outgoing sound. You then integrate thought, breath, movement and sound.

Sirens/pitch glides onto text – intoning then speaking

`1.20.6`

- Do some pitch glides and then begin to intone a line from a text – try chanting 'Shall I compare thee to a summer's day?' several times. Then speak the line.

- Roll over with a chanted line, going into speaking it as you sit up.

Articulation ☉

`1.20.7`

Repeat all the articulation work from last time (1.19.8 and 1.19.9) and use the DVD workout to help you (the 'figure of eight' and 'oop-poo' sequences with different consonants).

Text: sonnets

`1.20.8`

It may help to refresh your memory of the form by looking at the sonnet section in Part 3. This session we begin looking at a Shakespeare sonnet.

'Sonnet 18' by William Shakespeare

Shall I compare thee to a summer's day?
Thou art more lovely and more temperate.
Rough winds do shake the darling buds of May,
And summer's lease hath all too short a date.
Sometime too hot the eye of heaven shines,
And often is his gold complexion dimmed;
And every fair from fair sometime declines,
By chance or nature's changing course untrimmed.

But thy eternal summer shall not fade,
Nor lose possession of that fair thou ow'st,
Nor shall Death brag thou wand'rest in his shade,
When in eternal lines to time thou grow'st.
So long as men can breathe or eyes can see,
So long lives this, and this gives life to thee.

- First, physicalise it.

- Then talk through meanings, and look up anything you are unsure of.

As before, I will give a couple of suggestions for meanings, as a starting point. Say the first line. Talk about the image of a summer's day and people often talk about blue skies, neither too hot nor too cold, big smiles appear and it sounds like a state of perfection. Then you read the second line, and now the summer's day appears less than perfect, perhaps? Then there are rough winds, so even less so. Does this elevate the beauty of the youth, or reduce the beauty of the perfect day?

Look at the antithesis, for example rough winds and darling buds (antithesis is explained in Part 3).

Start to find the balance of the line. Beat out the rhythm and look at the rhyme scheme, and see what these elements give you as a speaker.

Choose a Shakespeare sonnet to work on for next time, as for the next few sessions we will be applying all the work learnt so far to a chosen sonnet.

Session 21

Keywords: *Developing resonance; sonnets*

Warm-up, capacity, placement, resonance and pitch   1.21.1–1.21.6

Repeat all the exercises from last session (1.20.1–1.20.6).

Additional resonance work for more depth   1.21.7

- Lie in semi-supine, allow the spine to soften, lengthen and spread across the floor.

- Do some gentle spine raises, with the feet flat. Lift the pelvis, rolling the spine gently up as far as your shoulder blades. On an out-breath and a slow 'f', let the spine roll down to the floor again.

- Ensure that you engage the abdominal muscles and pelvic floor to support you. Repeat this many times, going on to use 'sh' then 'v' and a hum, and finally come down through the spine on a long easy 'huh' or 'her', rather like a long relaxed sigh but on full voice as you descend.

- To aid your descent of the spine, lift the heels first and then come down – notice how much more clearly the spine articulates.

1.21.8   Supine sounding

- Still lying down, resonate and sound in different areas, first with humming and then with vowel releases, trying out 'mah' in your chest area, 'mee' in your mouth and on a higher note in your skull, drop through the chest with 'mah', sound out on 'moh' in your solar plexus, and 'moo' in your lower belly.

Just see what happens and what this means to you. This is a taster of deeper resonance work, which we will do more extensively in the second part.

1.21.9   Articulation ☉

- Sitting or standing in alignment, prepare with some massaging of the lips, cheeks, and tongue. Go through lip exercises – duck lips, Elvis lip curls, etc., and then with the tongue – the aerobic and ballet sequences. Remember to keep checking for release by shaking out and lolling the tongue in particular. Stroke down and soften the jaw occasionally, to ensure no tension has crept in.
- Do some consonant drills – 'bbb', 'ddd', 'ggg' (see DVD).
- Go through the 'figure of eight' (1.12.11) on 'ptk', 'bdg', and so on. See the handout and go through the sheet.
- Look at Appendix TIV3b – go through the sequences 'oop-poo ohp-poh', etc., physically and orally, and *then* with the sheet.

1.21.10   Text: sonnets

a. Meanings: If you have chosen a sonnet, go through the physicalising process. Then look up anything you don't understand by using a New Penguin or Arden edition, for example, and refer also to David and Ben Crystal's *Shakespeare's Words* to help you. You can then use this sonnet to apply all the voice and speech work ongoing throughout the next block of sessions, and really get to grips with one short poem.

If you have any uncertainties, look also at the nouns and verbs for clues, and first and last words for structure.

b. The iambic: go over the rhythm, marking up the text to ensure you have understood its scansion. Beat it out physically, and then mark up the text (underline or put a strong score mark over the strong beats, for example). If a line appears to be irregular or has an inversion, then mark in the weak beats as well.

Try out the sonnet, feeling the pulse of the iambic supporting the thought process. Apply all your vocal work – support the voice and the word, breathe each thought, and articulate each element.

Session 22

Keywords: *Muscularity; resonance; sonnets*

1.22.1–1.22.7 **Warm-up and preparation**

Repeat the whole preparation sequence of the last two sessions. By now it should be relatively easy to do as you will be familiar with this work, both physically and intuitively, through ongoing practice.

1.22.8 **Physicalised resonance**

This is the sounding of vowels through the body that we did in the last session (1.21.8). This time, ensure that your sound is easy and internal – what I mean by that is that, as you sound out your 'mah' or 'moo' for a few minutes, check that you are not pushing your sound. If doing this in a group, don't 'compete', but imagine that the sound is very much inside of you. Ensure that you don't retract or pull back the sound (the sound is still to be placed forward), but that the impulse is very much from your centre, and the sound vibrates your body. It will then automatically resonate into the room.

- Begin to add in some words, perhaps the name of a character you are working on, and then a line or two of text. You can, of course, use some lines from your sonnet, but if you also use character work, then it helps you integrate and inform all the other areas you are working on.

- Repeat all this standing.

Articulation ⊛

Repeat the work from last time, and as you become more familiar with the sequences (keep using the DVD to help you) then you
can begin to mix them up a bit or make up your own.

Text

If necessary, go over any meanings that you may be still unsure
of. In group work this can be very useful as you can help each
other, and at the same time become familiar with a large number
of sonnets, which is invaluable for the future.

- Try out your sonnet and, this time, begin to integrate and
  use the resonance work. If a particular line or word is
  troubling you, try out different pitches and resonances
  (speak it up in your head, or only in the oral space, for
  example) to see if that can free it up.

Use this to explore the antitheses in the sonnet as well.

Session 23

Keywords: *Muscularity; resonance; articulation; sonnets*

1.23.1–1.23.4   **Warm-up**

As in Session 20 (1.20.1–1.20.4).

1.23.5   **Placement and resonance**

See 'angel wings' in Session 15 – lie in semi-supine and release the sound as your hands reach towards the ceiling.

1.23.6   **Play with the floor for extra support and resonance**

- Roll to one side on a sound, and sound yourself to kneeling. Now move around using your hands, knees, sit bones – really roll around and play with the floor, getting weight and support, whilst sounding through 'v', 'z', hums and so on.

- Continue playing in this way and release those sounds into open vowels. Continue playing and try out some words, and a line of text.

- Bring this all to standing, taking the sensation of that extra support gained from the floor. When you come to standing, go to a solid surface and push away, if it helps, or use each other to give and release sounds through body weight and counterbalancing.

Articulation

- Prepare with some massaging of the lips, cheeks, and tongue. Go through lip and tongue exercises – see the handout sheets if you want reminders. Stroke down and soften the jaw occasionally, to ensure no tension has crept in.

- Do some consonant drills, the 'figure of eight' on 'ptk', 'bdg', and so on. See the Appendix and also go through the sequences 'oop-poo ohp-poh', etc., physically and orally and *then* with the worksheet (Appendix TIV3b).

- Soft-palate work – do a variety of yawns (open mouth, behind closed lips and so on). Then do the soft-palate drills (on 'g', 'k', 'ng') opening them out into vowels.

- Work through TIV3b, getting someone to call the sequences in turn, so you are not constantly reading but just 'doing'.

Text: sonnets

- Read through your chosen sonnet (standing up) and apply the support, resonance and pitch work from the sessions so far.

- Look at the breath points if you are unclear about the thought progression – breathe and speak each thought (to a full stop, or semi-colon, normally).

Whisper and speak

- Physicalise your sonnet again. Then get into pairs and whisper your poem to each other; then speak the text quietly to your partner. Make observations about any new discoveries.

- You can now learn the sonnet, doing this by imagery and thought (that is, not 'by rote'). You may well find that you know much of it already, through the ongoing processes, which is the best way to learn a text – you integrate your learning as you go along.

Session 24

Keywords: *Sounding and filling the space in the body; articulation; sonnets, falling inflections and line endings*

1.24.1 **Warm-up**

- Begin today with a gentle shake-out. Roll down through the spine several times, finding all-round expansion at bottom of your ribcage on a new in-breath, and then using the breath and a voiceless sound to come up. Repeat many times, using different sounds.

- Go through the sequences you have now become very familiar with.

1.24.2 **Pour and sweep**

Add in some extra floor work, do the pouring work and 'sweeps' of the body with sounds. You will be very loose and released, and the sound will be going right through your body.

- Sweeping: as you pour your body over to one side, bring yourself into a gentle fetal position. On the out-breath, pour over onto your back and as you do so, allow your legs to lengthen and your arms to open out on the floor, almost in a soft 'star' position, so that you are opening out the whole body. Continue moving and sweeping the body over onto your other side, into a slight fetal position again. You might also think of the image of a flower opening and closing. Move on the out-breath, take the new in-breath on your side, and move again, using sounds. Begin with 'sh' and then take it onto 'v', and 'z', and a sweeping hum.

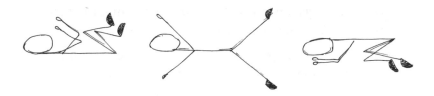

Sweeping and initiation points – these are suggestions to help you really integrate movement with voice, body with sound, and ultimately the whole into acting. I introduced 'initiation' (*where* a movement begins) in Session 13, and we now revisit the idea as a reminder.

a. Try sweeping by beginning with an impulse to move from your centre.

b. Try by beginning the whole movement from the extremities of fingers and toes – as if that is where the sequence begins. You may well find that this opens out the body much more

c. Notice the difference and now try doing both simultaneously – the first one is more in your imagination (thinking you start the movement from your centre) and the other is clearly very physical. All this will give you a really good stretch but keeping a sense of lightness at the same time. The sound follows accordingly.

- Pour or sweep up into sitting whilst sounding.

Floor play

`1.24.3`

Do some playing with the floor, sounding through feet, hands, knees, bottom/sit bones and even the tops of the feet against the floor, for strong support and resonance work.

1.24.4 Placement and pitch

- After pouring, sweeping and playing with the floor, come to standing, and open out into easy vowels.

- 'Mah' into 'ah' in your chest area, repeat lots of times. Then glide up onto a slightly higher pitch of 'ah' or 'mah' into the oral space, gliding into an 'ee' sound in the mouth, then pitch up again easily into an 'ee' in the head.

- Glide down through the mouth, and into the chest on 'ah', then glide down into 'oh', then 'aw', then 'oo'.

- Glide back up to the chest, around the middle of your range. The sounds should be free, easy and strong.

This is a lovely, easy way to get the voice warm, supported, resonance, forward and open. It also warms up the whole body.

1.24.5 Placement and resonance

- Standing easily in alignment, let in a breath and 'mah' out, sensing the sound coming out of your back and at the same time imagining it going forwards in an arc.

- Place one hand on your centre front, the other on your back. This will encourage you to find 'back' resonance, which has the wonderful effect of placing your voice very forwards into the space. It achieves a big sound with as little effort as possible.

- Keep repeating this until you feel ready to add text – use your sonnet. Put the sound and your text into the space. And as usual, walk this, try stepping back then forth as you sound and speak out, and keep walking and moving as you speak.

1.24.6 Articulation

- Do a quick massage of the articulators, do some drills and then go through the articulation sheets as last session.

Text: sonnets

Here is a whole raft of exercises for you to play with on your sonnet:

- Breath points – how and where does it breathe?

- Notes in register – play with your range connected to thought changes.

- Arc of the line – keep the thought up and through to the end.

- Rhythm – dance, step, tap, speak.

- Whisper it through. Then in pairs, speak the sonnet quietly to a partner.

- Falling inflection – 'and another thing' (see 3.14a).

- Line endings – finger click on word ends (3.14c).

- Antithesis – look for these, point them up by use of pitch and thought variations.

- Walk the journey of the thoughts.

- Vowels and consonants.

- Sing your sonnet.

- Pour and sweep with your sonnet – you will find the text pouring out of you without judgement.

Session 25

Keywords: *Filling the space in the body and in the room; articulation; sonnet work continued*

1.25.1 Warm-up

- Begin today with a gentle shake-out and spine roll as last time.

- Walk and move around the space using voiceless sounds and then onto gentle voicing, to find release and gentle support.

1.25.2 Floor work

- Lie in semi-supine, let in a breath, and for every breath, release on the following sounds at least two or three times each: 'f', 'v', 's', 'z', 'm', 'mah'.

1.25.3 Pour and sweep

- Do some easy pouring with 'sh' and then 'v', then try out some easy sweeping with the body, adding in voiced sounds (see the last session).

- As you sweep from one side onto your back and over to the other side, add in further sounds. When your voice feels really warm, begin to use some text.

Being heard in the space

At this point, it is useful to point out that, as your voice is now beginning to flesh out and gain some depth and weight, you can also feel more able to sound out and speak into a reasonable-sized space. If you are working in studios, it will all be very easy; if you are lucky enough to have access to a theatre space, then now is a good time to try out your developing voice for size. Don't expect it to be huge, and don't push or strain, but in a studio theatre you can easily be heard. Remember to shape the words and articulate clearly, as this makes a huge difference. Above all, as you speak into the room or space, think about sharing your sound with an audience. Being heard is no problem technically if you have a supported, resonant and forward placed voice with clear articulation. But if you push, no one will want to listen and you may sound hoarse or damage your voice. If you pull back on your voice it will retreat into you. In terms of getting that voice and text out to your audience, think only about sharing. Your intention is everything – if you connect breath and thought and add in all these technical niceties, and choose to connect the ideas of the text with your audience, then it will all be there for you.

- Stand in the space and hum to the wall, easily but clearly. Now try walking all round – if you're in a theatre space, include walking up into the seating area, behind the seating if you can. In fact, walk the whole space *and at the same time* breathe and release your breath on an 'f' as you do this. This means you are breathing the space, and making a familiar and easy connection to it.

- Come back to the central stage area or middle of the studio and just take it in. Now 'f' to your audience, to the walls, to the back. Remember, there is no need to push, just let it come out of you. As you let the next breath in, feel your sound returning to you from the space – this will give you a great sense of ownership and ease.

- Now hum and then release into a 'mah' towards the wall. Keeping that in mind, turn your back to the wall and continue to hum and 'mah' into the space, whilst at the same time imagining and feeling that your sound is coming from the wall behind you. This will not only help your back resonance, it will keep the sound placed forwards and give you a fuller sound out into the playing area.

- Hum and 'mah' to the walls, and walk around, sounding your voice throughout the room. Move the whole body, open out the arms, reach up and down and out, all the while maintaining a connection to your centre, and a sense of ease.

- Try out some bits of text following the same patterns, and/or lines from your sonnet.

1.25.5   Articulation

- Do a quick massage of the articulators, some drills and then go through the articulation pages (TIV3ab).

1.25.6   Text: sonnets and alliteration

Here is a further aspect of text to look at. Alliteration has two elements – the repetition of consonant sounds is called consonance, and the repetition of vowel sounds is called assonance. Point up the alliterative sounds (repeated sounds within a phrase). Here the consonance is shown in bold, and assonance is in italics – for assonance, the whole word or syllable may be in italics but it is the vowel sounds we are looking at.

> When I do **c**ount the **c**lo**ck** tha**t t**ells the **t**ime
> Nor *dare* I question with my jealous thought,
> *Where* you *may* be, or your af*fairs* suppose;
> But, like a **s**ad **s**lave, *stay* and think of nought,
> **S**ave, where you are how happy you *make* those.

Exaggerate to begin with, then speak more naturally – but feel the effect of the exaggeration so that you really use the alliteration. Find examples in your chosen sonnet and repeat the exercise. Notice what effect it has on the meaning and the feel of the poem.

Session 26

Keywords: *Physicalisation of sounds through the body; resonance; sonnet work*

Warm-up

1.26.1

- Gently shake out and roll up and down the spine with 'f' and 'sh'. Then walk and move around the space using voiceless sounds. This could take between five and ten minutes.

- Then go onto gentle voicing, to find release and gentle support.

Floor work

1.26.2

Repeat 1.25.7.

Pour and sweep

1.26.3

- Do some easy pouring with 'sh' and then 'v'. Try out some easy sweeping with the body, adding in voiced sounds.

Pour with text

1.26.4

- Continue to pour and sweep those open sounds, then start to bring in some lines from your sonnet. You will find that the text just pours out of you.

- Come to standing and keep moving with the sensation of pouring and sweeping as you walk, and add text.

1.26.5   Resonance

- Hum and 'mah' to a spot on the wall, move away and send the sound into the room. Feel your voice becoming an all-round sound.

- Stand and hum into 'mah', and imagine your voice coming out of your back, then coming from your front centre and going over you in a wide arc into the space.

1.26.6   Articulation

- Do a quick massage of the lips and tongue, and do some yawning. Go through lip and tongue stretches and exercises, then take it onto consonant drills.

- Go through the sequences in Appendices TIV3a and b. You may find that the consonant clusters on TIV3b are rather challenging – this is early second-year work, but it is a great introduction to the work on these clusters (where two or more consonants appear together, for example s+t+r gives you 'str', and s+k+t gives you 'skt'). Have a go if you feel ready, and notice how much is going on at the articulators, and how much tune you may hear from these complex sounds. They add many layers to the sound of a text.

1.26.7   Articulation race

If the group is ready for this (warmed up and very free), you can have some fun by having a 'race' with the sequence of 'patakah paytaykay peeteekee paytaykay pahtahkah' (the whole caboodle). I often say that none of the work in voice is a competition, and it isn't! Never compete with yourself or anyone else when acquiring technique or when applying it creatively, either. It does not matter if someone has greater capacity or a stronger tone than you, but do let those agile and strong voices inspire you. As for articulation, it's the same thing really.

And now for a total contradiction – be really competitive just for once. Get the whole group to do the whole sequence together, slowly, and then picking up pace until you are going as fast as you can, whilst still maintaining accuracy. Then you can try it out in pairs, and eliminate until you have found the fastest two, and find a 'winner'. Again, I do this for fun, and sometimes it has the effect of the so-called 'best' articulators/speakers going out in the first round, because they get so excited, and yes, so outrageously competitive, that it all goes wrong. What is important here is to just have a laugh. Because what often results is that those people who sometimes struggle will cast caution to the wind and find they can suddenly do a sequence that they had never been able to do before. And who cares if it all goes wrong? It's only one session in a lifetime! It is also a great way to use the trust you have built up in the group, so really support each other in this and become a great ensemble.

Text: sonnets

1.26.8

Speak through your sonnet and check that the breath is supporting the thoughts, and try out any exercises you feel you need to repeat.

Think also about this – who are you saying it to and for? Remember, these are intimate poems, so you might find saying your sonnet to one person is enough, as long as you share your sound and thoughts with the space and the audience, but keep the intention intimate. That way we will all hear it, but it will be very personal.

Session 27

Keywords: *Warm-up into resonance work; surround sound; articulation and text; revision, plenary*

1.27.1–1.27.4

Repeat 1.26.1–1.26.4.

1.27.5 Intoning into speaking

- Intoning with a count from one to ten, then one to twenty.

- Now intone from one to five and then make a smooth transition into speaking from six to ten.

- Intone a few lines of your sonnet. Repeat intoning, and make the transition into speaking.

1.27.6 Support placement and resonance

- Do some horizontal abseiling, and be really free, so that – as you bounce off the walls with your sounds, from 'v' to 'z' to humming and 'mah'-ing – you softly bounce away from the wall support, back into and across the space. This is great for being conscious of spatial awareness too, so that you don't bump into each other!

- Bounce from one wall to another, abseil off a door or a pillar in the room, or piano – any firm surface can give you an impetus to move and sound out. Your voice will become very free and really quite powerful.

- Stand and 'mah' and 'mooh' – you will be creating an easy but big sound. Now apply this to text – speak your sonnet into the space, without pushing, but freeing it out into the room.

Articulation

1.27.7

- Massage the lips and tongue, and do some yawning. Go through lip and tongue stretches and exercises, then take it onto consonant drills.

- Go through the sequences on TIV3a, b and c (further consonant clusters) if you feel ready for them. Use the bone prop.

Text: sonnets

1.27.8

- Speak your sonnet with the bone prop and then without.

- Remember to use your range, to point up the antitheses and speak with the balance of the line.

- Use the alliteration and the rhymes.

- Bring it all together.

If you feel something is not quite right, look at all the exercises for the sonnet that were outlined in Session 24.

If in a group, all the sonnets can be presented. You might then talk about the themes, the language, the very sensation of hearing all these sonnets together. Sonnets are like microcosms of text: mini-worlds of incredibly concise and dense language and thoughts. A mere fourteen lines create a whole world that you as a speaker and an actor have to portray with your voice. This is one of the reasons why they are such fabulous things for actors to work on.

If you now read through and speak aloud another sonnet from the sequence, chosen at random, you will find an amazing connection to your voice, to your body, to the words – let yourself be surprised and delighted at how accessible and easy this has all become.

- You might also now try out any piece of text from a play you are working on.

- Speak about your day, or your holiday plans, and be aware of how free and open your voice is.

The integration of all that you have done so far is intimately in your body, mind and voice, and is available to you for your acting and the everyday.

Recap of First-year Voice and Text – Vacation Work

Think about and discuss what you have learned from all the practical voice sessions, and for the last series of sessions think about what you learned from doing sonnets. What do you now feel about your own sonnet, and the sonnet sequence generally? How do you feel about your voice and concomitant speech and text skills, and how aware are you of the integration of those skills with movement and body practice, and the integration of all that into the actor's process? Are you aware of integrating these practices into everyday life, whether that is your everyday speaking voice, the way you move physically, the way you feel, and even the way your confidence may have changed.

Furthermore, you may want to consider what has been learned from ear training/accents work and other elements of voice if you are in training, and how these inform the integration *of all* your work.

Regarding your process in acting work – writing notes up in a formalised actor's notebook as well as keeping a voice journal is incredibly useful. You can plot your progress as well as simply keeping a record of the work you have done, and moreover how you are responding to it. It is so important to remember what's been done so you know what to work on between rehearsals or sessions. This is also very useful for future reference – when you leave drama school, you probably won't do this again, but it can help you enormously if you are struggling with something. You should always jot down the director's notes (and voice/movement/singing notes too), and then, of course, work on them.

Brief Summary of the First Year of Vocal Training

»   Release and relaxation.

»   Alignment – especially the head–neck relationship.

»   The sit bone–heel connection through the pelvis and the importance to voice.

»   A physically warmed-up body.

»   Breath – diaphragmatic and intercostal breath:
    1   Breath centring
    2   Breath capacity
    3   Breath support system
    4   Connecting breath and thought

»   Freeing and opening the channel – the open throat and clean onset.

»   Forward placement.

All of this is to be both technically understood and embraced, as well as creatively and imaginatively.

»   Theory of the voice – vocal anatomy and physiology. If in training, this will be taught as part of your ongoing process. Refer to the Appendix, so that you can now understand what all those parts are involved in. See how much you can work out for yourself.

»   Introduction to resonance – to flesh out the voice, placing sound in different parts, especially into the back and all around and through the body. This also gives you more choices, not just pitch and tone, but also the beginnings of a bigger voice to cope with varying spaces – being heard. This is developed further in the second part.

»   Introduction to articulation – release work into lip, tongue and soft-palate muscularity and precision. Shaping of the word.

»   Consonants are very important. Daily bone-prop work, including five conversations *and* application to articulation and text.

» Vowels also need to be clear, precise (differentiating between short and long vowels, for example) and above all, open. Playing with vowel sounds.

» Application to the word.

» Creative voice – imagery, pathways through the body.

» Text – this is summarised in suggestions for planning a course, in Part 3.

» Practical voice and text – application of all skills to acting *and* the everyday voice.

» Vocal health and the importance of hydration – maintain a good level of water intake. Also look at 'steaming' at the end of Part 4.

» Overview of integration – the physical body, using the body to support the voice and speech, can be seen on the DVD, so you get a clear sense of how it can all work together to integrate and deepen the experience of the work.

You might now have an extended vacation, so do keep up with regular voice and speech practice, so that you don't lose it!

Part 2

The Voice Gains 'Oomph'

Part 2a

'The voice gains "oomph".' By this I mean that, after a year or so of training, you can now begin to 'up the ante' and work progressively towards strengthening the voice and gaining good muscularity – but, as always, through an easy, released body and voice.

As your voice begins to develop and you begin your second year of training, you can also go right back to the start. This is not just a question of repetition, but you may well find that a revision of the absolute basics will really pay dividends. Go through the first two or three sessions from Part 1 – if you do this for a couple of weeks, you will find that the acquired physical knowledge in the body/voice responds very well. You can do this as a precursor to the sessions in this chapter. So start with plenty of release, breath centring, and gentle onset work.

Session 1

Keywords: *Revision of the basics; introduction to stamina*

First of all, check that you have understood what is meant by 'support'. There are so many ways to express this, and a subject of much discussion amongst voice teachers, but here follows one simple way to express the mechanics of it:

'Support' is the engagement of the abdominals and pelvic floor muscles *in conjunction with* the coming-together of the vocal folds to create a supported breath stream and vocal sound – the breath and the voice.

You need a constant stream of air at consistent pressure; this is achieved by use of the abdominals (and pelvic floor once you know what you are doing with the abdominal muscles) to support the outgoing airstream, on a sound that is produced by clean onset and closure/opening of the vocal folds. Being off-support can sometimes be easier to identify – generally, if a person is off-support, the voice sounds weak or weedy, or very pushed and constricted, and quite possibly rather 'creaky'. It is also not connected to the centre either physiologically or emotionally and, when it comes to speaking text, very often sounds unconnected and lacking in truth. So get that support system in place and it will help you both as an actor and as a speaker in life.

Clean-hands exercise; alignment and preparation for breath centring

- With very clean hands, stand easily and freely, shake out, then float your fingers up into the mouth and get them working the inside of the lips and cheeks. Also massage the cheeks and jaw from the outside, quite firmly but softening as you do it.

- Simultaneously, let the breath into your centre, and be aware of the breath coming in and out as you work the mouth into openness and ease.

Tapping to wake up the lungs and breath

- Stand freely, and tap all over the body. Pat with your hand all down one arm, hand, fingers, back up and all over that arm, whilst releasing the breath on a gentle continuous 'f'. Now do the other arm with an 's'. Go on to tapping up and down the legs, using 'sh'.

- Come back up and tap the top of the shoulder, the upper chest, lower-front ribs on that side, the side ribs, and as much of your back as is easy. Do this all with 'f' or 's', then do the other side with one of those sounds.

- Take your attention to your head, and tap lightly with your fingertips all over the head with a 'sh'. Tap the face lightly, massage the ears with little circular movements, ending by gently tugging the earlobes, all the while using voiceless sounds.

By now you should be feeling quite tingly, and the breath is well and truly centred and alive. It is also extending its capacity without any effort.

Capacity and support work

- Stand freely, let the breath in and release the outgoing breath stream on a constant, steady 's'. You can time this, to see how long your sound lasts, and then do the same thing whilst walking round the space, or doing an activity.

Keep the sound constant in order to engage your support muscles. Or engage the support muscles in order to keep the sound constant! It works both ways; it's the same thing.

- Do the same but with a baby 'f'. Notice any difference in ease, feel, and particularly the length of time you can sustain the sound. Spend a good ten minutes on these exercises.

- Repeat, this time with a gentle, continuous 'v' sound, standing still and then walking around. It is best if you can do both. Then explore this voiced version on 'z', then 'zh' (as in 'measure'). Most people find that the voiced sounds do not last as long, but there are always exceptions. Simply notice how much you can do easily, and then extend it over a period of time.

This is about gaining improved capacity, a more engaged support system, and increasing stamina.

- Try walking around the room on a hum, and do a bit of chewing whilst you hum, to ensure the voice is forward.

- Then take it onto a hum into an 'ah' sound – 'mah' – keeping the sound steady.

- Try different pitches and volumes, but within an easy range. By now you can hopefully tell if your voice is ready to extend itself – if you are not sure, then it probably isn't warmed-up enough, so keep to the middle of your range until it feels easy enough to go further.

- You can also try taking this 'mah' sound into sitting, lying down and getting up. Then try a line of text (something you know or what you want for dinner. It's just talking!)

2.1.4   Forward placement

- Place the voice as we have done previously (see 1.7 for more detail), by humming towards a point ahead of you, and sharing your hum, your sound, and your intention, with a point or object or person, somewhere in front of you. Feel the hum buzz onto your lips – this helps remind you that it is forward. As always, ensure that the sound is easy.

- Release that sound on some open vowels, remembering not to push the sound.

- Start to lengthen your sound, and ensure that you maintain engagement with support.

- Open it out into easy vowel sounds and challenge both ease of sound and increasing capacity at the same time.

- You can also play with these sounds in a group, going round the circle playing with different vowels and consonants. Share it with each other.

Articulation 2.1.5

Do a little articulation work – massage the lips, bite the tongue, have a few yawns, and then play around with some consonant drills learned from Part 1. This is just a taster to prepare your speech organs for a little text work.

Capacity with text 2.1.6

Before we begin applying capacity and stamina to complex text, remind yourself of the simple capacity work done on 'The House that Jack Built'. Take a look at that text again (1.20.3).

- Repeat this breath–thought and capacity work and remember to make it 'make sense'. In other words, don't read it monotonously as if it were 'just an exercise' by going into autopilot. Think about what you are saying, so that your thought and your voice create a picture of each element. Then try it out in a variety of accents – just have a go at some you may know already. If you have not done accent and dialect work yet, then you can always make something up – it's great fun to try and create a different way of speaking, even if you copy someone else's accent to just get a feel for something a little different. If you apply accent work to the capacity passage, one will feed into the other's work very neatly.

This not only stops you fixating or worrying about the capacity work itself, it also helps you integrate yet another skill as you go along.

In the following sessions we will be looking at capacity and the breath–thought connection in a more complex way, with some short contrasting extracts from Shakespeare.

Continue to have those five bone-prop conversations a day, preceded by some clean-hands work, or gentle massaging.

Session 2

Keywords: *Muscular capacity; support for stamina; resonance and articulation*

As with the last session, we begin with a revision of an important voice principle – this time it is about resonance. Check that you have understood what resonance is. What is it for? How do you know if you are resonating, and where?

As we saw in 1.11, resonance is vibration in a cavity or space. You can also feel sympathetic vibration through the body's structures. By sounding your voice and placing your hands on different areas such as the chest, skull, nose, etc., you can feel that vibration externally, and this in turn can help you feel those vibrations internally. By vibrating and resonating your vocal sound more fully and freely, you begin to 'flesh out' the voice, developing greater depth and range of pitch and dynamics. As you progress further in your training, you not only develop a stronger and much fuller voice, but those tones and dynamics you are developing will help you with character work. It is not just about being heard clearly in different spaces, or even about the overall quality of the voice for its own sake, but bringing life and variety to your sound so you are more able to make creative choices as an actor.

2.2.1 Centre the voice

- Go through some clean-hands work to release, soften and open the mouth and breath channel. Now place your hands at your centre, let the breath drop in and release on a gentle 'f'. Do this for a couple of minutes.

- Change the position of the hands – have one at the front over your navel, and one on your back in the equivalent spot. Feel or imagine the breath dropping into your centre, all the way round and through you, and imagine the sensation of breathing both into your tummy and into your lower back/lumbar region.

- Revise the sensation and physicality of the rib swing (1.6.5) by placing your hands (or the backs of your hands) on your ribcage at either side at the widest or most moveable point.

- Then one hand goes back to the tummy, the other stays on the ribs, all the while you are breathing and releasing on 'f', 's' or 'sh'.

- Swap hands. Move your hands so one is on the side ribs, and the other is at the lumbar region. Moving them around reminds you, or more importantly reminds your breath, to drop into the whole region and emanate a sound from there.

- You can then bring this all to standing if you were sitting and move around the room.

2.2.2 Tapping to wake up the lungs and breath further

- Go through some body tapping as explored often in Part 1, begin with a few taps released on 'f', 's', 'sh', and then add in voiced sounds like 'v', 'z' and humming.

2.2.3 Floor work for release, ease and warming the voice

- Lie in semi-supine, allow the spine to release and soften into the floor.

- Gently roll your head from side to side on an easy sound, and then gradually rock from side to side on a 'sh', rather like the pouring from the earlier chapter (1.12).

- Repeat for a couple of minutes, then take onto the usual voiced sounds of 'v', 'z', 'zh', 'm'.

- Roll over and come into the prayer pose and, again, release the breath on a variety of the sounds you have been exploring.

Here is a useful idea for changing the position and sensation through the body – try out the following different positions of the arms. Lie in child pose:

(i) arms out ahead of you with palms flat on the floor.

(ii) arms out ahead of you with palms facing (so the sides of the hands are on the floor).

(iii) arms out ahead of you with palms facing upwards.

(iv) arms behind you, palms facing down, and then up

All the while you are exploring, and you may find the breath dropping in slightly differently in terms of direction, place and feel, and the outgoing sounds may also change. There is no right or wrong here, unless a position causes you to constrict. Simply experiment and find the positions that help you and your voice.

- With an easy sound, perhaps a 'v' or a hum, roll up through the spine with a lengthening neck until you are kneeling up, then gently – with sound – bring yourself to standing. Have a very easy shake, and wave the arms around through extension as if they were wings. There will hopefully be a very free and open sensation through the body, and the sound will follow.

2.2.4 Place the voice forwards and resonate – a duvet of hum

- Walking around the room or space, feel the floor through your feet as you float up through the spine simultaneously, and sound out with 'vvv', 'zzz', etc. Then hum and do some chewing, massage the lips, and move with sound.

- Stand easily and hum, opening your hands out to the sides and at the same time *step back* into sound. Take a step or two forwards for the breath to drop in, then step back, whilst releasing the arms out on your hum.

- As you step back, imagine that your back is resting and easing into a nice, warm duvet, but instead of a feather duvet, it is just your hum – so it is like you have a duvet made of hums! Explore this for a few minutes, taking it onto a 'mah' or 'moo'. Your sound should start coming forward, be incredibly free, and very full.

- Play with pitch too.

2.2.5 Challenge muscularity and energy

- Walk around the room or space, this time with a good deal of energy and purpose, and let that sound out into open vowels, mixing and matching different combinations of consonants and vowels. This is not pushed, but it *is* muscular and energised work.

2.2.6 Articulation

- Do some preparation exercises, such as massaging then stretching the lips, and take on to a few lip sounds ('bbb', 'ppp', 'mmm', 'www') using the bone prop.

- Gently chew and massage the tongue, go through some big and then precise stretches, mix and match with vocal sounds, then take on to tongue-tip drills ('ddd', 'ttt', 'nnn', 'lll' and so on) with the prop.

- Go on to some yawning and releasing of the soft palate into sounds ('ggg', 'kkk', 'ng ng ng') with and then without the prop.

- Try out a few articulation sequences that you've already learnt, first with the bone prop and then without.

Text for capacity and the breath–thought connection (i)   2.2.7

We have already worked on breath capacity in a variety of different ways, and applied that work to text with 'The House that Jack Built'. We are now going to look not just at capacity on text as an exercise in extending the breath and voice, but applying this work to complex texts, to understand more deeply the connection between breath and thought. I use passages from Shakespeare because the writing exemplifies the importance of this principle so clearly. We will look at *Othello* this week, with two further extracts in the following sessions, and then bring them all together.

Capacity and the breath–thought connection in Shakespeare – what does each piece require and how do they differ?

Brief context: at this point in the play, Iago has manipulated Othello to such a point that he is now enraged and unable to hold back his anger. Iago has to say very little, and Othello is off like a raging torrent.

- Look at the length of thought. At the start of Othello's speech, there is a very short thought ('Never, Iago.') This requires only a very small (centred) breath, but it is a separate thought.

- You then take a deeper and bigger breath from 'Like to the Pontic...' (it is taken as easily as any breath). Just because you need more, you should not snatch in the breath or make it a big deal – but it *is* a new thought and therefore needs a new breath. This requires considerable skill and patient work.

  IAGO.
  > Patience, I say: your mind perhaps may change.

  OTHELLO.
  > Never, Iago. Like to the Pontic sea,
  > Whose icy current and compulsive course

189

> Ne'er feels retiring ebb, but keeps due on
> To the Propontic and the Hellespont,
> Even so my bloody thoughts with violent pace
> Shall ne'er look back, ne'er ebb to humble love,
> Till that a capable and wide revenge
> Swallow them up.

Read this through on your feet, physicalising it as much as possible, and then look up any words you don't know. Think about the antitheses, the contrasts, such as 'icy current' with 'compulsive course', and 'bloody thoughts' with 'humble love'. Notice how passionate this piece of text feels, and see how that one long thought drives through to the final stop. You could, in theory, take a breath just before 'even so' – but what this does is effectively to stop the flow.

Try the text by speaking on one breath through to 'Hellespont', take another breath and carry on from 'Even so' to the end. Now try taking more breath, and motor on past 'Even so' – and even if you only get to 'violent pace' on that one breath, you will notice the relentless nature of this big thought. You can then work on it bit by bit, until able to take the whole thought on one breath. This is just an exercise but is also about options for you as an actor, so that you can try out what is written by the author before deciding to do it another way.

Another point to mention here is about understanding text and looking things up – if you have established that the Pontic Sea is the Black Sea, the Propontic is the Sea of Marmara, and so on, you may know what these words are. But if you then look at an atlas, or go online to find these bodies of water, you will see something quite amazing – look at how one large body of water flows through and is squeezed into a narrow channel, and then... look for yourself, and then try out the text again. It is quite a thrill!

Practise this speech over the coming days (and weeks) so that soon you will be able to cope with the whole thing on those two breaths.

Session 3

Keywords: *Muscular capacity and support for stamina; nasal and oral resonance; articulation*

Centre the voice first

`2.3.1`

Have a little shake, massage and open up the oral space, and then centre the breath with some easy 'f' sounds for a minute or two. Place your hands at your centre, front and back, to remind your body if necessary.

Sun salutation and the voice ⊚

`2.3.2`

We are now going to use a well-known sequence based on a part of yoga practice. I would advise you to watch the sequence on the DVD before starting this exercise, as it's much simpler to understand visually how to achieve it. If you have any injury or condition that might make this difficult, use another sequence, or devise a simple routine that gets the body moving, and apply the vocal work to it. If you are in training, you may have been taught something similar, and you may be able to get someone to check that your alignment, positioning and body usage are helpful to the exercise. I would certainly not use this in the first year of training unless the students are being taught this kind of work formally, and it is quite demanding on the body, so work with a real sense of ease and awareness. However, it is a wonderful workout in its own right, and if you apply breath and voice to the sequence, the

191

body will be helped by the breath and sounding work, and your voice will learn to become stronger and much more consistent. It may sound a bit 'wavery' to start with, so this teaches you to establish and maintain a clean, smooth sound.

Go through the whole sequence once or twice without any sounding, to establish what you are doing. Then, on each complete cycle, release the out-breath on 'f', and do this at least three times. Then do three cycles on an 's', and three on a 'sh', and start to notice how easy the movement feels, and how the breath starts to really flow through the body.

I find it is better not to be too prescriptive about when to breathe in and when to breathe or sound out. The start of the sequence is definitely on an in-breath as your arms reach up, and the out-breath accompanies the first downward phase. On the DVD, the breath sequence is guided to get you started, but you can find your own pattern eventually.

You may find that is enough for today, but if you want to explore this with voicing, do the whole sequence with a 'v' and then 'z' and a hum.

The sun salutation will have warmed up and stretched the whole body, and the voice will have been expanded, capacity work challenged, and the support system thoroughly engaged. If you feel your capacity is still not there, do something like the beach-ball sequence or just taking the baby 'f' or 'v' for an extended walk.

2.3.3   Walking with sound

- Walk around the space whilst sounding out on 'vvv', 'zzz', etc., and at the same time do some chewing, massage the lips, and play with the buzz and vibrations.

2.3.4   Place the voice forwards and resonate

- Repeat the 'duvet of hum' from the last session (2.2.4).

Nasal resonance

We are going to start looking at specific placements for different resonances. Nasal resonance is a very important element to the voice – too little and the voice sounds 'bunged up', as if you have a cold; too much and it is overly strident and quite unpleasant. However, a lot of strong, bright nasal resonance can be very useful in certain situations, both in life and as an actor, because it gives an incredibly loud sound almost 'for free'. It can also give a potentially humorous or 'annoying' quality to a character voice. This is about further choices, so that you integrate the technique into artistry and have something extra to play with.

- Hum up into your head, ensuring that you are connected to your support system. Place your hands on your skull as you hum, then place a hand on the back of your skull and feel the buzz there. Now place your fingers on your forehead and see if that is buzzy, then onto the cheekbones. Now place your fingers on your nose and massage the bridge of the nose in particular. Feel and hear the vibrations in your nose.

- Continue to hum and buzz your nose, then bring the fingers away and reach slightly forwards and out to the sides (so you initialise a 'v' formation with your arms, and they can then open out more) as you release the sound into an 'ah' or 'mah' – this will help the sound open out.

- Play with this for a good few minutes.

- Begin to notice the sound as you experiment going from 'mmm' or 'nnnn' into 'ah' or 'oo'.

What you are looking for here is a nasal resonance on the hum of 'm' or 'n' (or 'ng') and then a very open sound on the vowel. This is to get the soft palate to do its work efficiently – so that it is down in order to get the sound (the passage of air) up into the nose for the nasal consonants, and then it jumps back up so the passage of air comes out of the mouth with the vowels. Using the hands to guide the sound into the nose with a massage, and then springing them away from the face for the vowels, will help this process.

- Open your throat and speak a few words up into your head. It may sound rather strange, possibly very 'bright' and loud. It may not be a particularly 'pretty' sound, but just go with it without judgement and see what happens.

2.3.6   Oral resonance

- Do a little humming and then really open up into the oral space, sounding a very free 'ah' or 'oo' and see how light and open your voice can be. This will bring your voice away from that strongly nasal sound into the mouth and give it a lighter feel. Try out a few words here.

- Now a little humming and bang the chest at the same time, and then open out into a 'mah' from the chest area. This should bring the voice down in pitch a little and restore a kind of balanced and warmer sound.

2.3.7   Resonance and articulation

- Go through the 'hah hey hee hey' sequence.

- Do a quick massage of the lips, bite the tongue a little, and try out some articulation drills – 'bbbbbbbbb-ba', 'dddddddd-da', etc.

2.3.8   Text for capacity and the breath–thought connection (ii)

Having worked on the *Othello* passage last session, we now take a look at an extract from *Richard III*. This passage also has quite a complex structure in terms of breath management, but places different demands on your technique.

Brief context: Queen Margaret is talking to the Duchess of York (Richard's mother) about the 'creature' that the Duchess gave birth to and the horror that he has become. It is an awful speech in some ways, with some incredibly strong images.

- Go through the speech physically, moving it very clearly and strongly as you speak, so that you get a real sense of her passion and anger, and also the enormity of what she is saying. Connect to the image – right from the start of this passage, she talks to an almost broken woman and describes her womb as being like a kennel producing this dog from Hell. It is strong stuff.

QUEEN MARGARET.
>From forth the kennel of thy womb hath crept
A hellhound that doth haunt us all to death.
That dog that had his teeth before his eyes
To worry lambs and lap their gentle blood,
That foul defacer of God's handiwork,
That excellent grand tyrant of the earth
That reigns in gallèd eyes of weeping souls,
Thy womb let loose to chase us to our graves.
O upright, just, and true disposing God,
How *do* I thank thee that this carnal cur
Prays on the issue of his mother's body
And makes her pew fellow with others' moan!

Queen Margaret's thoughts are very different from Othello's, with different lengths. Note that there are three thoughts here – from 'From forth' to 'death'; 'That' to 'graves'; and 'O' to 'moan'. So you have two lines, then six, and then four. That might sound easier than Othello's charge of seven or so lines, but in fact it is hugely demanding because of the sheer size of her thoughts.

At the same time, start to really engage with the language – with a passage like this, you can really chew it up. When you say 'crept' ensure that the voiceless 'p' and 't' are crisp – there is something very unpleasant in this. In 'dog', the 'd' and 'g' are very muscular and precise. Open up to the possibilities of the 'O' – this is not a small prayer! Also use the iambic – I have italicised 'do' because, although it is possible to stress that line 'HOW do I thank thee', I feel it is much stronger as a regular iambic – 'How DO i THANK thee'. Try them both aloud and see how they feel. The word 'issue' is so much better if you say 'IS-yoo' and not 'ISHoo' – the hissy 's' gives that extra unpleasant side to what Margaret is saying.

Practise this speech over time, in addition to Othello's speech, so that soon you will be able to cope with his speech on two breaths and Margaret's on three.

Session 4

Keywords: *Muscular capacity and support for stamina; resonance; articulation*

2.4.1   Centre the body and voice

- Do a few shakes and massages, using gentle voiceless sounds.

2.4.2   Warm up the body and voice with the sun salutation ⌖

Go through the sun sequence without sound initially, in order to establish good practice and to ensure that you are centred and soft through the joints, and that your directions or pathways through the body are clear.

Do the sun salutation and release your out-breath on 'f' for an entire cycle, then on 's', 'sh', 'v', 'z', 'zh' and a hum for each complete sequence.

2.4.3   Sun with open sound

You may be ready to do the whole sun exercise on an open sound. As you have let in the breath on the upward reach, you drop down on the hum, and if it feels comfortable in the throat (and head and nose) you can release onto a 'mah' sound.

You may find this is unpleasant, or you might love it. Be prepared to play and keep trying things out. If it doesn't feel or sound right when chanting 'mah' whilst effectively upside down, you can just hum on the way down, and when you come up to standing, then you release your hum into 'mah'. You may find 'mah' is good in the prayer position, not so good in the downward-facing-dog position. It is trial and error, so experiment and see where your body and your voice *want* to sound out.

Baby 'f' and beach-ball sequence   2.4.4

This is a good time to revise some basic work, and see how the whole mechanism responds – so do some baby 'f' work, and perhaps the beach-ball sequence, either as an additional help, or instead of the sun salutation.

Forward placement – clean fingers!   2.4.5

This is also a reminder about forward placement with a little extra.

- Ensure that you have clean fingers and hum a little, then bring it onto a 'mah'.

- Place the knuckle of your index finger onto the alveolar ridge (the roof of your mouth, just behind the upper-front teeth) with the finger bent, and hum. Keep humming for a minute, and then whilst humming, bring your finger out of the mouth and forward fairly quickly, making sure that you don't bash your teeth in the process! It may need to be a slightly downward motion and then out ahead of you.

- Repeat the process, with the middle finger joint on your alveolar ridge. Now sound out on 'mah', humming with the knuckle in place, and then opening out into 'ah' as you take your finger out and away. Repeat many times until you feel the buzz on your ridge.

- Do it again, this time with 'n'. Then repeat with 'b' so that you 'bah bah bah', as your knuckle presses the ridge and then comes away.

- Repeat with 'd d d' ('dah dah dah').

- Now, without the knuckle there, hum then 'mah', and 'nah', and 'dah dah dah'. You will hopefully get a strong sensation of the sound and your voice whacking forward and out into the space, without any need to push.

- You can also try using your thumbs to lift the upper teeth (or feel as if they are lifting), creating space and forward sensations.

- Hum and 'mah' to the space around you, to the walls and to other people. Then take it onto speaking a few words, your sound reaching out effortlessly and strongly.

2.4.6 Nasal and oral resonance

Repeat the resonator work from last session (2.3.5 and 2.3.6).

2.4.7 Resonance and articulation

- Do the 'figure of eight' (1.12.11) on 'mah may mee may mah maw moo maw mah'.

- You can also use this sequence for capacity, by going round the sequence on one breath, then twice round on one breath, and so on.

- Try intoning or chanting part of the loop of sounds, and then speaking the next part, so that you integrate the sung into the spoken.

Go over Appendices TIV3b and c. Chomp and taste those sound clusters.

2.4.8 Text for capacity and the breath–thought connection (iii)

We now look at a speech from *Hamlet* – Ophelia's thoughts here are all over the place, like her mind. Notice the very different requirements of capacity and stamina here, and how easy and flexible your breathing needs to be to handle the shifts and turns in this speech.

Brief context: She has seen Hamlet in a state of turmoil, and fears he may be going mad. She is utterly confused and unable to comprehend the changes in his personality, and the change in his attitude.

OPHELIA.
> O, what a noble mind is here o'erthrown!
> The courtier's, soldier's, scholar's, eye, tongue, sword;
> Th'expectancy and rose of the fair state,
> The glass of fashion and the mould of form,
> Th'observ'd of all observers – quite, quite down!
> And I, of ladies most deject and wretched,
> That suck'd the honey of his music vows,
> Now see that noble and most sovereign reason,
> Like sweet bells jangled, out of time and harsh;
> That unmatch'd form and feature of blown youth
> Blasted with ecstasy. O, woe is me
> T'have seen what I have seen, see what I see!

Take a look at the chaotic nature of her lines – for example, in the second line, look carefully at her ordering. You might expect that the courtier's tongue and the soldier's sword would go together, and yet see the order of the 'types' and then the order of their accomplishments – they do seem totally muddled up, which are great character clues within the text.

Look up anything you don't understand, physicalise the text. And then go again, paying attention to how this speech breathes. If in any doubt, speak the text as you walk round and change direction on every punctuation point, whilst maintaining the integrity of the breath supporting the whole thought, so that you use one breath from the start of a 'sentence' or thought and go right through to the full stop or exclamation mark, whilst simultaneously switching directions at each comma, dash, stop – this is quite tricky!

- Read all three passages, and see if you can feel, then understand, the different requirements of breath management, and what these different capacities ask of you as an actor. What do these differently breathed speeches give you as a creative artist? What clues is the writer giving you as to meanings, state of mind, and so on?

Continue to practise these each week, so that you build up your technique, your stamina, and your continuing pursuit of integration into acting.

Session 5

Keywords: *Capacity and support for stamina and agility; resonance and articulation continued*

Centre the body and voice

2.5.1

- With clean hands, massage the mouth and tongue.
- Do a few shakes and massages, using gentle, voiceless sounds.

Centre and warm the voice with the sun salutation

2.5.2

- Go through the sun sequence, and release your out-breath on 'f' for an entire cycle, then on 's', 'sh', 'v', 'z', 'zh' and a hum for each complete sequence.

Sun with open sound

2.5.3

- Do the whole sun exercise on an open sound, from humming into 'mah' or 'moo'.

Constructive rest

2.5.4

- Lie in semi-supine in 'constructive rest' – what I mean by this is that, when you have been working through a physical sequence like the sun salutation, it can be very useful to then lie in the supine position, and notice how released the body and breath are. Because you are very present, this resting is more than usually active and constructive.

- Release the spine, then let a breath in and release the out-breath – using one breath, release it on a continuous 'f-s-sh', gliding and merging from one to the next. On the next breath, repeat.

- Then on one out-breath, release on 'sh-s-f'. This should be an easy glide, with the placement of sound going from back (past the alveolar ridge) then sliding forward onto the ridge, and finally gliding into the labio-dental (lip and teeth) position with the 'f'.

- Repeat on voiced sounds, going from 'v-z-zh' on one breath; then coming from back to front on 'zh-z-v'.

Notice the effect of lying and gently releasing sound after the strenuous sun salutations.

2.5.5 Further capacity and support

If you feel you want more support and capacity work, come up to standing and walk around the space whilst releasing on the continuant voiceless and voiced sounds. Your body and voice will tell you what you may need at this stage.

2.5.6 Forward placement and resonance

- Do the knuckle work (2.4.5) from the last session.
- Take it on to humming and 'mah-ing' into the space around you.

2.5.7 Nasal, oral and skull resonance

- Repeat the resonator work again from 2.2.4.
- Bring this into some skull-resonance work – hum using 'm', 'n', or 'ng', whilst at the same time rolling up and down the spine. As you come up, release the sound into free, easy and high pitches of 'ah' and 'ooh'. Reach and release upwards with the hands at the same time, to encourage the sound to come out of the top of the head.

- Standing, tap the head all over as you hum, then lift the fingers up and away from your skull as you 'mee' and 'mah'.

- Drop down on a hum and, as you hang upside down, let some free and easy sounds pour out of your head towards the floor. It may feel and sound odd, which is just fine. Then let in a new breath, come up on an 'ng' and as your head comes up into alignment, release an open vowel sound out of the top of your head.

- Do this all again, playing with pitch range, ensuring it is always easy and open.

- Finally, standing tall, let in a breath, and hum into your chest. Then sound out a 'mah' from your centre, and see just how full your sound can become. Bang your chest too, as this can really help relax the soft palate, tongue and throat. Shake and sound out of the whole body.

Articulation   2.5.8

- Prepare the lips and tongue with massaging, chewing, kissing, grinning, lip curls, stretching and releasing, thick and thin, tongue rolls and so on.

- Do some simple consonant drills 'bbbbbbbb-ba', 'dddddddd-da', 'gggggggg-ga', etc., using the bone prop.

- Go through the 'patahkah' sequence quite quickly.

- Do the entire sequence 'patakabadagamanalathafasathavaza', etc., using the prop.

Restoration extracts   2.5.9

We are now going to use some texts from the latter half of the seventeeth century. This is a period known as the Restoration, which is both a political and social term. The king (Charles I) had been ousted from the throne and beheaded, and there followed a period of rule under the Cromwells, when no monarch ruled and theatres were closed. In 1660, Charles I's son and heir, who had been in exile in France, was returned to England and became

Charles II – hence the 'Restoration' of the monarchy. At about the same time, the theatres were reopened. Charles II brought with him many influences from France, and it was a period of lavish costume, great spectacle and, for the first time in England, women were allowed on stage as actors (there were female performers, such as dancers, before this, but not actresses). The extravagance is also seen in the language of Restoration comedy. Here, following the very visceral, emotional and gut-centred Jacobean theatre, the emphasis is on wit and sex. If Elizabethan and Jacobean text might be described as living in the heart and guts, Restoration comedies may be said to live in the head and the groin. The plays and style were very elegant and witty, but also uninhibited, bawdy, and highly 'theatrical'. This language uses ten words instead of one; the love of words is paramount, but this is not superficial stuff. Everything costs, so it is not style for the sake of it. There is a poignancy in Restoration that is very real, underneath all the style, gloss and wit.

As with the Shakespeare extracts used for capacity and breath management, we are going to look at three short pieces from the Restoration era. These will make demands on the breath, but also on articulation and range in the voice. These extracts not only help you to work on capacity, range, pace, clarity, agility of thought and articulation, they also serve as an introduction to a more sophisticated type of text. This may help propel you towards a period in training as an actor that makes greater intellectual as well as technical demands on you.

We begin this session with a piece by George Etherege, in a classic Restoration comedy called *The Man of Mode, or, Sir Fopling Flutter* (the clues are in the names!), Act One, Scene Two.

> EMILIA....Tell us, is there any new wit come forth – songs, or novels?

> MEDLEY. A very pretty piece of gallantry, by an eminent author, called *The Diversions of Brussels* – very necessary to be read by all old ladies who are desirous to improve themselves at questions and commands, blindman's buff, and the like fashionable recreations. / /

Then there is *The Art of Affectation*, written by a late beauty of quality, teaching you how to draw up your breasts, stretch up your neck, to thrust out your breech, to play with your head, to toss up your nose, to bite your lips, to turn up your eyes, to speak in a silly soft tone of a voice, and use all the foolish French words that will infallibly make your person and conversation charming; with a short apology at the latter end, in the behalf of the young ladies who notoriously wash and paint, though they have naturally good complexions.

You will have noticed that Medley has very long thoughts, with many twists and turns, so your voice needs the dexterity to cope. In particular, play with your range in order to help you create a picture through the list of qualities he talks about.

Session 6

Keywords: *Capacity and support for stamina and agility; resonance and articulation continued*

2.6.1   Centre the body and voice

- With clean hands, massage the mouth and tongue.

- Do a few shakes and massages, using gentle voiceless sounds.

2.6.2   A timely reminder about jaw tension

- Lightly place your fingertips over the jaw joints and gently close the teeth together. Notice the muscles engaging over the jaw joint. You might find they bulge out or feel quite tight.

- Gently but firmly massage your scalp on either side of the head. Ensure your fingers and shoulders don't tense up. Keep massaging and gradually bring your fingers down to massage just above and then over the temples. Gradually draw your fingers over the jaw joints, massaging as you come down the jawbone. Massage the whole face gently.

- Drop the head forward and gently flop your cheeks and jaw. With the head dropped, softly massage the jaw joint again, then slowly bring the head up, and stroke down the jaw with your fingers. Let the jaw hang open.

- Repeat the first stage of the exercise. You may find a great difference in the feel of the muscles overlying the jaw joints. They will hopefully be much softer and easier.

Centre and warm the voice with the sun salutation   2.6.3

- Go through the sun sequence, and release your out-breath on 'f' for an entire cycle, then on 's', 'sh', 'v', 'z', 'zh' and a hum for each complete sequence. Then into 'mah'.

- Drink some water!

Forward placement and resonance   2.6.4

- Go through the knuckle work (2.4.5) with 'mmm-moo', 'mmm-mah'.

- Use also the thumb to lift the upper teeth and ridge as you sound out.

Nasal, oral and skull resonance   2.6.5

As with everything in voice, plenty of repetition is required for your body and mind not just to 'get' the work, but to integrate it, so do all the humming and massaging of nose and head, spine rolls down and up, and releasing from nasal consonants into open-vowel sounds in various positions of the body, both down and up.

Articulation preparation   2.6.6

- Repeat 2.5.8, including the entire sequence 'patakabadagamanalathafasathavaza'.

- Work through Appendices TIV3b and c – use the bone prop.

Text – Restoration extracts   2.6.7

The Way of the World by William Congreve is arguably the jewel in the crown of Restoration comedies. Here, in two short extracts, Lady Wishfort (take note of the name, again) reveals her impatience and tyranny over her maid, as well as her rather sad state of mind (Act Three, Scenes One and Three).

LADY WISHFORT. Merciful, no news yet? I have no more patience – if I have not fretted myself till I am pale again, there's no veracity in me. Fetch me the red – the red, do you hear sweetheart? An arrant ash colour, as I'm a person. Look how this wench stirs! Why dost thou not fetch me a little red? Didst thou not hear me, mopus? / Not the ratafia, fool – grant me patience! I mean the Spanish paper, idiot, complexion darling. Paint, paint, paint, dost thou understand that, changeling, dangling thy hands like bobbins before thee? Why dost thou not stir, puppet? thou wooden thing upon wires.

A pox take you – fetch me the cherry brandy....

What a cup thou hast brought! Dost thou take me for a fairy, to drink out of an acorn? Why didst thou not bring thy thimble? Hast thou ne'er a brass thimble clinking in thy pocket with a bit of nutmeg? I warrant thee. Come, fill, fill. So – again.

As with Medley, your voice and speech need to be highly dexterous, light and quick. The breath patterns here are seemingly quite short, but very chaotic and change at lightning speed. Use plenty of range, and don't be afraid to go right up into your 'head' at times. If you stay truthful to the thought and the text, you can take a lot of risks, and it will work if you believe it. Even as an exercise in itself, this will encourage you to expand your vocal range.

Session 7

Keywords: *Stamina and agility; resonance and articulation continued; resonating a playing space*

We are going to consider now the notion of resonance in the playing space. So far, resonance work has been about discovering the different placements in the body, such as head, nasal and oral resonance, and the sensations of sympathetic resonance throughout the body's structures.

Resonance also applies to the space, room, theatre, wherever you are working, acting, speaking. All spaces resonate to some degree (with the obvious exception of a vacuum), and they resonate in different ways: if you are in a huge hall with high ceilings, brick walls and marble floors, you will be aware that the sounds are very 'echoey'. The voice bounces around and off the walls, and sounds are very 'bright' in tone and loud. If you then go into a recording studio with acoustic tiles and carpets and so on, the sound seems 'dead' – it seems to stop right in front of you. In a room or theatre with lots of velvet drapes, curtains, carpets, and indeed a large audience, all these will soak up sound. The voice has to be able to cope with these different spaces, and now that you are developing a much greater range of resonance, pitch, articulation, and deeper awareness of how your voice works in your body, you can explore the possibilities of that voice into different spaces.

Simply put, if you are in a fairly dead space acoustically, you need to balance the voice with lots of bright sounds, placing your vocal awareness into the skull, the mouth, and especially useful are bright nasal resonance and the mask of the face. Tapping your cheek and jawbone as you hum and open into vowel sounds simultaneously will aid the sound in coming forward but also in sounding bright.

If you are in a space that echoes or is loud, you usually need much warmer, 'chest' tones. Articulation also plays a very important part in allowing your sound to be heard in different spaces, so that bright, muscular consonant work and very clear and sharp vowel sounds will be helpful in dull spaces, for example. You also need to shape the words and end them – if word endings drop away, the effect is far worse in a space that is difficult acoustically.

Ultimately, you can only find out how this works by doing it. You must experiment, and because you have spent a long time in training the voice (and continuing to train it over years), you will have an enormous range of possibilities to play with. Try out as many different spaces as you can – if you are in training, you will already know how different your voice sounds in the different rooms and studios. Whenever you get the chance, start to experiment and play with the palette of sound in space. If working in a new theatre for the first time, you simply have to warm up in the performance area, or at least do a soundcheck, and get the company to listen to each other from lots of different places. You can then work out what your voice and speech skills need to do to adapt, as necessary. This is quite complex and you may not be ready for it yet – but as we have been working on resonance in some detail, I think it helpful to consider what you can eventually use it for, apart from the need to explore texts and genres and your character, vocally and verbally.

Warm-up and resonance 2.7.1–2.7.4

Repeat exercises from last session (2.6.1–2.6.4) – centring, jaw-tension release, sun salutation, forward placement.

Articulation preparation 2.7.5

Repeat 2.5.8.

Text – Restoration extracts 2.7.6

The Critic by Richard Brinsley Sheridan is technically not Restoration, as it is much later (the 1770s), but it sits well alongside the earlier pieces, as you will see from these extraordinary flights of verbal fancy and dexterity.

In Sheridan's critique of advertising (Act One, Scene Two), Puff tells Sneer that he is 'a Professor of the Art of Puffing' and a master of self-promotion – he is basically a copywriter and an author who teaches advertisers how to exaggerate their writing so they may 'enlay their phraseology with variegated chips of exotic metaphor' and so on. He may be the source of the modern advertiser's 'puff' (although the word itself is of Old English origin).

> PUFF. Even the auctioneers now – the auctioneers, I say,
> though the rogues have lately got some credit for their
> language – not an article of the merit theirs! – take
> them out of the pulpits, and they are as dull as
> catalogues! – No, sir; 'twas I first enriched their style –
> 'twas I first taught them to crowd their advertisements
> with panegyrical superlatives each epithet rising above
> the other like the bidders in their own auction rooms!
> From me they learned to inlay their phraseology with
> variegated chips of exotic metaphor: by me too their
> inventive faculties were called forth. Yes, sir, by me they
> were instructed to clothe ideal walls with gratuitous
> fruit – to insinuate obsequious rivulets into visionary
> groves – to teach courteous shrubs to nod their
> approbation of the grateful soil! or on emergencies to
> raise upstart oaks, where there never had been an
> acorn; to create a delightful vicinage without the

assistance of a neighbour; or to fix the temple of Hygeia in the fens of Lincolnshire!

Note not only the varying demands placed upon breath management, but also just how much range it is possible to use. On a thought like 'with panegyrical superlatives each epithet rising above the other', your voice can rise (or descend) with similarly exotic nuances. The only way it will be too much is if you are not centred and not true to the text and the character. Just have fun with this and relish the increasing stamina that all this demands from, and gives to you.

Session 8

Keywords: *Stamina and agility; resonance and articulation continued*

Prepare the body and voice
2.8.1

- With clean hands, massage the mouth and tongue.

- Do a few shakes and massages, using gentle voiceless sounds.

Centre and warm the voice with the sun salutation ☉
2.8.2

Go through the sun sequence, as 2.6.3.

Further body–voice integration and awareness – the dyna-bands of sound
2.8.3

Here is another way of discovering pathways through the body, those connections between different parts of the body, and how to use your voice to integrate and join them. The body awareness will in turn integrate the voice into movement.

- Stand freely upright, then drop through the spine and find the connection between your sitting bones and your heels. If you are unsure of your sit bones, you can stand and feel them with your fingers – place your hands on your bottom with the fingers curving downwards and you will be able to feel those sitting bones, especially if you bend and straighten slightly.

213

- Drop down, bend the knees slightly (and, if it helps, hold on to those sit bones), and imagine there is an elastic band between those bones and your heels. As you straighten and bend, feel the elastic stretching between the two points. If you release your breath on an 'f' or a 'v' or a hum, imagine the sound going between the two. As you then come back to standing, try out the sound again, and you may find it very strong. It gives you a real sense of grounding as it is coming up from the heels, through your sit bones and up and out.

- Here are two more great connections through the body. Become aware of your sacrum and place a hand there. Now put the other hand on your occipital lobe (the bone at the back of the skull). Now hum and 'mah' between the two hands and the two places on your body and see what happens. This will benefit from a lot of repetition.

- If you continue to hum and 'mah' and bring your hands away from the two points, see how much your voice will resonate both through the body, and into the space.

- Place a hand or fingers on the forehead and the other at your pubic bone. Gently bend and straighten between the two, with the notion of a dyna-band connecting them. Find the connection without collapsing – it is done with as open and released a body as possible, so you don't 'collapse' over but maintain line through the body. Hum it and 'mah' it, and again, repeat, play and discover those sound connections.

2.8.4 Forward placement

Go through the knuckle work (2.4.5).

- Try out the 'duvet of hums' (2.2.4) – hum into a 'mah' as you step back into your sound and let the hum and 'mah' sound out forwards across the space.

- Walk backwards as you hum and 'mah', then forwards, maintaining a clear stream of sound from your centre.

Nasal, oral and skull resonance

2.8.5

- Repeat all the humming and massaging of nose and head, spine rolls down and up and releasing from nasal consonants into open-vowel sounds in various positions of the body, both down and up.

- Hum and glide your sound down from your skull into the oral cavity and open out, using 'mmm-mah' into open-vowel sounds, then use bits of text.

Articulation

2.8.6

- Go through a quick massage of the tongue (gently biting if your hands aren't really clean), the lips, and soft-palate exercises. Use a mirror to look at the specifics of your tongue exercises.

- Repeat the ballet and aerobic tongue exercises.

- Go through the entire sequence 'patakabadagamanalathafasathavaza'.

Apply to text

2.8.7

You can now try some 'troubleshooting' with a piece you are working on, such as a project or play, and apply all this work to your ongoing rehearsal process.

Session 9

Keywords: *Capacity and support for stamina and agility; resonance and articulation continued*

In the last session before a break, it is a great idea to revise the work of the last few weeks or so, and bring yourself to a realisation that you have come a very long way. Your voice should by now be feeling much stronger, freer and more open. So now is a good time to recap.

Have a look back over the last eight sessions and create a revision session for yourself.

Go over the fundamentals, and now give yourself a little test. In Session 2, we looked at those three Shakespeare breath-management passages, and if you have been continuing to practise, you may now find them quite easy to manage. Don't worry if you can't do it yet, but note where you are, so that you know what you need to work on.

Play with all the range and resonance work we have added in, too, so that you take the technical work and play with it creatively. Play with resonating the voice in discrete areas – it's quite hard, but have a go at isolating sounds. For example, speak with an almost exclusively hyper-nasal resonance. Add to that a New York accent and you approximate the vocal choice of the character Janice in *Friends*. Speak with only pharyngeal resonance and a heightened RP accent and you might discover

Patsy from *Ab Fab*. Speak with oral resonance, a slight breathy onset and a general American accent and Marilyn Monroe may appear.

Revision and Vacation Work

If you are in formal training, you will have been working on all sorts of different elements in voice – the technical voice, practical voice and its application, detailed articulation and speech work, accents and dialects, not to mention text! It's a lot, but very exciting and rewarding. It is a great idea to have a rest now, but also to devise either a new or revised routine for daily practice. Ideally, twenty to thirty (or even ten to fifteen) minutes a day, and remember to have those regular bone-prop conversations too.

Remind yourself of the relationship between the skeleton/spine /its alignment, your voice/speech/articulation and the text. If studying dialect and accents, how does it all relate to voice work, and vice versa? These are valuable questions to ask at this point.

The other areas of training as an actor can also be considered, whether it is movement, singing, dance – what is their relationship to your voice, and how can you use your vocal skills in other areas of the training, as well as your life?

Part 2b

These sessions (which equate roughly to the second term of year two in actor training), will deepen the work on resonance and articulation, with the introduction of some deep body work, sounding through the structures of the body, and the use of very visceral and 'chewy' text. There should be no doubt that the voice really is gaining that 'oomph' factor!

Whilst we are going to further expand the body and weight of the voice, and apply that to some more weighty classical language, it is also useful at this point to look at some more modern text, and for this I have chosen some short passages from *Under Milk Wood*, a play written for radio, but which is now a stage play too. It is highly descriptive and demands use of all those resonators we have worked on, and great clarity. It can be a wonderful complement to your training if you are working in radio at this point in training. We will then return to the more visceral text of an epic piece translated and adapted in the late-twentieth century. I intend this to bridge the gap between ancient and modern, and it is a further accompaniment to other text work in training (or indeed for working actors), if and when you are working on Jacobean texts, for example.

For actors in training, there are other voice and text classes alongside each other, and over the next eight weeks I also work with second-year students on rhetoric in Shakespeare. This can be done at most points in second year (or the second 'chapter') but I generally place it alongside the biggest classical-acting project. Some suggestions for classical rhetoric can be found in Part 3.

Session 10

Keywords: *Revision; playing with sounds; articulation; modern text*

2.10.1 **Clean-hands exercise; breath centring**

- With clean hands, stand easily and freely, shake out, then float your fingers up into the mouth and get them working the inside of the lips and cheeks. Massage the tongue. Remember to keep aware of the breath coming in and out as you work the mouth into openness and ease.

2.10.2 **Tapping to wake up the body, lungs and breath**

Repeat 2.1.2.

2.10.3 **Release swings in shoulders and hips, adding sounds**

In order to free up the body, and therefore your voice, try this wonderful release work.

- Stand in parallel, with your feet slightly wider than hip-width apart, and step your left foot forwards. Swing the right arm behind you as you let in a breath, turning your head and eyes to follow the direction of your fingers. On the out-breath, swing the arm forwards, follow through with your whole arm, fingers reaching up and out ahead of you, with the head and eyes following through.

- Do all this and release your breath on an 'f', allowing the sound to carry on as you swing back and forth. If you can breathe in on the back swing, that's good, but once you have got going it doesn't really matter. Just notice at the start that breathing in as you swing back really opens up the intercostals and chest. The sound is continuous until you need the next breath.

- Swap sides. Repeat all this with 's' and 'sh', then take it on to 'v' and 'z' and then hums.

This is a great way to open up the whole body, and if you allow the knees to bend slightly, soften, and bounce through as you swing back and forth, you should notice that pretty much every part of the body is involved. It's a great way to warm up the body and integrate breath centring, breath capacity, vocal warming and releasing, all at the same time. It will also place the voice forwards, so when you do the forward placement this session (2.10.5), it should be pretty easy and almost instantaneous.

Capacity and support work

2.10.4

Here is some further work to improve capacity, gaining a more engaged support system, and increasing stamina. This is further repetition, but it is important to keep this element of the work 'topped up', if you like, so that it is a constant physical and mental reminder or support to your developing process.

- Stand freely, let the breath in then release the outgoing breath-stream on a constant, steady 's'. You can time this to see how long your sound lasts, and then do the same thing whilst walking round the space, or doing an activity. Constancy of sound and engaged support muscles intertwine and are codependent.

- Now do the same with a little 'f', and then repeat with a gentle 'v' sound. Again, you can stand still or walk around. Explore this on 'v', then 'z', then 'zh', extending the length of the sound. Spend a good ten minutes on these exercises.

- Walk around the room on a hum, and do a bit of chewing whilst you hum, to ensure the voice is forward.

- Then take it onto a hum into a 'mah', keeping the sound steady.

- Try different pitches and volumes. Take this 'mah' sound into sitting, lying down and getting up. Then try out some text.

2.10.5 Forward placement

Repeat 2.1.4.

2.10.6 Pitch glides and sirens to really warm the voice

A pathway isn't just a track in the forest or your route to work – a pathway is a route and a direction of energy (and breath and sound) through the body. For example, when you release your arms into a wide, 'angel wing' stretch, the movement begins deep inside the spine and tracks a pathway right through to the ends of the fingertips; breath and sound follow this track. This can also be expressed as a path for the voice through the space, such as the studio or theatre you are in.

- Do a few pitch glides (sirening the sound) on 'm', 'n' and 'ng'.

- Add in some movement to find pathways through the body. Having done the arm swings and hip opening, this should seem simple. Then allow the voice to find its path through the space. Don't think too much about what this means – just do it, experiment, and see what happens.

2.10.7 Deep resonance and range – extensive sounding into the body

This is an exercise to expand not just your resonating possibilities but the range of pitch as well. It is extensive and deep work, and if you can get someone to lead this, so much the better. It can be done on your own, but just don't 'clock watch' too much. It is wonderful done with a group of people, as you harmonise and resonate off each others' sounds. If you all happen to land on the same note and keep going with it, you will hear 'harmonics'.

We are going to lie down and sound out on a variety of vowels, imagining that they are each placed in different parts of the body. Every placement can be explored for a couple of minutes, and then build up over time, playing for a good four or five minutes with each vowel. You will then be exploring range and resonance for twenty to thirty minutes, and this kind of extended repetition really pays off.

- Lie in semi-supine with a book under your head. You will need to visualise each place in the body first, then sound the vowel into that place.

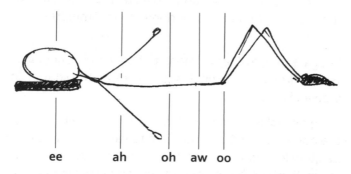

ee   ah   oh aw oo

This gets an 'imprint' of sounds deep inside the body.

- Begin by *visualising* the shape and sound of the vowel 'ah' (as in 'calm' or 'heart') and imagine that it lives, or is placed, in your chest or heart area.

- Start to sound out your voice on 'ah'. Find a pitch that is around the middle of your range. Keep with this, staying on the *same note* for at least a couple of minutes.

- Stop, listen to the room and let the effect of the sound stay with you for a few moments.

- Imagine 'ee' is in your mouth. Let the pitch rise gently, and explore 'ee' for a couple of minutes. Stop, listen, be still.

- Imagine 'ee' again, but this time it is up in your skull or the top of your head. Sound it there for some time. If you are doing this in a group, it probably won't sound very nice. It doesn't matter, just go with it, but don't overextend the pitch – it shouldn't be a strain. Remember that, once you have found a good note, stay on that pitch for a few minutes.

- Gently siren down your voice through the mouth 'ee'.

- Now visualise the shape of 'ah' again, imagine it in your chest, and sound it again, gliding down to the middle of your range.

- Imagine the shape of 'oh', and see it in your mind's eye around the solar plexus, just below the ribcage and above the navel. Let the pitch drop down a little and sound out the 'oh' into this area, exploring for a few minutes. Stop and listen.

- Imagine that 'aw' (as in 'more' or 'jaw') is in your belly. Gently drop down in pitch again. Explore the sound. Then stop and listen.

- Imagine 'oo' is in your lower belly or groin, deep and low in the body. Gently drop down in pitch again. Your voice may be quite low now, but don't go so low that there is creak or strain. Explore this lower end, and as the voice eases, try going a bit lower. Stop and listen.

- Begin to glide up through the body and the voice – 'oo' again, then siren or glide up into 'aw' in the belly, then up to 'oh' in your solar plexus. Glide again, up into the 'ah' of your chest, so that you are at about the middle of your natural range.

So:

1) Visualise the places first.

2) Then sound into them.

3) Place words in those areas if you feel ready to.

Slowly roll over and come to sitting. Stand when ready and then try out your voice on abstract sounds, then a few words. Have a chat. Notice how full and easy your voice feels!

Articulation

Do a few lip and tongue exercises, and some consonant drills. This
is a brief but helpful link into doing a little text this session.

Text: *Under Milk Wood*

Read through this opening passage from Dylan Thomas's *Under
Milk Wood*, a play for radio.

FIRST VOICE. To begin at the beginning.

> It is spring, moonless night in the small town, starless
> and bible-black, the cobblestreets silent and the
> hunched, courters'-and-rabbits' wood limping invisible
> down to the sloeblack, slow, black, crowblack,
> fishingboat-bobbing sea. The houses are blind as moles
> (though moles see fine tonight in the snouting, velvet
> dingles) or blind as Captain Cat there in the muffled
> middle by the pump and the town clock, the shops in
> mourning, the Welfare Hall in widows' weeds. And all
> the people of the lulled and dumbfound town are
> sleeping now.
>
> Hush, the babies are sleeping, the farmers, the fishers,
> the tradesmen and pensioners, cobbler, schoolteacher,
> postman and publican, the undertaker and the fancy
> woman, drunkard, dressmaker, preacher, policeman,
> the webfoot cocklewomen and the tidy wives. Young
> girls lie bedded soft or glide in their dreams, with rings
> and trousseaux, bridesmaided by glow-worms down
> the aisles of the organplaying wood. The boys are
> dreaming wicked or of the bucking ranches of the night
> and the jollyrodgered sea. And the anthracite statues of
> the horses sleep in the fields, and the cows in the byres,
> and the dogs in the wetnosed yards; and the cats nap in
> the slant corners or lope sly, streaking and needling, on
> the one cloud of the roofs.
>
> You can hear the dew falling, and the hushed town
> breathing. Only *your* eyes are unclosed to see the black

and folded town fast, and slow, asleep. And you alone can hear the invisible starfall, the darkest-before-dawn minutely dewgrazed stir of the black, dab-filled sea where the *Arethusa*, the *Curlew*, and the *Skylark*, *Zanzibar*, *Rhiannon*, the *Rover*, the *Cormorant*, and the *Star of Wales* tilt and ride.

Listen. It is night moving in the streets, the processional salt slow musical wind in Coronation Street and Cockle Row, it is the grass growing on Llareggub Hill, dewfall, starfall, the sleep of birds in Milk Wood.

It is almost enough at this stage to simply read that passage aloud, and reflect. Today's session is long and extensive, but just observe how it feels to read this velvety text after all that deep body work. Next week we can look at this in more detail.

Session 11

Keywords: *Advanced resonance, voice into structures of the body; modern text with resonance and clarity*

Clean-hands exercise

`2.11.1`

*   Prepare as usual with the mouth/tongue massaging and releasing.

Release swings in shoulders and hips, adding sounds

`2.11.2`

Warm up the body and centre the voice with the swing work (2.10.3).

Sirens

`2.11.3`

*   Do some easy sirening/pitch glides to really warm the voice on 'm', 'n', 'ng'.

*   Add movement and pathways through the body – drop through the spine, play with the hands leading the body, or the toes leading you with the sound following.

*   Add pathways through the space – let the body lead you around the room, pitch gliding, dipping and rising physically, and releasing the sound into the space.

2.11.4 **Deep resonance and range – extensive sounding into the body**

Repeat this work from the last session (2.10.7). If you can do this work for about twenty minutes or more, once or twice a week, it will give enormous weight and depth to the voice, and is particularly helpful for people whose voices are still on the light and high side. For those who tend to sit in the lower or bass end of their voices, spend a bit more time on the chest, then especially the mouth and skull work here.

2.11.5a **Skeleton work – introduction to sounding through the structures of the body**

At this stage in vocal training, I use work that goes into very specific structures of the body. This work is inspired by Patricia Bardi's[6] *Vocal Dance and Voice Movement Integration.* I am using only a small but a significant element of her vocal and physical practice, to explore the skeleton and organs as a means of extending and deepening resonance and vibration of sound in the body. I highly recommend seeking out Bardi's work, as it has had a profound effect on many vocal users. I have found it invaluable in exploring resonance and particularly vocal character choices.

We begin by considering the skeleton. If you can look at a model of a skeleton so much the better (I have a miniature model, which is a great teaching and learning tool, and well worth the investment), or you could look at an illustration.

Begin by looking at the ribcage. It is surprisingly large when looked at just in skeletal form. The bones appear quite light, and form an open cage or basket structure. Because of the cartilage between the lower ribs in particular, it looks very springy and bendy, and there appears to be a lot of space inside. Of course, there are organs and flesh and everything else that makes up your body, but concentrate just now only on this bony structure.

- Place your hands on your ribcage and explore the way it feels underneath your hands, moving around as you do so.

- Take a look at the pelvis. There is a similarity to the ribcage in that there is a circular nature to its structure. Look at the bones of the sacrum, pelvis, hip crests and sit bones. Note how much more solid this area appears to be in comparison to the ribcage. Place your hands and fingers on your sacrum, and then on the hip bones, moving around and getting the feel of these bony structures.

Rather like the process we went through in deep sounding and exploration of vowels through the body, we will now visualise something, move it, then sound it.

Skeleton work – ribs and pelvis shake

2.11.5b

- Lie in semi-supine on the floor and take a few moments to release and relax.

- Visualise your ribcage. See it in your mind's eye, taking a little while over this.

- Shake your ribcage gently. Don't make any sound just yet. Shake it and rest.

The shaking must be very fluid – this is not a rigid or stiff shake, it wants to move on from the pouring and vibrating your body and sound with great ease. When you shake, the area or region concerned is moving as if you were lying on a wobble board. This is not tension or constriction work, it is physically quite strong but gentle at the same time. So you shake your body from the inside (not using your hands to move or shake it externally).

- Shake the ribcage again. Other parts of you will move and go along for the ride, but just ignore them and concentrate on the movement and sensations occurring only in the ribcage. Rest.

- Gently shake it again and rest.

- Visualise your pelvis. See it in your mind's eye. Shake your pelvis.

- It can sometimes help to gently roll around on the floor, visualising and feeling the structure. Shake again then rest.

- Shake the pelvis again, rest.

- Now return to the ribcage, shake it and rest. Notice the difference in the feel and weight. Spend another minute or so shaking first the ribcage and then the pelvis.

- Become very aware of how they feel.

This work may seem strange at first, and it can take a long time for the body to understand it, but just go with it. As with a lot of the work, you may not 'get it' today, but as you repeat the work it will sooner or later come to mean something.

2.11.5c   Skeleton resonance work – rib sounds

- Visualise your ribcage. Shake it. Now – as you shake it, begin to let the ribcage *sound itself*. This is a slightly odd instruction, perhaps, but the idea is that you let out whatever sound is released, because of the shaking and your imaginative tie to the structure. If you decide in advance what kind of sound to make, it is likely to be imposed and untruthful. So, let the ribcage sound out.

- Rest and listen to the space.

- Repeat several times – visualise the structure of the ribcage, shake it, and let it sound out.

2.11.5d   Skeleton resonance work – pelvis sounds

- Visualise your pelvis. See it in your mind's eye. Shake your pelvis.

- Rest and repeat.

- Now – as you shake it, begin to let the pelvis sound itself.

- Rest and listen to the space.

- Repeat – visualise the structure of the pelvis, shake it, and let it sound out.

- Repeat the process with the pelvis and ribcage. You may find that they sound the same, or they may sound incredibly different. It doesn't matter at this stage. If you are doing this work in a group, it is important not to be influenced by others' sounding, or to try copying them. Just go with your own experience, then let it go.

- Come to sitting and reflect.

Next session we'll try out some words.

Articulation

As always, do a little more preparation on the speech organs, with a little massage of the cheeks, lips, jawbone. Gently bite the tongue and get it mobile. Do some lip stretches – puckers, etc. – then some tongue stretches – big, elastic stretches, then some precise, smaller movements.

- Do a few drills with 'bbb bbb bbb bah', 'ddd', 'ggg'.

- Add in a few sequences – 'oot too oht toh' and so on.

Text: *Under Milk Wood*

Look again at the passage from *Under Milk Wood* – read this through using the bone prop. As you have been doing extensive resonance and body work, the voice will be responding to the physical and resonant demands of the piece. Using the bone prop will not only open up the back of the oral space, but the mobility of the lips and tongue will also bring the sound forward. This will encourage real clarity with the words.

Look up words you don't know, or think about what they mean to you. Pick apart some of the phrases – here are a couple of examples.

Compare the long soft consonants and vowels of the girls:

> Young girls lie bedded soft or glide in their dreams, with rings and trousseaux, bridesmaided by glow-worms down the aisles of the organplaying wood.

Really exaggerate the dreamy, sensual quality of 'girls' ('errr') and 'aisles' ('eye', 'lllzzz'), with the short sharp rhythms of the boys 'wicked' (short vowels) and 'bucking' ('ʊ-i'):

> The boys are dreaming wicked or of the bucking
> ranches of the night and the jollyrodgered sea.

If you can do a Welsh accent, that helps with the rhythm, but have a go at this anyway – look at the slowing-down of:

> the sloeblack, slow, black, crowblack,

– into the motion of the sea moving the little boats around on:

> fishingboat-bobbing sea

If you can get hold of an audio version, have a listen to the original with Richard Burton. Close your eyes and listen. Now read the passage again. Make choices.

Session 12

Keywords: *Advanced resonance, playing with sound; voice into skeletal structures; modern text with resonance and clarity*

Clean-hands exercise

2.12.1

Prepare as usual.

Release swings in shoulders and hips, adding sounds

2.12.2

Warm up the body and centre the voice with the swing work (2.10.3).

Gentle release and capacity

2.12.3

*   Let the breath in and release on sustained and elongated sounds of 'f', 's', 'sh', 'v', 'z', 'mmm'. You can apply this to text by trying out a short speech that challenges your capacity.

Sirens

2.12.4

Repeat 2.11.3.

Deep resonance and range

2.12.5

*   Revise a shortened version of this work from previous sessions, going through each vowel for a minute or two. Come to standing and try out your voice.

2.12.6a Revise the skeleton

- Lie in semi-supine. First of all, repeat 2.11.5b, where you simply shake the ribcage without sound, and then the pelvis, without sound, noticing the difference in weight and feel.

2.12.6b Skeleton resonance work – rib sounds

- Visualise your ribcage. Shake it gently. Don't make any sound, just shake it and rest.
- Shake the ribcage again. Rest and repeat.
- Shake it again and let it sound out.
- Keep playing with the sounds of your ribcage, without judgement.
- Shake it, sound it, and now stop shaking but keep sounding. Then rest.

2.12.6c Skeleton resonance work – pelvis sounds

- Visualise your pelvis. See it in your mind's eye. Shake your pelvis. Remember the image of the wobble board if that helps keep this gentle and internal – so there is as little *doing* as possible.
- Rest and repeat. And again. Be patient and just explore the sensations.
- As you shake it, begin to let the pelvis sound itself.
- Rest.
- Repeat – visualise the structure of the pelvis, shake it, and let it sound out.
- Shake the pelvis, sound it, then stop shaking but keep the sound going.

2.12.6d Ribcage and pelvis sounds

- Repeat the process with the pelvis and ribcage.
- Come to sitting and reflect.

Words in ribs and pelvis

Think of a line of text you know, or try the first short line from *Under Milk Wood*.

- Visualise the ribcage, shake it, and let it sound out.

- Repeat, stop the shaking, but keep the sound going.

- Repeat, and now after sounding, try out a line of text.

- Go through the whole process again with the pelvis.

Try your text, odd words and everyday phrases. Relish and taste the sound of the words either in your ribs or your pelvis.

- Take a moment to reflect. This will be repeated next session.

Articulation

- Prepare the speech organs, with a little massage of the cheeks, lips, jawbone. Gently bite the tongue and get it mobile. Do some lip stretches, then some tongue stretches.

- Do a few drills with 'bbb bbb bbb bah', 'ddd', 'ggg'.

- Go through 'pah pay pee pay pah paw poo paw pah'; and with 'b', 'd' and 'g'.

- Try it with 'tch' (as in 'chip' or 'cheese') 'tcha tchay tchee tchay', and 'dj' (as in 'judge' or 'jelly'), 'dja djay djee djay'.

Text: *Under Milk Wood*

Read through the *Under Milk Wood* passage.

Notice how your voice feels with the text after all the resonance and body work. See if you can bring in the experience of the skeleton work. It may be too soon to notice this, so just imagine it. Your voice will certainly feel warm and ready to fire up the language. Make choices, play with it.

Session 13

Keywords: *Advanced resonance; voice into structures of the body, organs; text*

2.13.1–2.13.4

Repeat 2.12.1–2.12.4.

2.13.5   Support work

Support on 'z' – check for ease of intake and a strong muscular support through the abdominals, pelvic floor and engagement through the back.

2.13.6   Warm and place the voice forwards

Hum to a point in the room, then 'oo' into the space, then 'mah' and 'ah' for a few minutes.

2.13.7   Spine curls and voice work on the floor

- Lie in semi-supine, allow the spine to lengthen and widen (think it, don't *do*), then let in a breath and do a few pelvic tilts and curls.

- After this initial phase, you can try some spine raises – on an out-breath lift up from the tail bone and raise or uncurl the spine up as far as the lower edge of the shoulder blades (don't go any higher, this is not a shoulder stand). Let in a breath and slowly come down on an 'f' or 'sh'.

- Repeat several times, ensuring that you engage the abdominals – this should happen automatically if you are using sounds supported from your core.

- It is not about 'crunching the abs' or squeezing in any way. A gentle engagement is what is required, so that the breath, the voice and the body aid each other.

- Repeat with 'v' and then some hums.

An image to help you: imagine that your spine is a string of pearls, and as you come down, you are placing one pearl at a time down onto the floor. Soften as you do so.

- As you descend, raise the heels so you work through the balls of the feet – this can really stabilise you and it helps the back/spine come down a bit at a time.

- Repeat and as you descend, sound out on a 'huuuuh' like a long, grounded sigh, whilst imagining that someone is gently pressing through your sternum (you can get someone to actually do that, or try it yourself with one hand or your fingertips). This may get a very grounded and solid sound out of you. It should feel very released and easy. Stop if you feel any discomfort.

- Roll over, come to sitting, then standing, and try some sounds standing and walking around.

Body structure work – revise the skeleton resonance work   `2.13.8a`

- Lie in semi-supine. Before going on to organs, we will do a quick revision of the skeleton – visualise the ribcage, shake it and sound out.

- Keep playing with the sounds of your ribcage, without judgement.

- Shake it, sound it, and now stop shaking but keep sounding. Then rest.

2.13.8b

- Visualise your pelvis. See it in your mind's eye. Shake it.

- Rest and repeat. And again. Be patient and just explore the sensations.

- Now – as you shake it, begin to let the pelvis sound itself.

- Shake the pelvis, sound it, then stop shaking but keep the sound going.

2.13.9 Body structure – the organs

Patricia Bardi works on four regions of organs in the body, and we will look at two during this session. This is my adaptation of the work, and the areas to look at today are the lungs and guts (the small and large intestine).

2.13.9a Visualise the lungs

- Visualise your lungs, come up with some images (examples that may help include balloons, upside-down trees, sponges, bubbles – ask a group for ideas and it's amazing what some will think of! Use whatever helps you).

- Gently shake your lungs then rest. Shake them again. As with the skeletal work, other stuff will move too – ignore it and concentrate on your lungs. If it helps, roll gently from side to side, feeling and engaging with the weight/lightness of the image.

- Rest and repeat the shaking. Rest and observe.

2.13.9b Visualise the guts

- Come up with some images. Now either gently roll from side to side, or shake the guts. Rest and repeat. You might find it helps to imagine your intestines are shaking like a jelly on a plate – it gives that sense of ease and fluidity again.

- Shake the guts again, explore this, rest, and repeat. Rest and observe.

Shake the lungs and guts

- Repeat the process by visualising then shaking first the lungs and then the guts.

- Begin to notice the difference in feel, and the difference in weight.

Sound the lungs and guts

- Visualise your lungs, shake them. Now, as you shake, begin to let the lungs sound themselves. As with the skeleton, it may seem slightly odd, but just let out whatever sound is released and don't decide in advance what kind of sound to make.

- Rest and listen to the space.

- Repeat several times and rest.

- Visualise your guts, shake them. Now, as you shake, begin to let the guts sound themselves.

- Rest and listen to the space.

- Repeat several times and rest.

- If you feel ready, compare the two sounds again by sounding one after the other, both whilst shaking, and then whilst still. You might also try some words in these areas, these vocal qualities.

You can also try this:

- Shake the lungs and guts.

- Roll and feel the different weight on your side, then on your front, the other side, and then on your back.

- Repeat and add sound.

- Come to sitting and reflect. Then stand, hum and 'mah' on a good, long and easy breath a few times and notice how your voice feels.

2.13.10 Articulation – alveolar and post-alveolar

- Do some tongue-preparation exercises, using a mirror to observe – go through some aerobic and ballet exercises. Apply this preparation to the following sound sequences, with and then without the bone prop:

  'Oot too, oht toh, awt taw, aht tah ayt tay eet tee
  od doo ohd doh awd daw ahd dah ayd day eed dee.'

- Repeat with 'n', 'l', 's', 'z', then onto 'tch' and 'dj'.

- Now go through this:

  'Tch-tchah tch-tchay tch-tchee tch-tchay.'
  'Dj-djah dj-djay,' and so on.

2.13.11 To some text work

Use and apply all this work to either a piece or character you know, or take a look at this further extract from *Under Milk Wood*. This is a great contrast to the opening section. The voice now goes from narrative to character, and from night to day – don't overthink about that last idea, just try out the text to see what might be meant by a 'day' voice.

> CAPTAIN CAT. All the women are out this morning, in the sun. You can tell it's Spring. There goes Mrs Cherry, you can tell her by her trotters, off she trots new as a daisy. Who's that talking by the pump? Mrs Floyd and Boyo, talking flatfish. What can you talk about flatfish? That's Mrs Dai Bread One, waltzing up the street like a jelly, every time she shakes it's slap slap slap. Who's that? Mrs Butcher Beynon with her pet black cat, it follows her everywhere, miaow and all. There goes Mrs Twenty Three, important, the sun gets up and goes down in her dewlap, when she shuts her eyes, it's night. High heels now, in the morning too, Mrs Rose-Cottage's eldest, Mae, seventeen and never been kissed ho ho, going young and milking under my window to the field with the nannygoats, she reminds me all the way. Can't hear what the women are gabbing round the pump. Same as

ever. Who's having a baby, who blacked whose eye,
seen Polly Garter giving her belly an airing, there should
be a law, seen Mrs Beynon's new mauve jumper it's her
old grey jumper dyed, who's dead, who's dying, there's
a lovely day, oh the cost of soapflakes!

Session 14

Keywords: *Voice into structures of the body, organs; visceral text*

We now go deeper into resonance and relish, moving onto some very gutsy, visceral text.

2.14.1–2.14.7

Repeat warm-up and preparation as in the last session 2.13.1–2.13.7.

2.14.8 Extensive sounding into the body

If you feel like further preparation, do the extended vowel placement and sounding work (2.10.7).

2.14.9 Organs – lungs and guts

This week, repeat the organ work from last time (2.13.9).

It pays dividends to take time with this work, particularly as it may seem very esoteric to some students. Even for those who find they respond to it immediately, it is necessary to go slowly, and repeat and repeat.

- So visualise, then shake and sound the lungs. Do the same with the intestines. Repeat each area several times.

- Notice how easily you access the work and the sounds following the repetition.

Articulation

Prepare and exercise the speech organs as usual, using a mirror. Do some aerobic and ballet exercises, this week paying extra attention to the soft palate and back of the tongue – so include lots of yawning with mouth open and then behind closed lips.

- Now to some drills:

  'Oog goo, ohg goh, awg gaw, ahg gah ayg gay eeg gee.'
  'Ook koo ohk koh,' etc.
  'Oong ngoo ohng ngoh,' etc.

- And then this:

  'G-gah g-gay g-gee g-gay,' etc.
  'K-kah k-kay,' etc.

Text: *Beowulf*

Here is the first of three extracts from a visceral, epic poem, *Beowulf*, in a wonderful translation by Seamus Heaney. This is the beginning of the poem.

> So. The Spear-Danes in days gone by
> and the kings who ruled them had courage and greatness.
> We have heard of those princes' heroic campaigns.
> There was Shield Sheafson, scourge of many tribes,
> a wrecker of mead-benches, rampaging among foes.
> This terror of the hall-troops had come far.
> A foundling to start with, he would flourish later on
> as his powers waxed and his worth was proved.
> In the end each clan on the outlying coasts
> beyond the whale-road had to yield to him
> and begin to pay tribute. That was one good king.

And what a beginning! Heaney, in his introduction (which is itself a great read), explains how he translated (or 'rendered') the first word of the Old English 'Hwaet', which in previous versions had been, variously, 'lo', 'hark' 'behold', but in:

Hiberno-English... the particle 'so' came naturally to the rescue, because... (it) obliterates all previous discourse and narrative... and (is) an exclamation calling for immediate attention. So, 'so' it was.

As an actor, you need to make that simple 'So' work to call attention. Now pick out one of the many wonderful descriptive images – 'whale-road', which is the sea. So simple, so ancient and yet so prescient. This is great stuff for an actor to use. Get the feel of the words rolling around your tongue and in your mouth, and at the same time get your storytelling skills going.

Pay particular attention to word shape and use very muscular articulation. Make every element of the word really count.

Session 15

Keywords: *Organs; visceral text*

2.15.1–2.15.7

Repeat warm-up and preparation as in Session 2.13.

Extensive sounding into the body

2.15.8

For further preparation, do the extended vowel placement and sounding work (2.10.7).

Organs – all four regions

2.15.9

Lungs and guts

2.15.9a

Go through a repetition of shaking and sounding the lungs and guts, either way round, comparing the different sounds.

2.15.9b

We will now look at two further areas, beginning with the central organs.

We will concentrate now on the larger organs that sit in a band roughly around the central area of the body: the liver, the stomach and the kidneys. The thoracic diaphragm is resting on top of these organs. Remind yourself of where these are, get others to describe the placement in the body, or look up some pictures if you're unsure. We will go through the same process as before.

- Lie down in semi-supine. Visualise, then shake, then sound the central organs.

- Repeat, with a rest, several times.

This area can be quite tricky to locate and sound, and may elicit very little, or a great deal of odd noise. There is no way of knowing until you try it. Sometimes people have a similar sound quality to the guts in this area, but the tempo will radically alter. Others have no change at all in sound. Observe what happens.

- Repeat.

2.15.9C

The fourth region we shall explore vocally is the sexual organs. This is, of course, where women and men part company for a while! Whilst male and female voices will differ anyway, and whilst our body structures are generally different in weight, size and so on, here we have very different bits – therefore different experiences. It is a good idea to talk through what you have – this may seem facile to an adult group, but it can be surprising how complex a woman's body is, or how not everything is entirely external for men, or entirely internal for women.

- Lie in semi-supine and chat it through, then release into an easy breath.

- Visualise first, then shake gently. Rest, visualise, shake, and rest. Repeat this several times. I find that with this area, people can be tempted to make up a sound or decide in advance perhaps more than any other area, so the visualisation and shaking without sound is very important.

- Visualise again, then shake, and now let those organs sound themselves.

Do this several times. Let yourself be taken by surprise – because this can produce some really startling effects.

Repeat all four regions of organs several times.

You can also bring this onto text – try out a line of text that you know (or use a line from *Beowulf*). If you keep repeating the same line but in different organ areas, you get a good sense of how differently the voice (and speech) behave and respond to the different areas of sounding.

You can also try it out with a line of text from a character you are currently working on – you may find a difficult line becomes free, or just that a line you are happy with takes on new possibilities.

Gently come to sitting then standing, and try out the whole lot whilst standing. Shaking your organs in an upright position will bring your experience into the everyday, but it will also help you apply it to your acting – which for much of the time is done upright!

Articulation

- As usual, prepare and exercise the speech organs. Do some drills – use these and make up other combinations. Do these both with and then without the bone prop.

  'Oot oht awt aht ayt eet
  ots ohts awts ahts ayts eets
  oos ohs aws ahs ays ees
  oost ohst awst ahst ayst eest
  oosts ohsts awsts ahsts aysts eests.'

- Repeat each sequence with:

  'Ook ,ooks, ookst ookt, ookts, oosk, ooskt, ooskts'.
  ooth-t ooth-ts oof-th ooks-th.'

- And finally, as a relief, with:

  'Ood ohd awd ahd ayd eed.'

(I say a relief, because after all those 's', 'f' and 'th' sounds, it is lovely to come back to ground with a strong, firm 'd.')

2.15.11 Text: *Beowulf*

- Speak the section from last time (2.14.11) and then the following, which is another short section for you to play with (lines 99–105):

  So times were pleasant for the people there
  until finally one, a fiend out of hell,
  began to work his evil in the world.
  Grendel was the name of this grim demon
  haunting the marches, marauding round the heath
  and the desolate fens; he had dwelt for a time
  in misery among the banished monsters,

Speak this with and without the bone prop.

2.15.12 Troubleshooting

If you are working on a play, scene study, poem, or pretty much anything you want help with, you can try troubleshooting any difficulties or challenges you have. Look at voice, speech or text issues and queries, and look at vocal choices to create character, based on all the experimental work we have been doing. Integrate everything you do.

For a long time, you have to learn the basic 'technique' and then try to apply it all to text, your acting and your everyday voice. Now your acting and text work can have a direct bearing on voice work, they are inseparable in many ways.

Session 16

Keywords: *Voice into structures of the body, organs and skeleton; visceral text*

`2.16.1–2.16.7`

Repeat warm-up and preparation as in Session 2.13.

Extensive sounding into the body `2.16.8`

- Do the extended vowel placement and sounding work (2.10.7).

Organs – all four areas `2.16.9`

- Revise all the organs, with visualisation, shaking then sounding, of the lungs, the guts/intestines, and a little more on the central organs and the sexual organs.

- Compare and contrast all your sounds.

- Try it all in a sitting position, then standing.

Organs – the brain `2.16.10`

Here is a rather odd one.

- Lie in semi-supine and think about the brain for a moment. Now, you won't want to shake this around too much, so just very gently roll the head from side to side and imagine that you are rolling the brain around, very softly. If you feel okay with this, you can try a gentle shake too.

Be soft and careful – only you can know if this feels fine, but if it does, go with it and try sounding the brain. It may add to your palette of vocal colours, and your characterisation through voice.

2.16.11 Skeleton

- You can fairly quickly revisit the skeletal sounds (2.11.5), shaking and sounding the ribcage, then the pelvis.

If your voice is responsive to this work, and you want to make further discoveries, you can try out the following:

- Shake and sound your arm bones, your leg bones. Try the finger bones and the toe bones (this is great if someone is struggling with the top end of their voice, i.e. a bass who tends to rumble around the lower end a lot of the time). If ready, you can try for even lighter or higher sounds – I have found students make great leaps by shaking the fingernails and 'sounding' them. Conversely, if a voice needs more depth of pitch or weight, sound those leg bones or the pelvis, or try out the guts again.

2.16.12 Articulation

- Go through a little preparation if the speech organs feel they need it, and try out some consonant clusters (see Appendix TIV3c).

2.16.13 Text: *Beowulf*

Here is the last extract to look at – the section where your voice and speech organs can really express the text, respond to the weight and scope of the imagery, and relish the viscosity and viscerality of the monster's rage. Jump into this and move around with it, feeling the swoops and dips in the rhythm and its strong pulse. Really hit the 'd' of down, and the hard strong 'g's of God and Grendel. If those consonant sounds are weedy, it won't give you the guttural hard edge you need. Contrast these with the softness of 'off' and 'mist', and so on.

> In off the moors, down through the mist-bands
> God-cursed Grendel came greedily loping.
> The bane of the race of men roamed forth,
> hunting for a prey in the high hall.
> Under the cloud-murk he moved towards it
> until it shone above him, a sheer keep
> of fortified gold. Nor was that the first time
> he had scouted the grounds of Hrothgar's dwelling –
> although never in his life, before or since,
> did he find harder fortune or hall-defenders.
> Spurned and joyless, he journeyed on ahead
> and arrived at the bawn. The iron-braced door
> turned on its hinge when his hands touched it.
> Then his rage boiled over, he ripped open
> the mouth of the building, maddening for blood,
> pacing the length of the patterned floor
> with his loathsome tread, while a baleful light,
> flame more than light, flared from his eyes.
> He saw many men in the mansion, sleeping,
> a ranked company of kinsmen and warriors
> quartered together. And his glee was demonic,
> picturing the mayhem: before morning
> he would rip life from limb and devour them,
> feed on their flesh; but his fate that night
> was due to change, his days of ravening
> had come to an end.

An additional articulation exercise – 'And-er…' 2.16.14

The inestimable musical director and singing coach Kate Edgar told me about this one – it is very useful if you are struggling with word endings, especially with really weighty text.

- Take a line of text, and where any word ends with a consonant phoneme (that is to say, a word that ends in a consonant you pronounce) you say 'er' ('uh') at those endings. I will use 'uh' so that rhotic speakers don't sound the 'r'.

251

In off the moors down through the mist bands
God-cursed Grendel came greedily loping

Becomes:

In-uh off-uh the moorz-uh down-uh through the mist-uh
bandz-uh
God-uh cursed-uh Grendel-uh cam(e)-uh greedily loping-uh

- Say each line with the 'uh' several times, then repeat it
  without, as normal. You can get amazing results with this
  simple idea, but it takes a bit of practice and perseverance.

Session 17

Keywords: *Voice into structures, compare skeleton and organs*

Clean-hands exercise   `2.17.1`

As before.

`2.17.2–2.17.7`

Repeat preparation as in Session 2.13.

Sounding vowels through the body   `2.17.8`

Here is a reminder of the extensive sounding of vowels into different placements in the body. Lie flat or in semi-supine and sound the vowels for a few minutes on one note each, at a time.

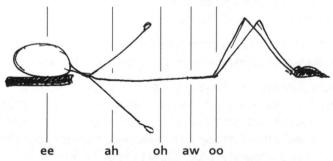

ee   ah   oh aw oo

- Visualise each place first, then sound it.

- Place words in those areas.

253

2.17.9   A revision and comparison of the skeleton and organs

- Go through all the processes of visualisation, shaking, then sounding, into the ribcage, the pelvis, then the lungs and the guts.

We will now make some comparisons between the sounds in different combinations:

- Compare ribcage and pelvis: shake, sound and speak in each area, first one then the other. Speak some text in each area.

- Compare lungs and guts: do the same process of shaking and sounding one then the other. Speak the same line of text in each area.

- Compare the ribs and lungs: so shake the ribcage, sound it. Shake the lungs, sound them. Repeat with text.

- Now compare the pelvis and guts: so shake the pelvis, sound it. Shake the guts, sound them. Repeat with text.

One of the most frequent discoveries I have noticed is that the bone structures equate to the consonants, and the organs equate to the vowels. It is not really surprising, since the bones are the framework and structure of the body, and the consonants are the architectural framework for the word. The organs are where our emotions sit (my heart was in my mouth, I had a feeling in the pit of my tummy, butterflies in the stomach, it was gut-wrenching, and so on), and the vowels of a word hold and convey the emotion. Aaahh!

If you don't find this happening or it doesn't make sense, then just go with any useful experiences you gain from the work.

You can play with all these areas and qualities of sound. Apply it to any text you are working on, and particularly to character work. It can be fantastically useful on both classical text and modern, and really frees you up to experiment, to work right through the body and integrate every aspect of your work.

Further ideas for experimentation

Sometimes when students don't easily respond to big range changes we do skeleton work on ribs and pelvis, then try out the arm bones, leg bones, finger bones and toe bones; and shake and sound the fingernails for guys who don't access the top end or the lighter tonal qualities in their voices.

With organ work, you can try out the brain too. Very gently move the head and then imagine you are moving the brain around, and then let it sound, and you might find a very strange ethereal quality.

Articulation

2.17.10

Go through a little preparation if the speech organs feel they need it and try out some consonant clusters (Appendices TIV3b and c).

'And-er...'

2.17.11

Repeat this from the last session (2.16.14).

Text: *Beowulf* and *Under Milk Wood*

2.17.12

Revise the texts we have looked at over the last eight sessions – *Under Milk Wood* and *Beowulf*. Take a few sections and try them out. Talk through your discoveries, and compare the texts. Whilst they seem very different, and come from entirely different eras, you may make some very useful connections between them. I leave it to you to discover for yourself what these might be.

You could also apply the work to Shakespeare, classical text, to television or film scripts, and see what happens.

Revision and Vacation Work

Have a rest and a break now, but continue either with your own devised outline for daily practice, or develop something new, based on the work of the last eight sessions.

Consider what have you learned during this last couple of months or so, regarding the changing language, types of language and word usage, and the challenges these pose for the actor. Think about vocal choices, the possibilities introduced by the notion of the breath–thought connection, and how resonance and articulation integrate and relate to each other.

Part 2c

In this last block of sessions, which equate to a third term, or the last part of a second year of training, everything comes together and all that hard work pays off. You are hopefully now ready to shout, scream, laugh and cry at will, with an ease and openness that comes of all that practice. I am going to give a few suggestions about the extreme vocal states, rather than go into great detail, because this is very demanding work and it requires absolute control of technique and a really free body and voice. It is far easier to learn in the moment – shouting can be taught extremely easily at this stage in a few minutes! It can be hard to glean from the written page, and there may be no one there to check you are doing it safely, but a few clear suggestions will certainly get you going. If in doubt, work with a professional coach. If at any point it feels wrong or uncomfortable, don't do it. Just occasionally, a person is not ready at this stage to scream or shout, so we just say no – it's simply that some voices take longer to be available than others. Conversely, I have had first-year students who would be ready for the work, but most people are only now about ready to go with it.

Much of the work you already know – extreme voice needs a released body, an awareness of how to keep open and not tense, an ability to engage support strongly without undue tension; it needs good breath support, an open channel, placement, muscular articulation and a grounded body and voice, coupled with very clear intentions and objectives. Everything you have learned, therefore, but now you use it all, with a stronger impulse.

When it comes to text, this is where I introduce Greek dramas – it's a funny thing, but at the end of the formal training in voice, body and speech, we go right back to the origins of much of Western drama. Chronologically, one might start there in terms of an academic learning environment, but physically and emotionally it is so huge that actors are normally ready for it only after all that preparatory work of two years. The text is inherently straightforward (you don't need to spend hours trying to decipher basic meanings in the way that you do for Aphra Behn, say), but the scope is so vast that you need a big voice and a very open body and emotional centre. Any holding back will mean you cannot do it justice and may simply be unable to cope with it safely, physiologically as well as emotionally. The chorus element also works well at this stage because actors/students are by now so good at listening! You cannot breathe and speak in unison if you do not listen well, and I mean listening with your ears and your body and all your senses. This is what I call the 'yummy' stage in training.

Session 18

Keywords: *Revision workout; begin extreme voice or heightened vocal states – to laugh and cry*

Student-led warm-up and feedback

2.18.1

For these last sessions, ideally the student/actors work in pairs to lead the warm-up. This is so that there is total ownership of process, and they get feedback not just from a tutor or coach, but more importantly from each other. Any gaps in process are discovered, and what really works is shared. This element, of course, often comes much earlier in training, and it really depends on the programme, but I include it here as a reminder that you are ready to take complete possession of your work.

Warm-up and revision workout

2.18.2

Construct your own warm-up or take one from previous sessions or Part 4.

Additional release and resonance

2.18.3

- Lie in semi-supine. If in a group, have all the heads in the centre, feet facing out, so you are in a circle.

- Set up some humming, and when warm take it on to extended 'mah'-ing around the middle of your range.

- Hum and slide up into 'mee', down through 'mah' and down easily into 'moo'.

The beauty of doing this in a group, with your heads near each other, is that you should feel as well as hear some great resonance happening, especially if you have a lovely wooden floor to work on. Whatever the surface, sense and feel the vibrations and work off each other.

- Speak some text, and if each person goes to lie in the centre of the circle at a time, everyone in turn will give and receive vibration, resonance.

- Slowly come to sitting, then standing, and try out some sounds and bits of text.

2.18.4 Sirens and pitch glides to cry

This comes from an idea based on the work of Lise Olson[7] (have a look at her work on the Voice of Violence, truly wonderful stuff).

- Lie down again and do some pitch glides or sirens, first on an 'm', then 'n', then 'ng'.

- Siren again, starting on a middle note and rising up in scale to the high end of your voice (only go as far as is easy and released).

- Now siren up and then release out into 'mah' or 'mee'. So 'mmm-mah'. It should be very free, released, open, and a high sound – not too loud, that is not the point. Try this also starting with an 'n', and then 'ng' – you will probably find one of them is easier, so do whichever is best for you.

- From that high rising 'm' into 'mah' or 'mee', let the sound and the pitch drop down a little and it will sound like you are crying. In a group, this can sound very eerie, or unsettling. It may make people laugh, just let it go.

- And now whimper – so let in a little breath, and 'm-mah, m-mee' or 'n-nah, n-nee', and so on. Try out 'ma-ha-ha' or 'na-ha-ha' then 'muh-huh-huh', 'boo-hoo-hoo'.

- Extend your hum a little, then whimper into a vowel. It will sound truly pathetic.

- Try it all out sitting and standing.

At first this is all done without facial expressions, so it is properly centred and rooted in technique. When you have got that, then you can bring in the 'acting' and emotional release. This lays the foundations for safe shouting and screaming – work it all out technically, then bring in the emotion. It will work, you will be able to do it safely and at will.

- Talk about crying – when and why we do it, as with laughing. You can then ensure that you make different choices, a cry can be many things, as can a laugh. Find the variation from the impulse of your text/character. This enables you to find layers and bring extra dimensions to the work.

Sirens and diaphragmatic bouncing to laugh

`2.18.5`

Here are two approaches to laughing on cue:

`2.18.5a`

- Lie down and say 'tee hee hee' quite high in your range – this seems so simple yet is incredibly effective. Then come down to your centre note and say 'ha ha ha'. Drop down your voice and say 'ho ho ho'.

- Repeat all three in different pitches and placements. Then when you have tried it all technically – and this is so easy it will take very little time – you then think of something funny and try them again. Try with a bit of text. Stop and start the laughing at will.

`2.18.5b`

- Another way to find your laugh is to lie down and place your hands on your centre around your navel. Then let in a little breath and say 'hah' – very lightly, just imagine you are touching it off your centre. Repeat. Now let a little breath into your hands and say a light little 'hah'. It is important not to have too much 'h' – check that your channel is open, there should be no constriction. Hardly any 'h', just light and easy. Do this a few times.

- Let in a little breath under your hands and say 'hah-hah'. Repeat.

- Same again, with 'hah-hah-hah'. Build up to four in a row, then five, then six, until you are doing as many as you can. Do this without facial expression, and then, when you know it is totally free and centred, just laugh!

- You can now let go, laugh high, low, belly laughs and just the feeling of being tickled pink into giggles.

2.18.6 Cry and laugh

This is also inspired by Lise Olson – now you cry and laugh alternately.

I like to do this in a group – a thumbs-up signal means everyone laughs, thumbs down means everyone cries. Do this without facial expressions first, and then give yourselves permission to make all the faces you want. If you alternate really quickly, you can tell if it is coming from technique (in other words, it is not self-indulgent or out of control) – and best of all, it is really funny to do and to watch!

2.18.7 Text

Try out some bits of text and apply the laugh and cry techniques.

2.18.8 Articulation

In Appendices TIV3a–c. If you have time, go through all this weekly.

2.18.9

Repeat some of that text again.

Session 19

Keywords: *Heightened vocal states – laughing and crying, abuse and shouting*

Warm-up

2.19.1

As in the last session, construct your own warm-up. You need to be very open, released and totally on-breath. If in any doubt, go through the whole extended warm-up in detail from Part 4.

If your voice is not completely ready and warm (and by now you will absolutely know what that feels like), add in some further resonance and humming work, lying in semi-supine and then taking it into rolling, sitting and standing.

Remember to include jaw-release work, and be soft and released.

2.19.2

Further work on warm-up, resonance and power support

1   Lie in semi-supine and feel the spine and whole body release, widen and lengthen.

2   The 'frog position' – lie on your back with the knees up, feet on the floor, then let the knees fall out until the soles of the feet are touching each other (as if praying with the feet).

   •   Let the breath in and out on 'f', 'sh', 'v', hums, etc. The longer you do this and use the breath to relax, the more your hip joints, knees and ankles will soften and release. You can then feel the breath coming deep into the body.

- Imagine that you are breathing through your groin area. Great work if you let it just be. If there is any discomfort beyond a bit of tension or muscle ache, then engage and use your core (abdominal) muscles to bring yourself back into semi-supine. But that bit of ache, as long as there is no pain and no sharpness, will be eased by the exercise – especially by doing it with breathing and sounding into any muscles, tendons, or joints that feel the ache.

- Let the breath and your voice soften the joints. At the same time, this position enables you to get a fantastically free and deep breath into the body.

3   Side to side – return the knees to the upright, feet flat, then gently rock and roll the knees to either side. As you do so, breathe and sound out on a hum, then into 'ah' and 'oo', several times.

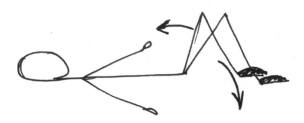

4   Roll to lie on your front, face down.

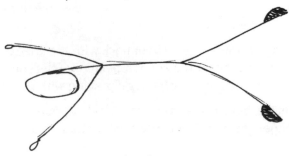

- On the out breath, hum and press down into the floor with your hands, feel the abdominals engage, and use as much of your body, easily but as firmly as you can, to power your support system and the hums. Take this on to any sounds that feel easy.

- *Variation:* press also with the tops of your feet, and you should get quite a bit of extra 'oomph' – this is a fun way of discovering how much grounding and power you get from really working with the body.

- *Variation:* try this with little 'fists', with the same pressing-down for sound.

- *Variation:* bring your hands back until they are roughly under your shoulders (as if you were about to do a press-up) and then use the 'v' and hums, pressing through your hands (check you are released through the shoulders, and avoid any tension in the upper chest or back). Again, you will feel a strong support and powerful but easy sound.

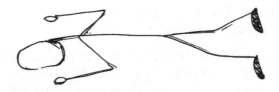

Then as you continue to 'v', push up with your hands to all fours into kneeling. Then push back with your hands so you are kneeling up, and have a shout. Now play with the floor whilst 'v'-ing, finding support through your hands, knees, sit bones, feet. Roll around, keep sounding, then come to standing and with the memory of all that strong engagement, continue sounding with your 'v' and hums, and 'mah's. The support will continue to be intensified and remembered as you stand and continue to sound.

2.19.3 Revise laughing and crying

- Try this lying down first – going through the sirens on 'm', 'n', 'ng', into 'ma-ha-ha' and the diaphragmatic bounces for laughter.

- Come to standing and do the whole lot again, upright.

- Drink a little water.

2.19.4 Shouting

- Do some lovely yawns to remind the larynx and channel to open up and stay free, and do a little easy chewing. Stay soft.

- Standing very easily, let a breath in and just call out from your centre. Go to a wall and do a bit of horizontal abseiling with 'v', a hum, and into 'mah' and 'moo'. Increase the volume gradually until it is fairly loud. This should feel very easy. Come away from the wall and try it – with the muscle memory of the abseiling, and the support from both the wall and the floor work earlier – still very clear, rooted and centred. Do a little hum on 'm' or 'n', around the middle of your range, shake about a bit, and then just have a shout – 'HAH!' or 'NO!'

Once you are fully warmed up and in a good state of conscious release, it will all be very easy. The main thing is not to pull back in any way. Be open, be free, keep everything engaged, alive and soft, and let it out. If you are teaching or leading the group, then you may need to check that no one is constricting (chin jut is a common default) so ensure the head/neck relationship is good and that there is no collapsing through the back of the neck. I find that – when everyone is warm and has done all the strong support preparation, followed by a little hum – by just demonstrating with open arms and shouting, while signalling that they should just join in, no one has time to stop themselves or constrict! Once people have been 'kidded' into doing it without stopping, they realise how easy it is. Furthermore, at this stage in training, people always know if they are straining or constricting in any way, and have a pretty good awareness of whether they need to stop and check or can carry on and sound out in a very released manner.

If you feel any strain, stop and check that nothing is tensed up. Have another go. Yawn again, and do a few little hums. Sip some water.

Try out some phrases – use something from any text you have.

Abuse – swearing

I began to teach a class in swearing because I noticed that, when actors have to swear with a given text, they sometimes become very disconnected or overemphatic. If you do not swear in your everyday life, then, as with any character work that is very different from yourself, you have to go to a new place physically and emotionally. And if people do use swear words habitually, they sometimes overdo them when acting, so that the language of abuse sounds somehow tacked on. So either an actor doesn't quite want to commit, or they overcommit and it becomes technically tense or emotionally untruthful – and often both. Of course, you have to use the language, and if a character is very angry or in some other extreme emotional state, then the language needs to be allowed to go there, but always from a safe state, and with a connected and truthful impulse. Like a stage fight, you work it out and then integrate it.

Here is a progression to play with – you may have come across something similar before, as it is quite a common way into abusive language. It is best done in a group.

There is no need to be loud either, do this sequence on normal volume.

- Swear with everyday words – look at someone in the group and say: 'You door!' 'You radiator!' 'You wall!' (This is the best bit, in a way, because it is really funny, and also somehow more abusive than the worst of scatological language and expletives.)

- Add in some adjectives – 'You yellow door!' 'You stupid radiator!' 'You plastic paintpot!', etc.

267

- Swear using children's swear words – think of your own, share ideas.

- Now swear using adult swear words – again, share ideas and try them all out.

Do all this without too much emotion, then, ensuring you stay released and open, add in some venom. This is fun and very empowering. It is not personal! If you find there are words you don't like, then talk them through. If anyone is struggling, go back to the ordinary words and flip between 'fff-ancy coat' and 'stupid arsehole' (or whatever it is you don't like) until it is just another word. Then when it comes to the context, it won't jump out or be held back, and it will be integrated and truthful.

2.19.6 Warm-down

Drink some water and do some gentle humming around the middle of your range. Check all is well by humming and 'ah-ing' up and down, and then rest.

2.19.7 Articulation

Go through some massage and release exercise then a few articulation drills (Appendices TIV3a–c).

2.19.8 Text

- Try out some Shakespeare curses – on normal volume, then raising the level. There is no need to overdo the volume, as the language itself holds the power, but you need all options. These insults are wonderful.

  'Thou reeky flap-mouthed hedge-pig!'
  'Thou beslubbering sheep-biting measle.'
  'You clack-dish.'
  'Thou elvish-marked, abortive, rooting hog!'
  'Thou rag of honour!'
  'Curse this poisonous bunch-backed toad.'

- And now really use the consonants. Take that last one – Shakespeare makes you slow down, because to get the full effect you need to use and let us hear the 'ch' of bunch, the 'b' then the 'k' then the 't' phonemic sounds in 'backed', and the 't' and 'd' in toad. Spit it out quietly and see how much venom you can muster. I also like 'rag of honour' because it seems so innocuous. One of my favourite insults as an actor is from a Restoration play, where a character calls a servant 'thou fragment of the shop' and 'thou thing' – what a put-down!

- Warm down again, gently humming around the middle of your range, to bring everything back into equilibrium.

Session 20

Keywords: *Heightened vocal states – anger; application to Marlowe text*

2.20.1 Warm-up

Do an extensive warm-up as before.

2.20.2 Repeat the extended resonance for further warming

As in the previous session, including the frog position, and side-to-side release and sounding work.

2.20.3 Power support

- Again, repeat the floor work, and the power support taken from lying on your front. Place your hands on the floor by your shoulders – this should engage the core muscles very readily.

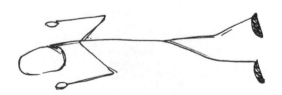

- Bring it all to kneeling and then to standing.

Sirens and pitch glides

- Release the jaw with some massages and stroking down. Have a few easy yawns. Now do some sirens on 'm', 'n' and 'ng', and take them into 'mah', 'nah', 'moo', 'noo' and 'ng-ah', with a little crying and laughing for good measure.

- Try all this standing and walking around the space, ensuring all is free, forward placed and easy.

Anger

The voice of anger is a big one – not only can it sometimes be very loud, but even quiet anger can get tense. Also, this work tends to bring up emotional memories and so you need to work very dispassionately and technically. The process allows you to be totally in the moment and utterly released because it gives you a safe place to work from.

- Talk about anger – be objective – and think about what makes people angry and why, and what happens to you. Always connect each part of this with a breath.

We are going to use a methodical progression.

- Begin on all fours.

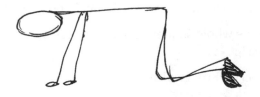

Ensure that your head is in good alignment with the rest of the spine so that you are looking at the floor. Your shoulders are soft, everything is easy, released and aligned. Remember to keep soft in the hands (soft kitty paws, or tiny hot-air balloons under the palms) to prevent any jamming up through the arm and shoulder joints.

This sequence works in two parts. The first is the progression from calm through to anger; the second part is the application to increasingly percussive/sonic choices. You have an *impulse*, which is your emotional state or thought, and your *sound*, which responds to that.

- For each of the following, you let in a little breath and release it towards the floor. The channel is open so there is no sound on the in-breath or the out-breath, for the first sequence (breath only).

  a) Think of something slightly irritating – send a breath towards the floor.

  b) Get a little annoyed – send a breath towards the floor.

  c) Get very annoyed – send a breath towards the floor.

  d) Now you are angry – send a breath towards the floor.

- You now repeat the whole sequence with a voiceless fricative, so it looks like this:

  a) Think of something slightly irritating – send a baby 'f' towards the floor.

  b) Get a little annoyed – send a baby 'f' towards the floor.

  c) Get very annoyed – send a baby 'f' towards the floor.

  d) Now you are angry – send a baby 'f' towards the floor.

- Repeat the whole sequence with a voiceless plosive – do it all with a 'p'.

- Repeat all four parts with a 'v'.

- Then do it all with a 'b'.

- Think of an innocuous word like 'potato'. So you say 'potato' normally, and then with a slightly irritated thought, then with a little annoyance, progressing to real anger. Keep checking that everything is free.

- Do this all without emoting. The thought of annoyance or anger is there, and the sounds will be strong, but you are in total control of what you are doing. Like the flipping between laughing and crying, you 'f' and 'b' and 'potato' at will, with anger, pleasure, whatever you want. There is no doubt that you may feel some of the emotion because your body has a psycho-physical response (the connection between emotional and physical states), much in the way that, when you technically laugh with a bounce from the diaphragm, or cry technically with a pitch glided 'm' into a sob, you may well feel sad, or burst out laughing. But the point is that you can start and stop yourself at any moment. It's acting!

You are planning all this much as you would a stage fight or dance sequence. The emotional truth comes from the context, and the text.

- Direct your anger to the floor.

- Sip some water.

- Drop into prayer position or child pose, relax and release, and have a little rest.

- You can try out the whole sequence in prayer position, if it feels good, and rest again.

Do not do this or indeed any extreme vocal state for more than ten minutes in any one session.

- Come back to all fours, and, if feeling relaxed and in no way tired, massage and stroke down your jaw very softly, and repeat.

Check and observe your own physicality to ensure that no excessive tension has crept in, and that no self-indulgence takes you into unsafe (and boring, untruthful) practice.

Before trying out some text, sit and breathe out, then breathe in the image of a perfect spring day, or take yourself to a place that makes you feel very relaxed and comfortable.

- Try out the whole sequence standing.

- Have a rest and do some gentle humming. Sip some water.

- Bring it on to text.

2.20.6 Text

Choose either something that you may be working on, or a bit of the cursing in Shakespeare.

I also suggest you look at Christopher Marlowe's *Tamburlaine, Part 1* for huge and powerful speeches. Look at Tamburlaine himself, and at Zabina and Bajazeth. In Act Four, Scene Two, Tamburlaine orders that the captured king Bajazeth is taken out of his cage and forced to kneel for Tamburlaine to use as a stepping stool – 'Bring out my footstool' – this is a king he is talking about. Bajazeth curses him, and the following exchange 'Base villain, vassal, slave... Stoop villain, stoop!' and 'Fiends look on me, and thou dread god of hell...' – is heady, angry stuff, and you need all that technique in order to go to what Ben Jonson called Marlowe's 'mighty line'.

Later in the play you can look up Act Five, Scene Two, where the king and his wife Zabina kill themselves – 'Now Bajazeth, abridge thy baneful days, / And beat thy brains out of thy conquered head', following which his queen rages herself into a frenzy – 'O Bajazeth, my husband and my lord, / ...Hell, death, Tamburlaine, hell, make ready my coach, I come I come!' and she runs against the cage and bashes her head into the bars, braining herself to death. It doesn't get much bigger than this, so you can see how far you have to be prepared to let go.

Use this sequence:

- Read through as normal.

- Whisper the consonants only.

- Whisper the vowels.

- Speak both.

- Speak both with anger.

Warm-down

Do a little gentle humming around the middle of your range to bring everything back to equilibrium.

Keep hydrating for twenty-four hours – you will hopefully be in the habit of taking in sufficient daily fluids, but after any extreme vocal states, it is particularly helpful to remind yourself to keep drinking, warm water being the best option. This not only hydrates your whole system, but the action of swallowing relaxes the musculature of the larynx, as I mentioned early in the first chapter. Avoid ice-cold water, as this can cause the throat to contract and restrict, causing possible tensions. Do some steaming too (see end of Part 4).

Session 21

Keywords: *Heightened states – anger, screaming; choric text*

2.21.1 Warm-up and preparation

- For at least twenty to thirty minutes, go through a full warm-up preparation as in the last sessions. Ensure that you include plenty of easy pitch glides, humming and finding power support on your front.

- Take a few sips of water.

- Do some yawning.

2.21.2 Revise anger

You can go quite quickly through the progressive sequence for anger, from the last session (no more than three minutes should cover it). This acts both as a reminder and helps you ensure that you are totally free in the breath channel with a fully supported voice.

Drink a little water.

2.21.3 Rest

- Lie in semi-supine, and as the breath comes in, imagine you are breathing in the air of a perfect spring or summer day. Do some gentle humming.

If you feel the need for further release work, release your breath on sounds using images.

- Release on 'f' and imagine your stream of 'f' as a delicate, fluffy cloud.

- Release on 's' and imagine it as a halo of light forming around you.

- Release on 'sh' and imagine it as a vapour trail.

- Repeat with voiced sounds of 'v', 'z' and 'zh', using those same images.

Screaming (i)

This is easy if you have all that basic technique under your belt.

- Massage your scalp, temples, face and jawline, stroke it down softly and let go.

- Lie in semi-supine, do some easy mid-range humming. Do a few pitch glides/sirens.

- Glide up and down on 'm', 'n' and 'ng', but limit your pitch range – not too high or too low.

- Release those glides into 'mah' and 'nah' and 'ng-ah'.

- Gently humming, come to sitting and then standing.

- Do some very gentle abseiling – so connect with a wall or door, and very softly push yourself away, whilst sounding on a 'v'. You will still get the support and a sense of grounding, but by doing it softly through the hands, everything in your body will remain open and easy. Check that you have a good head–neck relationship (by ensuring that you don't throw the head back at all).

- Walk around the space, floating your arms around in a very loose 'dance', whilst sounding out on 'vvv' and 'mmm-ah'. The feet stay grounded but all is easy and free.

- Come to standing, maintaining that freedom of movement, have a little yawn, soften the jaw. Then open the mouth, let in a breath and let out a scream. If you really just do it, with all that warming, placement and freedom, there should be no problems at all.

At the time of writing, I have just taken my current second-year students through this progression. Everyone in the group let out a wonderful, free and released scream. When I asked what enabled them to do this, they rattled off a list of the 'usual suspects': alignment, support, open throat, ease and release, forward placement, warm voice, connection to the centre. Then one of them summed it up perfectly and succinctly. He said: 'No reticence.' So, as was said, all you need to think about is to have no reticence. Let it go.

That's really it. If you have the fundamental technique integrated into your body and voice, then after a thorough warm-up you think, 'I'll scream' – and you scream. You let it out. The lightest and briefest of hums immediately afterwards brings you right back to 'normal'. This is, in fact, easier than an angry shout for most people. It is such a freeing sound.

To add an extra layer, for example if you are working on a play where several characters scream, or one screams several times, you can mix it up with variations on pitch and tone. Experiment. A very powerful sound is achieved when a male actor screams high in his voice, or even in falsetto. If he is technically proficient and free, the sound will be safe and clear, and can be awesomely disturbing!

Don't overdo this work, though – in a two-hour class that includes a full vocal warm-up and workout, each person will do these heightened states for no more than about ten minutes, spread out in short bursts over the period of an hour or more, with plenty of rest, light hums, and sips of water between each extreme sound. When in rehearsals and performance, ensure that you always warm down. If any damage is going to occur (and there is no reason why it should hurt your voice at all if you know what you are doing), then it is usually not during a performance but afterwards. Without a warm-down, if you rush out to a party and start shouting or talking too loudly, you might overdo it without realising. So warm down, take care of yourself. Integration is not just for acting, it's for life!

Screaming (ii) – the released tantrum 2.21.4

Here is an alternative exercise:

- A further physical gesture you can use is to jump around like a jellyfish, so you are very free and soft in the body. Then open out the arms and bring them down firmly but gently, as if saying 'ta-dah!' – as if you are presenting something. You might think of this as a relaxed or released tantrum, as a student of mine recently called it – so it's like stamping your foot and bringing the hands down and forwards, keeping them open and strong like a big bunch of bananas. This opens the body out and helps to bring the sound forward, but with an incredible sense of freedom, softness and ease.

This works for a shout as well, of course.

- Drink a little water, and have a mid-range hum, very gently, to bring everything back into equilibrium.

- Do a warm-down by either standing easily or go into semi-supine and do a little humming.

- Have a rest for a few minutes.

Articulation and text 2.21.5

As usual, do some articulation work to keep it all trotting along-side your vocal development.

- Try out some text. If you feel up to it, by all means have a little easy scream with bits of text. If you are in any way vocally tired, then just speak a little, at normal volume.

- Go on to some chorus speaking – see Part 3 for exercises on ensemble movement and breath. Then try out the following wonderfully visceral and very direct chorus from Liz Lochhead's *Thebans*. Students commented that it is stirring, 'beautifully truthful' and said 'it feels like the author has been affected and is a part of the story.' Try it in a group, and then split sections between male and female voices; see what works and discover why.

CHORUS.
> fear   that's the god that rules us now
> our hammering hearts won't stop
> a tiny pulse of agitation beats behind every temple
> little incendiaries of anxieties ignite
> till fullblown terror catches fire and overwhelms us
>
> we are quaking
>
> any moment now the noise of battle
> loud alarms and sirens
> drowned out in louder clash and screaming
> our city's finest   our bravest men
> are on the very battlements
>
> what will happen to us all
> to our prayers and our hopes?
> from the enemy skies a hail of missiles
> comes whistling down   raining on us bullseyes
> targeting our defenders with terrifying accuracy
>
> cities stand so tall
> we live in them forgetting they can be broken
> brought down in flaking ashes   smoke and horror
>
> the broken city is a forest that offers no shelter
> no shelter for the   screaming baby
> starving on the breast of the murdered mother
> for the raped girl splayed beneath the laughing soldiers
> for the old men herded like beasts
> for their mutilated corpses
> for the old women dragged by the hair like animals
>
> for the skulls cracked like egg-shell
>
> now is the time
> time for our terror that has been so long growing
> to be harvested
> nightmare may be tomorrow's news
> but at least   at last
> for good   for ill
> the battle will be over

those among us who are men
or remnants of men   must fight
adrenalin and terror   a tidal wave
sweeps each to a fateful city gate

and those who are women
must cower at home and pray and wait

It is a dark, horrible piece, described by another actor as being 'like a diary entry' – which I think is a good way in, as it seems so personal. Look at the spaces within the text and use those pauses. Feel the beats and work for the choric voice, using the breath to aid your speaking as a group. Find the changes, and you can start to orchestrate the piece with pitch and tone, volume and differing dynamics. It is powerful stuff.

Session 22

Keywords: *Breath and resonance; extending range; revise the scream; wail*

2.22.1 Warm-up and preparation

For at least twenty to thirty minutes, go through a full warm-up preparation, as in the previous sessions.

2.22.2 Rest – image work

Repeat 2.21.3.

2.22.3 Resonance and placement

Do plenty more humming and 'mah'-ing on the floor with pouring, and then bringing it to standing and moving round the space.

2.22.4 Revise the scream

As usual it is good to revise from a previous session, so go over the processes for screaming from last time.

2.22.5 Gentle scream into a wail or lament

Screams are not always loud. If you take the volume right down, you can imagine you are lamenting some terrible sadness or loss. You need only use the gentle sirens/pitch glides to release out into 'mah', 'nah' and 'ng-ah', adding in a little sobbing quality. Let the diaphragm bounce a little for the sob. It is like a very sad laugh.

You can also try this:

- Release your voice with a gentle 'oo' sound on a mid- to high pitch. Then choose a lower note, and 'sing' between the two notes.

- Speed up so that you are going quickly from one to the other, high to low and back again.

- Speed up again so that you are oscillating the sounds. The faster you do this, the more strange the quality, until you are wailing and almost ululating. (Ululating is also a sound achieved by fast movements of the tongue, and can be used both in celebration and as a howl or wail of grief. The sounds are commonly associated with Arab cultures in particular. Ululation was used in ancient Egypt and in ancient Greece – in *Agamemnon* it expresses ecstasy and joy, as well as rage and grief.)

As with all these states, experiment, and see how many different qualities you can find. Get the group sounding out on a gentle hum and then 'oo' or 'ah', and have individuals trying out these oscillations – it's rather like a yodeling quality. Take it gently and it can be very mournful and disturbing, and fantastic for deeply sad texts and atmospheres. I used wailing and lamentation to create soundscapes in both *Widows* by Ariel Dorfman and *Phaedra's Love* by Sarah Kane. By choreographing the laments, using variations of pitch, tone and volume, lamentation in the former was an unbearably sad sound; and in the other was grotesquely disturbing and chilling.

- Try some text – a great example of lament in Shakespeare comes in *Richard III* when Queen Elizabeth mourns for her lost babies:

Ah, my poor princes! Ah, my tender babes!
My unblown flowers, new-appearing sweets!
If yet your gentle souls fly in the air

And be not fixed in doom perpetual,
Hover about me with your airy wings
And hear your mother's lamentation.

- Or from *King John* when Constance is lamenting her dead son:

O Lord, my boy, my Arthur, my fair son,
My life, my joy, my food, my all the world,
My widow-comfort, and my sorrow's cure!

Speak these texts, and see where you might wail or lament. Use this lament quality as you speak the words, choosing just a few to do it with. It doesn't need to be loud, or used throughout on every word (and indeed is better used in moderation) but a sob quality and a ululated hover, 'ah', or sob on the words 'hear... lamentation' will evoke the most extraordinary sounds and sensations in the speaker and the listener.

- Warm down with some gentle humming.

Session 23

Keywords: *Extending range; opposing extremes – the outdoor voice and voice for television and film*

In this session we will look at the outdoor voice, and then go to the opposite extreme, if you like, to consider voice for television and film. The same vocal equipment, but the application is different.

2.23.1–2.23.3

Repeat 2.21.1, 2.21.3, 2.22.3.

Articulation

2.23.4

• Warm up the articulators, and then go through the sequences on Appendices TIV3b and c, with a great deal of released muscularity and agility.

Really challenge yourself on these sequences and sounds, and go for both precision and pace.

The outdoor voice

2.23.5

Working in the open air presents its own challenges. The main factors to consider are where you are – if in a wonderful amphitheatre, your voice is likely to go out and come back to you

285

with relative ease. If, however, you are in an outdoor playing space that is very open and has no walls or structures to bounce your sound off, then you need to be very specific about how and where you place the sound. Other factors to consider include ambient noise, which can be from the weather, or aircraft, traffic or people talking – all sorts of noise may compete. The weather affects your voice – if it is a cold day, then you may tense up and your voice and body may need a lot more warming up than usual to ensure safe usage. If it is hot and humid, this can affect the vocal folds, so you will want to ensure you have a very open channel, with lots of hydration to help. And if it is windy, then your voice can literally get carried away.

You need to support your voice absolutely, surely and strongly outside; your articulation is paramount, and your intention and direction must be very clear. Directional sound becomes important – in many open playing spaces, you simply can't let your head wander or 'float around', and so you may need to make adjustments. It is likely you will need to physically change certain moments – a casual turn of the head is not normally enough in an open-air space with a large audience. You need to turn the whole body in the direction of your gaze. You then guide or direct the audience very clearly and they will follow your voice. Think about directing your speech very clearly to the audience. Clarity of expression through strong and muscular articulation makes an enormous difference, far more so on a windy day or when you're outside competing for the audience's attention (they get more distracted outside) – so dropped word endings and sloppy consonants won't cut through.

- Go outside and try speaking at a normal, everyday volume, and just see how it feels. Ideally working with a group, chat to each other and become aware of the sensation of voice outside. Then choose somewhere as your 'audience' and speak to them. Listen to each other, and notice whose voice and speech carry most and try to work out why. Pitching, clarity, volume and placement all have a bearing.

- Now look at your environment more specifically and see if you can try different directions. For example, you may be on a housing estate – so speak your text to the nearest wall; if there is a more open space, speak to that; if there are trees, speak to the nearest tree and then the furthest away. This really is all about intention. If you are in a very big, wide-open space, then you will certainly need to up the volume.

- If you are in a car park or a narrow street with a high wall, you can use this as an 'amphitheatre', where you will get a lot of your voice coming back to you, bouncing back off the surfaces of the wall. This is a great sensation and gives you confidence.

- Imagine you are in an outdoor theatre (maybe you are lucky enough to actually be in one!) and speak to your audience. Look at the sweep of the seats, take in the nearest, and speak to them, then take in the furthest away, and without pushing, just imagine you are speaking to friends with whom you really want to communicate.

- If it is very noisy and too much, then just give yourself a break and don't try and compete with it. You can speak over people chatting, you can use more 'oomph' from your support system and engage a bit more muscularity and shape, and be heard over some extraneous noises, but some you just can't. If an aeroplane goes high overhead, you might cut through it. If, however, a helicopter clatters past, there is very little chance that you can top it, so don't try! Just wait a moment. Everyone knows you are in the open air doing a performance in the twenty-first century, so you may as well acknowledge that – it doesn't mean you are coming out of character or out of the moment. It's just part of life.

The main thing here is to experiment – because there are so many variables, there isn't a complete list of what to do. You just have to use every ounce of your technique, integrating it totally into your body and connecting it to your intention. Be specific – if you are in any way woolly or unclear, whether physically, vocally, or in your thoughts, it won't carry. If you place yourself physically in the arena, open up your body and really use the space, connect to your support system and use all the dynamic range of voice and speech, it will happen for you. Help each other out, as you have done in other work, by doing a soundcheck for yourselves, in just the way you do when in a new theatre space indoors.

Having worked on such extreme, usually very loud vocal states, it is a great exercise to switch into voice for television – because you have to be in total control of your instrument, and it is a good game to play. So if doing a session on shouting or anger, do a bit of television-voice work before and after it, as this will challenge every aspect of your technique, and it demands a fair bit of your brain too, which can't be a bad thing.

2.23.6 Voice for television and film

The reason that this is in the chapter for 'extreme' vocal states is that, whilst you need masses of energised and strong support for shouting and screaming, you obviously have to use less volume, generally, for television voice, but it still has to be supported. Speaking quietly on full support takes quite a lot of sensitivity and control, especially when you have spent so much time developing a big, full, resonant voice. The tendency is either to carry on with that big voice so that it is too loud and booming, or the opposite happens to the extent that the actor devoices (goes off support and is so quiet or so unsupported that they are either difficult to hear or the shape of the word becomes indistinct, and often the integration goes right out of the window). So here are a few ideas to get you going. You now use all that technique but with very fine tuning.

Here is a simple progression for speaking on low volume but with clarity and support – sometimes people devoice on television because they want to sound 'natural'. However, it is eminently possible to sound extremely natural and still be on support! You still need to be heard. The main thing is to keep every part of your technique, it is just less obvious.

- Lie in semi-supine. Release your out-breath on some 'f' and 'sh' sounds, very gently. Really engage the support system and create a lot of space in the body with your breath.

- Repeat with 'v' and 'z' and a hum. Now try the 'v' and humming, sounding as quietly as you are able, whilst still supporting from your abdominals. Keep the sound constant and consistent.

- Come to sitting and then standing, and try out the above in each position.

I am indebted to Alex Bingley for the wonderful light image and 'volume control' in the following sequence for finding true support at quiet volumes.

1   Lie in semi-supine and imagine a ball of light inside you and think of it as a volume control – it will do the work.

- Release on 's'. The ball of light expands and increases the breath pressure.

- Still releasing on 's', the ball of light decreases and reduces the breath pressure. Your sound goes from loud to soft.

- Then sound quiet to loud on one breath on a 'v'.

- Ensure there is no tension in the abdominals or throat. There is exertion but no tension.

- Come onto all fours and then into prayer position for a minute. Soften in the jaw.

2   Return to all fours — blow out or release the air on 'f' using the ball of light and play with different pressures on 'v'.

- Repeat with a hum as quietly as possible.

- Take it onto 'oo' very quietly, like a light. Then repeat with 'oh' and 'ah'.

All this is very quiet but not devoiced. You are still on support, engaging the abdominals, closing cleanly at the vocal folds, but just doing it very quietly. This takes quite a bit of concentration!

3   Repeat this on all fours with some television text — chant or intone the text, as quietly as possible, using the light-control knob inside you.

- Imagine the light is under your hands — the light is small and therefore quiet, as the light expands the sounds get louder.

- Gradually expand the light until your voice is loud enough to fill a large space, then reduce again.

Keep the placement forwards, and take the volume up and down at will, maintaining full support. This flipping between very loud, to normal, to very quiet, is a great way of gaining total control of your technique.

4   Check that your articulation is absolutely 'present' but is effortless.

5   Stand and speak your lines at normal volume, and then very quietly, maintaining full support. Really pay attention to integrating breath and thought, and engage with the articulation. A word like 'soft' will sound soft, and that final 't' will be very delicate, but it will be heard and is *present*.

Session 24

Keywords: *Breath and resonance; extending range; ideas for other extreme vocal states*

Warm-up

2.24.1

- With some pouring on 'f', 'sh', 'v', 'z'.

- Then take a baby 'f' for a walk then a baby 'v'.

- Notice how all this feels after training your voice for some time.

Physically involve voice and body

2.24.2

- Do lots of patting and tapping with the usual sequence of sounds. Bang the chest, tap each others' backs (ensure you avoid the kidney area) and get that 'surround sound' going.

- Walk around the space with these, picking up the pace again and again until you are getting very physical and warm. Jump up and down with sounds.

- Do some sirens and pattern these through the body, letting it spiral up and down, roll up and down, and sound this with 'm', 'n' and 'ng'.

2.24.3 Semi-supine for release and resonance

Release, widen/lengthen and sound out on easy sounds – you choose.

2.24.4 Resonate and place the voice

Bring yourself to standing and try some abseiling with sounds.

2.24.5 Articulation

Go through the preparation and then do a mixture of sequences. Really play with this now, and use the complex consonant clusters that give all that added texture to your sound.

2.24.6 Text

Try out one of the earliest poems or speeches you worked on, and see how it has changed, or what you can now bring to it. This can be incredibly satisfying. Then try out a speech from a play you are currently working on.

2.24.7 Ideas for other vocal extremes

And finally, here are some ideas for other extreme states that you might find helpful.

Physically restricted characters

If you are playing a character who is in some way physically restricted, you simply need to ensure that you compensate. For example, I worked with an actor who was playing a wheelchair-bound character who had a form of paralysis on one side, so that she was slumped and compressed on the left side of her body. We worked to find plenty of space in that side, so that when she 'slumped', she maintained a feeling of space there. She could then breathe fairly easily into the 'paralysed' side of the body, and at the same time, we worked on breathing much more fully into the right side. The rib swing on that side was more pronounced, and she was able to take plenty of breath into the side and the back of the ribs. This also had the effect of her taking good breath and space into the slumped left side of the body, whilst looking apparently 'un'-abled in that area.

To find safe vocal usage is to become very aware of how you are creating your character's physical life, so here is another example, which is absolutely about integrating movement work and awareness into your voice. An actor was creating a 'mouse-like', very timid character, and part of the physical choice involved stooping a little, and holding the head forwards – so there was that voice teacher's worry of major chin jut. When we looked, it was clear that she was moving into the physicality from the front of her body – leading from the front of the shoulders and her chin, and the voice inevitably sounded quite constricted. So I worked with her on finding the initiation of the movement so that it came from the spine. We came to the upright, softened in the upper back, opened out – and back – from the spine, and then created the stoop. In doing so, we found a great amount of space and release through the back of the neck in particular. The voice then responded because the channel was far more open, so the actor could engage much more easily with the support system, and not go on her throat. This kind of work really needs guidance, but it gives you some ideas to work with at least.

Safe coughing, shortness of breath

If you have to cough as a character, I think it's a bit like having to smoke on stage (if in places where you could be asked to). Set up the idea of it (and in the case of smoking, which I once had to do whilst actually in the throes of a really sore throat and cough!) by constantly having the paraphernalia of the smoker, always about to light up, cigarette constantly held, or the cigarette packet being handled, without ever actually smoking. Nowadays there are some nifty 'electronic' prop cigarettes, so if you are using those, these notes are less important.

However, if you need to cough (whether as a smoker's cough or because the character has a cough) then set up the cough safely and 'act' it. The action in itself can be imitated by appearing to shake and spasm the body without actually doing so. You can also make a lot of safe noise by using the mouth, especially the lips, with a puffed, wet breath. Experiment and improvise cough-ing noises using lips and tongue, then add in the spasm through the body. The occasional cough is fine especially if it's voiceless, as is a voiced cough with clean onset and plenty of release and ease through the action – the voiceless cough will carry in quite large performance spaces. Like anything in acting, if one's inten-tion is clear, it will carry to the audience. The main thing is to ensure that you are breathing down into the lower lungs and using the full extent of your diaphragmatic and intercostal breath, with good rib swing. You then act the spasm and appar-ent 'clavicular' breath – make it look like you are heaving up in the chest, but you are in fact breathing properly into your centre and lower-back ribs.

I think the same applies to shortness of breath – if you appear to be struggling to breathe, and signal it through the body, you can still take a good diaphragmatic deep breath, whilst making it look like you are gasping or can only take very short raspy breaths. Again, use the lips/teeth and tongue to make the sound, so none of it is done at the vocal folds. If any drying-out occurs, use the trick of rubbing the tongue tip quickly and quite firmly against the lower-front teeth – you gets lots of saliva very quickly and it keeps everything nice and moist.

If it helps, you can place your hands on your lower ribcage at each side, ensuring that you let the ribs swing out to take a good cen-tred breath. Keep the hands there and pretend to heave in the upper chest, or indeed do heave, but make sure that the ribs are swinging and the breath is low. The hands will guide you towards this safe usage. You can also really feel the back ribs opening out too.

Other 'extremes'

You will probably have to experiment and improvise, but now have plenty of techniques and imaginative ideas to get you started. A few examples:

- Sex noises – use your imagination! But do think about it – it's not just one sound or one pitch...

- Strangling – you can make some very impressive 'being strangled' sounds by using just your tongue. Get lots of saliva, raise the tongue sides and send breath through, to create gurgling sounds. All this is therefore done without using the voice itself. You can add in vocal sounds but by keeping them to a minimum you work safely and easily.

- Vomiting – there may be occasion when you need to 'vomit' on stage or screen. Rather like the strangling sounds, you can do a lot with the tongue. Also the cheeks – if you puff out the cheeks and make the movement of vomiting, you look like it's happening and the sounds are also effective, if you then release them through the lips.

- Giving birth – generally a lot of deep sounds, so get very open, and let out groans, etc., from your centre. The odd high shriek will layer the sound. And ask someone who has done it!

Try things out, always with a sense first of release, openness, support, and ease.

- Remember always to *warm down* – it is essential that you do this.

- Rest, relax, gently hum. Be easy, forward-placed and soft.

- Do gentle pitch glides on 'ng'. Hum again, getting smaller each time.

- If the show has been relatively straightforward both physically and emotionally, this can all be done as you are getting changed.

- If you have played a highly physically and emotionally demanding part, you may be very tired – take time to lie down in semi-supine, and do this gentle humming for five minutes. This will give you some energy back and restore you to equilibrium and ease.

What Next?

As you go into your third year of training, and then take the leap into a career as an actor, the temptation is to stop working on your voice, movement and acting skills, as if they were somehow 'done with'! But they are only just beginning. I strongly recommend that if you are no longer having formal classes, then you maintain your own daily workouts, and keep exploring the voice.

If you don't maintain your core skills, you really will lose some of them. It won't all go or disappear, especially if you are working as an actor, but now is the time to consolidate everything you have learned and worked on so far. The benefit is that the work will now go much deeper.

So if you are at the beginning of a third year in training, I think it incredibly helpful if you go right back to the start. I used to teach third-year voice classes, and at the start of the final year, I taught the students a first-term, first-year class. The now well-trained actors loved it, because they found incredible depth coming to and from the work. It was a wonderful surprise, but that's the great thing about this work – it never stops working for you and your voice.

As you go on, you will find much greater range and complexity to your voice and your acting. Part of this is due to ongoing work, part of it is just that, as you get a little older, your voice will gain more depth and range – as long as you use it, it keeps forming new layers through experience, life, and continuing muscular and cellular training.

Consolidate the work, keep working on the basics, and apply it all to repertoire. Now you can start to think very specifically about voice and speech and what you are working on. The warm-up chapter gives some ideas for this, but much of it is down to you thinking about what the work is about, and then adapting your voice accordingly. You have the techniques, so now find that artistry and put them all together. And keep going, because an integrated voice is a wonder.

Part 3

'This Way Please'
– ways into text

Part 3

'This Way Please' – Ways into Text

I am including a separate chapter on text in order to consolidate and put down a number of ways in which you can tackle text. Obviously, work on text could entail a whole book to itself, but here are some ideas to get you going. Each of these, whether a one-off, or the progressive series of exercises such as the sequences on 'demystifying Shakespeare', can be used as an adjunct to the lesson plans or warm-ups. There are many ways to get into a text and I think you need to try out as many as possible, particularly if you are having difficulties with a word, a line, or a speech. Never make assumptions and always do it physically first – this is a great way to begin inhabiting the language, to make a sensuous and visceral connection to words.

First-year work – let's begin with a big one.

Demystifying Shakespeare

First of all, why use Shakespeare in the first year of training? There are various schools of thought on this, but I think it's good to at least introduce him as soon as possible, certainly in the second term or semester, because he's a good writer, and good writing is much easier to work with than bad writing. Also, because the density and richness of the language deserves a very simple starting point, and you can build on that and go into much more depth in the second year and beyond. For people unused to speaking classical text or poetry, it can take a long time to become familiar with it, never mind good at it. By starting gently, then repeating and repeating, going into more detail and more depth each time, a build-up occurs. The only way to get really good at this stuff is to do it a lot. There are a few people who are natural-born verse speakers, but most of us have to work at it until it becomes 'natural' and easy.

I find that, presented in the right way, Shakespeare can thrill people who have never had much, if any, experience of his work. It can truly surprise students who may have had a negative experience or hold preconceptions, and it will appeal to those who already love the writing, because finding the 'simplicity in complexity' is a real eye-opener. The demystifying of Shakespeare's language, therefore, can speak to all.

Where to Begin

Let's start with the Prologue to *Henry V*. I begin with this because it *is* a beginning – a prologue is an introduction, a speech before a play, a scene-setter if you like. And this particular prologue is so much about theatre, actors and audience that it talks to us directly through the centuries, which is part of the surprise factor. It tells us right away that we are in the theatre – there is no pretence other than the imagination that we are going to need. It tells us that Shakespeare understood the world of the play and the theatre, and reminds us that he was an actor too. It also reveals just how directly Shakespeare speaks to his live theatre audience. I believe he was the model for much of Brecht's work, and certainly for many more modern and contemporary writers. There are direct comparisons between these writers – the way that they create highly complex characters and then surprise us and provoke thought in the audience almost in the same moment. Brecht asks us to come out of the emotion of a moment through direct address (among many of his techniques) and Shakespeare does the same thing. We know we are in the theatre.

This prologue is so enchanting, too, in how it practically begs the audience to forgive the actors their inadequacies. We've only got a few actors ('Into a thousand parts divide one man' – imagine that each actor playing a soldier represents a thousand on the battlefield), our theatre is tiny and we want to show you a whole country ('Can this cockpit [a little, round building] hold the vasty [huge] fields of France?') and just please, please, please use your imagination ('*Think*, when we talk of horses, that you *see them*'). What a brilliant way to open a play – ask or rather *tell* your audience to help you!

Physicalise the text

3.1

The first exercise is *physical*! Do not sit and read it, and don't look up any words, yet.

- Get up and physicalise the text. This means you read it off the page and at the same time you describe what you are saying physically. This could be very literal – 'O' is described and shaped by your hands and arms forming a big 'O' or circle, getting the whole body involved; or it can be as abstract as you like. Be big and bold – overdo it and have fun.

CHORUS.
  O for a Muse of fire, that would ascend
  The brightest heaven of invention,
  A kingdom for a stage, princes to act,
  And monarchs to behold the swelling scene!
  Then should the warlike Harry, like himself,
  Assume the port of Mars, and at his heels,
  Leashed in like hounds, should famine, sword, and fire
  Crouch for employment. But pardon, gentles all,
  The flat unraised spirits that hath dared
  On this unworthy scaffold to bring forth
  So great an object. Can this cockpit hold
  The vasty fields of France? Or may we cram
  Within this wooden O the very casques
  That did affright the air at Agincourt?
  O, pardon! since a crooked figure may
  Attest in little place a million,
  And let us, ciphers to this great account,
  On your imaginary forces work.
  Suppose within the girdle of these walls
  Are now confined two mighty monarchies,
  Whose high upreared and abutting fronts
  The perilous narrow ocean parts asunder.
  Piece out our imperfections with your thoughts:
  Into a thousand parts divide one man,
  And make imaginary puissance.
  Think, when we talk of horses, that you see them
  Printing their proud hoofs i'th'receiving earth;
  For 'tis your thoughts that now must deck our kings,
  Carry them here and there, jumping o'er times,
  Turning th'accomplishment of many years
  Into an hour-glass: for the which supply,
  Admit me Chorus to this history,
  Who, prologue-like your humble patience pray,
  Gently to hear, kindly to judge, our play.

- Don't worry if you don't understand it all – you probably won't at first, so just go with it and don't worry about the minutiae.

- Do it all again, and take your time. Overdo the words, 'chew' them, and see how your body and voice feel as you bow before your imaginary audience, in deference to them, as you beg their pardon for being so lowly, or as you point towards France, for example.

- Begin to see the *scope* and *size* and *space* conveyed in the speech. Shakespeare, I am sure, would have been a film-maker if he were living now. He is brilliant at visual pictures and at altering the perspective of a scene. Consider these 'shots':

  1 'the vasty fields of France' – do this very physically and as big as you can. Vast fields, the rural landscape of a whole country – this is the *panoramic shot*.

  2 'Agincourt' – the town and site of the battle in France – point to it. This is a different physical experience from pointing or sweeping your arms to indicate a whole country. You are probably pointing to somewhere more specific in or just beyond the space you are in – this is the *mid-shot*.

  3 'cockpit' – this little theatre – AND –'admit *me*, Chorus to this history' – me the actor – these are the *close-ups*.

- So now, see how you feel about the speech, and what sense it makes to you. You will certainly have a much better idea of its scope and you will also have a fair idea of the story it tells.

- Do this all again in further sessions, so that the repetition helps you become familiar both with the sensation of getting physical with the text, and gets the text itself inside you a little more each time. As you repeat this work, you can reduce the size of gesture, retaining the sense of it, and find a way to 'naturalise' and integrate the work into the words.

The next exercise can be done in the second session, or a week later.

<table>
<tr><td>**3.2**</td><td>**Find out the subject matter of the text**</td></tr>
</table>

If you are doing this a week or so later, go through the physicalising of the text to remind yourself what you discovered last time, then go on to the next way in.

We are going to look at the *nouns* in the speech. Find out what a noun is – simply, it's a word that is either a thing ('table', 'hound', 'invention' – this third example is called an abstract noun, whereas you could describe 'table' as a concrete noun) or a person ('Harry', 'I'), or a place (Agincourt, London); a naming word. It's surprising how many people don't have this basic grammatical knowledge (you're not alone!), but bit by bit you can learn new things. These are very useful to an actor – this is not just an intellectual exercise.

- Underline the nouns in the speech. It's easier and simpler if you leave out pronouns ('you', 'himself', 'this', 'us'). Just the main nouns. The speech is printed again below with all the nouns underlined. But do it for yourself first on the unmarked speech, in pencil, to see how you do, and then compare to the marked-up version.

> O for a <u>Muse</u> of <u>fire</u>, that would ascend
> The brightest <u>heaven</u> of <u>invention</u>,
> A <u>kingdom</u> for a <u>stage</u>, <u>princes</u> to act,
> And <u>monarchs</u> to behold the swelling <u>scene</u>!
> Then should the warlike <u>Harry</u>, like himself,
> Assume the <u>port</u> of <u>Mars</u>, and at his <u>heels</u>,
> Leashed in like <u>hounds</u>, should <u>famine</u>, <u>sword</u>, and <u>fire</u>
> Crouch for <u>employment</u>. But pardon, <u>gentles</u> all,
> The flat unraised <u>spirits</u> that hath dared
> On this unworthy <u>scaffold</u> to bring forth
> So great an <u>object</u>. Can this <u>cockpit</u> hold
> The vasty <u>fields</u> of <u>France</u>? Or may we cram
> Within this wooden <u>O</u> the very <u>casques</u>
> That did affright the <u>air</u> at <u>Agincourt</u>?

O, pardon! since a crooked figure may
Attest in little place a million,
And let us, ciphers to this great account,
On your imaginary forces work.
Suppose within the girdle of these walls
Are now confined two mighty monarchies,
Whose high upreared and abutting fronts
The perilous narrow ocean parts asunder.
Piece out our imperfections with your thoughts:
Into a thousand parts divide one man,
And make imaginary puissance.
Think, when we talk of horses, that you see them
Printing their proud hoofs i'th'receiving earth;
For 'tis your thoughts that now must deck our kings,
Carry them here and there, jumping o'er times,
Turning th'accomplishment of many years
Into an hour-glass: for the which supply,
Admit me Chorus to this history,
Who, prologue-like your humble patience pray,
Gently to hear, kindly to judge, our play.

• Read out loud all the nouns, in order as they appear in the speech. So what you have is this:

> Muse, fire, heaven, invention,
> kingdom, stage, princes, monarchs, scene!
> Harry, port, Mars,
> heels, hounds famine, sword, fire, employment.
> gentles, spirits, scaffold, object.
> cockpit, fields, France
> O [the circular wooden Globe theatre]
> casques [military helmets]
> air, Agincourt
> figure, place , ciphers, account,
> forces, girdle, walls, monarchies, fronts, ocean.
> imperfections, thoughts:
> parts, man, puissance [power]
> horses, hoofs, earth;
> thoughts, kings, times, accomplishment,

years, hour-glass: supply
Chorus, history,
patience,
play.

• Do this several times, speeding up a little each time until you can read the list fluently.

Reading this list will give you the subject matter of the speech, or the basic story. That is an incredibly simple and useful tool for understanding any speech. You can apply this to all texts, or at least ones you have difficulty in understanding.

3.3 Find out the action of the text

Having looked at nouns, we now look at verbs – the 'doing' words (which are more complex than nouns – verbs are divided into various forms, so you might have 'sit', 'sitting', 'to sit', 'sat', 'might sit' or 'would sit', and so on).

• Underline the verbs in a different colour. These are marked in bold in the next version, printed below.

These are slightly more complex, in that sometimes a verb is separated into two parts by other intervening words, and is sometimes inverted. Note, for example, that 'Then **should** the warlike Harry, like himself, **Assume** the port of Mars' means 'if Harry **should assume** [take on] the port [bearing] of Mars [the god of war]'. Read these two elements as one verb.

O for a Muse of fire, that **would ascend**
The brightest heaven of invention,
A kingdom for a stage, princes **to act**,
And monarchs **to behold** the swelling scene!
Then **should** the warlike Harry, like himself,
Assume the port of Mars, and at his heels,
Leashed in like hounds, **should** famine, sword, and fire
Crouch for employment. But **pardon**, gentles all,
The flat unraised spirits that **hath dared**
On this unworthy scaffold **to bring forth**
So great an object. **Can** this cockpit **hold** ['can hold?']

The vasty fields of France? Or **may** we **cram**
Within this wooden O the very casques
That **did affright** the air at Agincourt?
O, **pardon!** since a crooked figure **may**
Attest in little place a million,
And **let** us, ciphers to this great account,
On your imaginary forces **work**.
Suppose within the girdle of these walls
Are now **confined** two mighty monarchies,
Whose high upreared and abutting fronts
The perilous narrow ocean **parts asunder**.
Piece out our imperfections with your thoughts:
Into a thousand parts **divide** one man,
And **make** imaginary puissance.
Think, when we talk of horses, that you **see** them
Printing their proud hoofs i'th'receiving earth;
For **'tis** your thoughts that now **must deck** our kings,
Carry them here and there, **jumping** o'er times,
Turning th'accomplishment of many years
Into an hour-glass: for the which supply,
Admit me Chorus to this history,
Who, prologue-like your humble patience **pray**,
Gently **to hear**, kindly **to judge**, our play.

- Go through the whole speech, and read out the verbs only.
  It looks and sounds like this:

would ascend
to act
to behold
should assume
should crouch
pardon
hath dared
to bring forth
Can hold   may cram   did affright
pardon!
may attest
let work.

Suppose   are confined
parts asunder.
Piece out   divide   make
Think
See
Printing
'tis
must deck
carry   jumping   turning
admit
pray
to hear   to judge

You now have the action of the speech – what happens in it. This is a very quick way into a speech and gives you instant access to its dramatic action. After all, what people *do* is what matters. Drama means *to do*.

If you read that list again and again, a bit quicker each time, you discover something quite extraordinary. It starts off quite apologetically – '*may* cram' and '*should* assume'. When the speech gets to 'suppose', it becomes very insistent – 'think', 'see', 'carry' – it tells the audience, now, what they need to do. It is compelling and urgent. Right at the end, it almost stops us with 'to hear' and 'to judge' – and we are then set up for the opening scene. That change in use of verb forms, from the conditional, almost hesitant use ('we may', 'can we?') to the unconditional, instructional ('we will', 'do this', 'you think') gives the structure of the speech, it changes the pace dramatically, and even its atmosphere, and is another way to manipulate an audience. Draw them in gradually and then you've got them.

NOUNS = subject matter, the story

VERBS = the action, what happens

3.4   Vowels and consonants in text

Let's turn the attention to the sounds in the words. Vowels and consonants give words structure, emotion, meaning, everything. In time you will begin to see how vowels carry the emotion in a word, and how the consonants give the word its structure, its intellect, if you like.

Here is an example of what I feel is a 'long' big, expansive phrase:

'The vasty fields of France'

Vowels:

You may need a bit of help with this, but here is a starting point.

- Look at the word 'vasty' and say it aloud. The first vowel sound is a long 'aah' – 'v aahh stee'.

- Try 'fields' – this is a diphthong, a long vowel with two parts – 'f eee uh lds' – 'ee-uh'.

- And 'France' – its central vowel sound is 'aaahh' again.

- So the 'vasty fields of France' sounded with the vowels *only* is like this – 'Aaaah ee eeee uh o(f) aaaah'.

These are long, long sounds for the most part, and they convey the wide expanse of those fields in that great country.

Consonants:

This is where it gets really interesting.

- Look at and say 'vasty' again. The first consonant sound you actually say is 'v' – and it's a fricative, which means a continuant sound. You can go on saying 'vvvvvvvvv' for as long as you have breath.

- Try out 's' – and the same goes.

- Try 'f' – same thing, it's long.

- The 'l' of fields feels and sounds quite dark and full 'lllllllll'.

- What about 'ds' – if you say 'fields' and then just 'ds' you will find it sounds like 'dzzzzzzzz' – a long continuant sound.

- In the word 'of' you have 'vvvvvvv'.

- The 'F' of 'France' is 'fffffffff'.

- The 'n' is 'nnnnnnnnn'.

- The 'ce' is pronounced 'sssssssss'.

So you have lots of long sounds, which give a sense of space and expansiveness (notice how sensuous these sounds are, how physical and visceral they feel):

'Vvvvvvvv sssssssss t fffffffff lllllll dzzzzzzzzzzzz vvvvvvvv fffffff r nnnnnn ssssssss.'

And:

'Aaaah ee eeee uh o(f) aaaah.'

The whole structure of these words gives a feeling of expanse – the form exactly matches the content or meaning.

Let's look at a 'short' phrase.

'Can this cockpit hold...'

Vowels:

- Say 'can' aloud and then just the vowel – 'a' as in can.
- Now say 'this' – then just the vowel – 'i' as in 'this'.
- Say 'cockpit' – the vowels alone are 'o' and 'i'.
- And a slightly longer vowel in 'hold' – 'oh'.

So we have 'a i o-i oh.'

- Repeat it and find the short, staccato feel – 'a i o-i oh.'

Consonants:

- Say 'can' and it sounds like 'k' then 'n'.
- Say 'this' and you have 'th' and 's'.
- Say 'cockpit' – 'k-k' and 'p-t'.
- Hold – the first sound is 'h' – say this as lightly as possible – here it is tiny.

So we have 'k n th s k-k p-t'.

It's staccato and short. So the whole phrase is largely short and 'small':

'k a n   this   k o k p i t   h o l d.'

Rather like the cockpit of a plane (modern parallels work sometimes!) or the cockpits where fighting cockerels fought, or this little theatre – so can this small round pit (short staccato sounds) hold the enormity of a country (long continuant sounds). Accident or not, it feels great. Sometimes people ask if Shakespeare really intended his use of vowels and consonants to be this precise, they wonder if he knew and planned in this way. Well, as pronunciations were different then, the effect might not have been the same, or perhaps it *did* all work out this way. Did he know he was doing that, was it intentional? We don't know, but the point is, whether it was intentional, incredible intuition or lucky accident, it doesn't really matter. What I do know is that when this exercise works, it really does the trick.

If you then go back to the start of the speech, you get that great word 'O' – which in this case means something like 'if only' – if only I had a goddess of inspiration (a muse) to inspire me. So that 'O' is big. So many modern actors shy away from classical 'O's – it's as if they are afraid of the big emotion, or afraid of seeming over the top (what an awful phrase that can be) – how can you possibly be too big when you are asking to be inspired by a Greek goddess of inspiration? This doesn't mean you shout and bluster, but it *does* mean that you *commit* to it. Try it out, physicalising it again and again. When you bring it back down to a more realistic and truthful way of saying it, it will be in your body and in your thoughts. And if you are being truly truthful, it won't be too big.

First word, last word

3.5

- Read through the speech again, and this time read out only the first word in each line ('O The A And', etc.). Then read just the last word in each line ('ascend invention act', etc). You then read first and last words only ('O ascend / The invention / A act / And scene', etc.).

This is incredibly revealing, and by now you will really understand a lot of the speech, almost by default. This last exercise looks and sounds like this:

O, ascend
The invention,
A act,
And scene!
Then himself,
Assume heels,
Leashed fire
Crouch all,
The dared
On forth
So hold
The cram
Within casques
That Agincourt?
O, may
Attest million,
And account,
On work.
Suppose walls
Are monarchies,
Whose fronts
The asunder.
Piece thoughts:
Into man,
And puissance.
Think, them
Printing earth;
For kings,
Carry times,
Turning years
Into supply,
Admit history,
Who, pray,
Gently play.

You could also acknowledge full stops in the middle of verse lines, so instead of 'Crouch all' you would have 'Crouch employment' and then 'But all'. That would perhaps be more specific or just a different choice.

Application to Other Texts

All the exercises for text so far have been applied to one speech from Shakespeare, but they all work for pretty much every kind of text you will tackle. Just because it's an apparently simple, modern script, does not mean you don't apply the same care and attention to the words. You might not need to go into such detail in order to understand it – let's face it, a line like 'let's have a nice cup of tea' is hardly demanding on your intellect or even on your sensual connection to the words. So applying Text Exercise 5, for example, means that you now have 'let's tea'. It makes sense. The nouns are 'cup' and 'tea' – tells you all you need to know about the subject matter! This may seem like a facile example, and you won't have time to apply every single exercise to every single piece of text you ever tackle, but do try them out on seemingly easy scripts and it will pay dividends. Work is never wasted if it's done for the right reason and in the right way.

Rhythm 3.6

Really, this could be a whole chapter of its own, or indeed a whole book, because it is so important and complex. But an introduction to the concept and form of rhythm is a start and will be a helpful toe in the water. Quite simply, rhythm is meaning. There are many ways to discover the rhythm in a piece of writing, and many excellent references to help you, and among the best are Peter Hall's *Shakespeare's Advice to the Players* and John Barton's *Playing Shakespeare*. This work is so physical and so much about the experience, it is really helpful to be guided physically – but here are a few ideas.

Let's look at the iambic pentameter, because that forms the bulk of Shakespearean verse. You'll find it in many other writers, up to the present day, but I will go back to him for inspiration.

What is an iambic pentameter and what does it mean? 3.6a

'Iambic' comes from the Greek '*iambus*', meaning a foot of two syllables. Why 'foot'? It originates in early Greek drama, which was sung and danced – the foot would come down firmly on the strong beat. So when it says 'foot', it literally refers to the foot! So stomp out the i-**amb**, the de-**dum**. Dance the rhythm of:

> de-**dum** – de-**dum** – de-**dum**
>
> weak-**strong** – weak-**strong** – weak-**strong**
>
> light-**hard** – light-**hard** – light-**hard**

Or even just:

> left-**right** – left-**right** – left-**right**

Don't pussyfoot around with this, *mean* it, do it clearly and obviously. You can also beat this out with your hands, but that is rather missing the point. It won't go into the body so strongly. The strong beat is the strong foot coming down on the strong beat. However, I will come back to the use of hands shortly.

What about pentameter? 'Meter' is fairly straightforward, literally meter or measure. And 'penta' means five, as in 'pentagon', a five-sided shape. So 'penta-meter' is five measures. Iambic is de-**dum**, which is in two parts (one weak and one strong), so then an iambic pentameter is a line of verse which has five measures each of two beats. To put it another way, do the sums: $5 \times 2 = 10$. Ten beats, ten syllables. That is a regular iambic pentameter.

> 'In **sooth** I **know** not **why** I **am** so **sad**.'
> 'I **hope** the **sun** will **shine** all **day** to-**day**.'

- Make some lines up yourself. They'll be better than this last one!

- Dance or hop this from one foot to the other. Do it slowly and deliberately. It is regular, rhythmical and makes you feel secure.

- Exaggerate your dance:

  de-**DUM** de-**DUM** de-**DUM** de-**DUM** de-**DUM**

  Ensure that as you finish your ten-line beat, you are strongly down on the DUM foot, and that the other foot is poised on the ball of the foot or toes but is not lifted. Both feet are on the floor. You may feel an impulse to move off with the next foot but just hold on. And then repeat several times. Now do two lines of ten, one immediately after the other.

• Tap out this rhythm with your hand on your chest.

pa-**pum** pa-**pum** pa-**pum** pa-**pum** pa-**pum**

As you tap this out again and again, see what you notice. What is this rhythm? What does it represent to you? You might feel it is like the rhythm of horses cantering. Tap it again on your chest. You might start to notice that this is the rhythm or the beat of your heart, and it is indeed – it is your pulse and it the pulse of the line. The significant thing about the heartbeat is that it can speed up and slow down.

• Stand or sit quietly and feel your pulse, then walk with that pace for a little while.

• Run around or jump up and down on the spot as fast and for as long as you can. Feel your pulse again. It will be racing. Now walk around to that pace.

So exertion changes the pace, but for actors, the real deal is that our emotions change the pace – think about your heart beating faster when you are angry, afraid, or just downright excited. Think about your pulse when you are chilling out. The amazing thing about the iambic pentameter is that it can do this within that fundamental structure of a ten-beat line. Quite *how* that is achieved is complex, and is generally to do with the distribution of different consonant and vowel combinations, and the distribution of syllables (monosyllabic lines are usually slow, multisyllabic lines tend to go faster). This will take practice to understand and use, but it will come in time, with guidance and experience. For now, be aware of that pulse.

• Dance it again, find a partner and see if you can dance the iambic pentameter together, speeding up and slowing down.

• On your own, try out one line then two or three at a time. After some practice, begin to make the beat less 'obvious', so that you gradually move or walk this beat in a more natural way.

- Walk around the room with the underlying pulse, and try out a few simple lines, first in the exaggerated way, and gradually reducing the exaggeration, so that you sound like a real human being, and at the same time are being driven or are simply feeling that beat.

- Find a speech and go through it very slowly and methodically, beating out, dancing out, stepping out that rhythm, again and again and again. You need to do this a lot – not everyone gets this stuff straight away, but when you do, and meaning is revealed, it is so rewarding.

3.6b Lines of irregular length

Lines of irregular length are there for many reasons. Sometimes they show that the speaker is rushing onwards. Often it is because they need to pause, they can't go on, or they stumble. Experience and practice, with help, will tell you which is which. Here is an example from a twentieth-century sonnet by WIlfred Owen:

What **pass** ing **bells** for **these** who **die** as **catt** le?

de   **dum** de **dum** de **dum** de **dum** de **dum** de

- Go back to the physical exercise of stepping from foot to foot, around the room. You should find that the eleventh syllable at the end means one foot is on the floor, the other foot is suspended, off balance.

Why the uncomfortable eleven-beat line at the start of the poem? He is talking about the young soldiers going to die like a herd of cattle, slaughtered before their time, the uncomfortable truth about that war and all its horrors. You are unsettled right from the outset.

- Repeat the dance of the eleven-beat line again. Then dance a ten-beat, then two lines of ten beats followed by the eleven, so you really feel the difference.

And here is an eleven-beat line from Shakespeare: 'To be or not to be that is the question.'

- First of all, just say the line aloud a few times without even thinking about the rhythm – say it as you might just naturally read it, or as you may have heard it.

- Exaggerate and beat it out as if it were a regular iambic pentameter.

  To **be** or **not** to **be**, that **is** the **ques** tion.

One of the most famous lines in Shakespeare is an irregular iambic pentameter. Why? Look at what Hamlet is saying – shall I live or shall I die? What is the point of life? What shall I do? He just does not know how to *be* in the world. His mind is in turmoil, he is shaky – the line ends shakily. If you slowly but surely dance the de-**dums**, then at the end of an eleven-beat line, your foot is in suspension, literally, whichever way you decide to stress it all.

There is something else that happens here. Very often actors will deliver the line with the strong emphasis on 'that' – '**that** is the question'. But if you beat it out as a regular iambic, it becomes 'that *is* the question.' Try out both and see how they feel. Somehow, for me, the stress on 'is' means that there is no other question to be considered but this one. It makes Hamlet's agonising all the stronger. *But* you don't have to be a slave to the rhythm, you can make your own choices. I think that we should first consider all the possibilities of a text, and see what we think the author wrote before deciding to do a rewrite. There are so many variables and so many opinions on this, and I love to challenge and break the rules, but it is more delicious when you know you are breaking them! It is also clear that it really depends on the line of verse. Sometimes, when you learn a 'rule' that you hadn't been aware of, you make the most startling of discoveries.

Inversions

3.6c

The iamb is de-**dum**. Sometimes that foot or measure of verse is inverted or swapped round and it becomes **dum**-de, also known as a trochee (i-**amb** / **tro**-chee). So you may get this:

dum-de de-**dum** de-**dum** de-**dum** de-**dum**

The trochee or inverted foot appears at the beginning of a line quite often, but you will also find it elsewhere. We'll look at this briefly here, and I would come back to all this irregularity in much more detail in a second year of training.

3.6d   How a character can manipulate through rhythm

Joan of Arc in *Henry VI, Part 1* is trying to persuade Burgundy to return to the French side. She says:

> Look on your country, look on fertile France.

Don't force the text into *your* way of reading – read it as it is written. It does not ask you to stress the first word. So many actors will decide it should be:

> **Look** on your **coun**try, **look** on **fer**tile **France**

But this, I think, may be missing something. Of course, you can and must make choices as an actor, but I believe that one should try and see if it is a regular iambic; see if you can work out what the author wrote and do it their way first. Then, when you fully understand the 'rule', you can experiment – you may decide to change it, and that is your choice. Many directors and actors ignore the iambic, but I cannot see the point in that. If a text is written in verse, there's a reason for it! Don't be slavish about it, but let it guide you. If the rhythm is so irregular as to be chaotic, it is usually telling you that the character is in chaos (Leontes in *A Winter's Tale* is a great example of a character descending very fast into chaos and mental turmoil). Look for the clues when you are more experienced and have done plenty of experimenting with the verse form.

Look again at Joan's line – the iambic tells you it is:

> Look **ON** your **coun**try, **LOOK** on **fer**tile **France**

- Read it this way several times (out loud) and you will find the meaning – she says 'look **ON**', or 'look **AT** your country', and then the second '**LOOK**' becomes so much more insistent – 'No, Burgundy, really **LOOK** at it! See what you've done.'

- Take the whole speech and read it through several times (physically, on your feet). Then look at the first pair of syllables in each line (only the first iambic down the speech). See below and read the first two syllables in each line (Look **on** / And **see** / By **wast**-, etc.). You find something very startling:

Look **on** thy country, look on fertile France,
And **see** the cities and the towns defaced,
By **wast**ing ruin of the cruel foe,
As **looks** the mother on her lowly babe,
When **Death** doth close his tender-dying eyes.
See, **see** the pining malady of France:
Be**hold** the wounds, the most unnatural wounds,
Which **thou** thyself hast given her woeful breast.
Oh **turn** thy edged sword another way,
Strike **those** that hurt, and hurt not those that help:
One **drop** of blood drawn from thy country's bosom,
Should **grieve** thee more than streams of foreign gore.
Re**turn** thee therefore with a flood of tears,
And **wash** away thy country's stained spots.
Be**sides**, all French and France exclaims on thee,
Doubting thy birth and lawful progeny.
Was **not** the Duke of Orleans thy foe?
And **was** he not in England prisoner?
But **when** they heard he was thine enemy,
They **set** him free, without his ransom paid,
In **spite** of Burgundy and all his friends.
See **then**, thou fight'st against thy countrymen,
And **join'st** with them will be thy slaughter-men.
Come, **come**, return; return thou wandering Lord,
Charles **and** the rest will take thee in their arms.

She drives on and on with regular monotony, until that word 'doubting'. It can only be pronounced with the strong stress on the first syllable, or it wouldn't make sense. You can't say 'doubt-ing', for that would be nonsense. So the first syllable stresses, and the whole speech is thrown out of kilter for a moment – it stops, almost lurches to a halt for a brief moment. So, what is she saying? 'France doubts you, and what's worse (for a noble lord) your very legitimacy is being doubted' – she brings him up short and is reeling him in. The abrupt change in rhythm is on the most hurtful or damaging thought of all. And the very last line gives you a choice, perhaps, but if you *do* stress the second word, the 'and' points up hugely the importance of not just the king (Charles) but *all* the people. Brilliant rhetorical tactics.

3.6e   How a character's thoughts can be revealed through rhythm

Here is a simple but powerful example of what happens when you really just use the rhythm as it is written.

Isabella in *Measure for Measure* is in turmoil. A novice nun, she has been told that the only way she can save her brother from the death penalty is to sleep with Angelo. She threatens to tell the world what he's said, but he uses his position to show her how no one will believe her. She is left alone:

> To whom should I complain? Did I tell this,
> Who would believe me?

Actors will sometimes stress this as:

>   **Did** I tell this
> **Who** would believe me?

Look now at it as a regular rhythm and you get this:

>   Did **I** tell this
> Who **would** believe me?

For me, the first way feels too confident, the second way (the reading of this as a regular iambic pentameter) reveals her despair and uncertainty. Try both aloud a few times, to see how each one feels.

3.6f   Short lines and shared lines

If a line within the verse is very short it means it is a short line – that means that there is something in the gap. It is called a pause!

Always try out what is written/printed in the text first. *Go to* the text, don't make it come to you. Look for these textual clues. Here are some examples.

In *Henry V*, the archbishop and bishop have virtually plotted to bribe the king in order to keep hold of their lands, and at the end of their private scene is a moment of pure suspension (a double forward slash (//) indicates missing lines):

ELY.
>   But, my good lord,
>   How now for mitigation of this bill
>   Urged by the commons? Doth his majesty
>   Incline to it, or no?

CANTERBURY.
>   He seems indifferent,
>   Or rather swaying more upon our part
>   Than cherishing the exhibiters against us;
>   **For I have made an offer to his majesty – //**
>   **to give a greater sum**
>   **Than ever at one time the clergy yet**
>   **Did to his predecessors part withal.**

ELY.
>   **How did this offer seem received, my lord?**

CANTERBURY.
>   **With good acceptance of his majesty;**
>   Save that there was not time enough to hear, //

ELY.
>   What was the impediment that broke this off?

CANTERBURY.
>   The French ambassador upon that instant
>   Craved audience; and **the hour, I think, is come**
>   **To give him hearing: is it four o'clock?**

ELY.
>   **It is.**
>   [*And here is that dramatic eight-syllable pause for effect.*]

CANTERBURY.
>   Then go we in, to know his embassy;
>   Which I could with a ready guess declare,
>   Before the Frenchman speak a word of it.

ELY.
>   I'll wait upon you, and I long to hear it.

That short line is just that. Don't rush in with the next line – Shakespeare has written in a pause for effect. Ignore that and you lose the point. How you play the pause is a matter for you to decide, but there are many possibilities – could they be looking at each other, signalling their agreement without actually saying so? Could they be uncertain? Find out, but use the pause you've been given to see what might be happening.

In *Macbeth*, there is one of the most exciting examples of *shared lines*. Here, the two characters are totally in tune with each other. Macbeth has just killed Duncan, the king. Both he and Lady Macbeth are highly strung, and start to become terrified by the night.

MACBETH.
I have done the deed. Didst thou not hear a noise ?

LADY.
I heard the owl-scream and the cricket's cry.
Did not you speak?

MACBETH.
[*Fast pace.*]   When?

LADY.
[*Fast pace.*]   Now.

MACBETH.
[*Fast pace.*]   As I descended?

LADY.
[*Total stop.*] Ay.

MACBETH.
[*Another stop.*] Hark!
Who lies i'the second chamber?

LADY.
                              Donalbain.

MACBETH (*looks at his hands*).
[*Short pause.*] This is a sorry sight.

LADY.
A foolish thought, to say a sorry sight.

The pace is very fast until the 'Ay' and then one can seemingly take all the time in the world. So they share that furiously paced line – the four speeches ('Did not you speak?' / 'When?' / 'Now.' / 'As I descended?') are all one line of iambic pentameter. They think they keep hearing noises in the dead of the night. When she says 'Ay', he stops dead and they both halt, listening. He then commands 'Hark!' and stops again to listen. You could put the pause at the beginning or end of the line – try it out – and see which feels right to you. Each of those two lines has a nine-beat or nine-syllable pause. This is an unbelievably tense atmosphere, created purely by the use of rhythm.

A shared heartbeat

Romeo and Juliet have an exchange and a sharing of a line that is achingly beautiful. It is a simple and astonishing feat of character and action clues from the author. Juliet is on her famous balcony, sighing in the night air about Romeo. He has crept into the garden, having scaled the wall, and is talking about her, sees her, but daren't speak yet, as he is in serious danger of being discovered. Here is a part of their scene:

ROMEO.
    She speaks, yet she says nothing. What of that?
    Her eye discourses, I will answer it.
    I am too bold. 'Tis not to me she speaks //
    See how she leans her cheek upon her hand.
    O that I were a glove upon that hand,
    That I might touch that cheek!

JULIET.
                     Ay me!

ROMEO.
                 She speaks.
    O speak again bright angel...

Romeo and Juliet are completely in tune with each other, breathing together in this exchange, made all the more exciting by the fact that at this point they are not actually talking to each other, but *with* each other. She doesn't even know he is there, and yet is right in the middle, in the heart of the line. They are totally in sync with each other, the pulse of the line is shared, it is one mind, one thought, one heartbeat – the heartbeat of the iambic shared, the heart of the lovers shared.

A choice from different editions

Sometimes different editions of Shakespeare's plays throw up some interesting choices. Here is an example from *King John* in which the king is ordering Hubert to kill the young prince Arthur. Here, just *one line* of iambic pentameter is divided between several speeches. In one version, 'Death' begins a sequence of five shared speeches that make up one line of iambic pentameter.

KING JOHN.
    Good Hubert! Hubert, Hubert, throw thine eye
    On yon young boy. I'll tell thee what, my friend,
    He is a very serpent in my way,
    And whereso'er this foot of mine doth tread
    He lies before me. Dost thou understand me?
    Thou art his keeper.

HUBERT.
                       And I'll keep him so
    That he shall not offend your majesty.

KING JOHN.
    Death.

HUBERT.
       My lord?

KING JOHN.
           A grave.

HUBERT.
                 He shall not live.

KING JOHN.
                           Enough.

In the second version, 'Death' is given just one line, which gives a very long pause, and the following four speeches follow on very differently as a result.

KING JOHN.
>Good Hubert! Hubert, Hubert, throw thine eye
>On yon young boy. I'll tell thee what, my friend,
>He is a very serpent in my way,
>And whereso'er this foot of mine doth tread
>He lies before me. Dost thou understand me?
>Thou art his keeper.

HUBERT.
>   And I'll keep him so
>That he shall not offend your majesty.

KING JOHN.
>Death.
>[*Single line followed by a nine-syllable pause.*]

HUBERT.
>My lord?

KING JOHN.
>   A grave.

HUBERT.
>   He shall not live.

KING JOHN.
>   Enough.

The only way to really discover what these different versions give you is for two actors to speak them aloud several times.

Shared lines can also signify that characters are incredibly impatient with each other, or that they are so in tune, they finish each other's thoughts like an old married couple. Infinite variety and infinite possibilities.

Rhythm in prose

3.6g

All text has rhythm. Every time we speak we are talking in one rhythm or another, but are generally much less of aware of it than when we use verse forms. However, rhythm in prose can be highly significant. It's a matter of trial and error, but here is one example of how to find the rhythm.

In *The Rover* by Aphra Behn, Hellena is determined to avoid becoming a nun, and wants to find out what might lie in store if she were to find a man. She says:

> Now you have provided yourself with a man, you take no care for poor me. Prithee tell me, what dost thou see about me that is unfit for love. Have I not a world of youth? A humour gay? A beauty passable? A vigour desirable? Well shaped? Clean limbed? Sweet breathed? And sense enough to know how all these ought to be employed to the best advantage? Yes, I do and will. Therefore lay aside your hopes of my fortune, by my being a devotee, and tell me how you came acquainted with this Belville; for I perceive you knew him before he came to Naples.

If you mark up the breath points by looking at the punctuation and speak this aloud, you will find its rhythm changes hugely between short, fast phrases and then long thoughts from 'And sense…' followed by the quick 'Yes, I do and I will' and then a longer thought from 'Therefore'. See if you can work out why the phrase length changes.

3.7   Antithesis

This is a hugely important element of any text, but particularly with verse, as it so often gives you the balance of a line, or even the balance of a whole speech. Simply defined, it is a figure of speech in which words or thoughts are contrasted or put in opposition to each other. So that 'rough winds' in Sonnet 18 oppose the idea of the 'darling buds of May' – one is rough and violent, the other gentle and lovely.

If you break down the word, you get 'anti' – which means against or opposed to – and 'thesis' – which means an idea or proposition. So 'antithesis' is an idea which is then opposed or reversed. 'Thesis' also means a setting-down or a down-beat, the strong beat in a bar of music or a foot of verse – so by understanding and more importantly *using* the antitheses, you get a stronger hold on the rhythm. One could then argue that a couplet or the resolve in the speech is the synthesis – the putting together or reasoning of the argument towards a conclusion. So, 'thesis', 'anti-thesis', 'synthesis', can give you the structure of a speech.

'To be or not to be' is one of the most obvious – to live or die, to exist or not. If you look at the whole of this speech, you can see it is entirely antithetical. 'She speaks, yet she says nothing', from the Romeo extract above, is antithetical. In *Julius Caesar*, Mark Antony says, 'I come to bury Caesar not to praise him', and this is then contrasted in Brutus' antithesis in prose.

Antithesis works in prose, too, but can be less obvious than in verse. Look for it whenever you read text, and if it is there, it should be used and pointed up.

You should use antithesis to balance one thought against the other. There are many ways to do this, but pitch changes, dynamic changes in voice (loud or soft, strong strident tone or breathy or gentle) are two straightforward ways of revealing those contrasting ideas. If necessary, exaggerate the antithesis with pitch or volume, and when it is much clearer to you and the thoughts are integrated, you can be more subtle – but the contrasts will be there in your work. Try this for when Brutus says, 'Had you rather Caesar were living, and die all slaves, than that Caesar were dead, to live all free men?'

The sonnet

3.8

Here is a little more information and guidance on the sonnet form, to accompany the sonnet work in Part 1d. I have included this here because I hope it will serve as a useful introduction to something that can be incredibly useful for an actor.

The term 'sonnet' comes from a Provençal word 'sonet' and the Italian 'sonetto', both meaning 'little song'. In the thirteenth century, it took on the sense of a fourteen-line poem that follows a particular rhyme scheme and structure.

The Italian sonnet (also called 'Petrarchan', after the most famous sonneteer of the time, Petrarch) normally comprised two sections, an eight line (octet) proposition, followed by a six line (sestet) resolution. The rhyme scheme was generally Alexandrine (which is six measures or metres, each line consisting of twelve syllables).

The English, Elizabethan or Shakespearean sonnet usually uses the iambic pentameter (five measures with ten syllables), and the structure is usually three quatrains (three sets of four lines) and a couplet.

The first one hundred and twenty-six of Shakespeare's sonnets were written to a young man, and the last twenty-eight to a dark-haired woman – the 'dark lady'.

His early sonnets urge the young man to marry so that his beauty may be perpetuated through having children. Then there is a section of sonnets about uncritical love, and gradually they become more anxious and critical. Common themes are time as a destroyer (of love, beauty, life) and self-doubt.

The rhyme scheme often takes on the ABAB / CDCD / EFEF / GG sequence. This is often called a Shakespearean sonnet, because he is its most famous advocate.

The form of the sonnet is a dialectical construct, or an argument, which allows the poet to examine contrasting or opposing ideas, emotions, beliefs, etc., juxtaposing those ideas, and usually resolving them at the end. The final rhyming couplet often resolves the poem, but sometimes it completely inverts or subverts it and takes you by surprise. So, as drama deals in conflict, journeys and complex text, sonnets are miniature masterclasses – and just great exercises for the actor. Sonnet writers include:

- Thomas Wyatt (1503–1542) (who introduced sonnets to England in the early sixteenth century)

- Spenser (1552–1599), Shakespeare (1564–1616), John Donne (1572–1631), Milton (1608–1674)

- Shelley (1792–1822), Keats (1795–1821), Dante Gabriel Rossetti (1828–1882), Gerard Manley Hopkins (1844–1889)

- Robert Frost (1874–1963), Edna St Vincent Millay (1892–1950), Wilfred Owen(1893–1918), Jean Toomer (1894–1967), W.H. Auden (1907–1973), Margaret Walker (1915–1998)

- Pablo Neruda (1904–1973), Seamus Heaney (1939–),
  Marilyn Hacker (1942–, who wrote a novel in sonnets), Dr
  Sonnet Mondal (1990–).

Looking up words you don't know

3.9

With Shakespeare, you need a good glossary (use the classic C.T.
Onions *A Shakespeare Glossary*, and the more recent and truly
excellent David and Ben Crystal's *Shakespeare's Words*) and a
good, *large* dictionary. A pocket dictionary simply won't give you
enough information. Many editions of the plays themselves will
have a glossary of words and phrases too, so look at a couple of
versions to get more information. Get to love searching for words
and phrases. If you are training to be an actor, words are your life,
and knowledge is essential to understanding and getting the feel
for language. If you are working on your voice for 'life', what could
be more rewarding than discovering new worlds through words.

With modern texts, you might still find those reference books
useful, but you still need a large dictionary. Get one that also has
the derivations of words at the end of each description. If you
know a bit of Latin or Greek, or Old French, for example, you will
appreciate the way words have come into our language. If you
don't understand other languages at all, it doesn't matter, but it
will begin to give you an insight into how words have come about.
One director I worked with said she knew professional actors who
had started to learn Latin – why not!

But a word of warning about looking up words: there is absolutely
no point in looking up every word in a speech, and then not making sense of those words in context. All you end up with is a list of
words making no more sense (or even, *less* sense) than your original text.

Here is an example of how *not* to use the dictionary to help you.
The following is a definition of a well-known phrase – read this
aloud:

> Great in number forefeet of quadrapeds construct the
> natural agent that stimulates the sense of sight
> expenditure of energy.

What?!

This makes absolutely no sense whatsoever, and you sound like someone who has swallowed a very unhelpful reference book. Here it is again, with the original word of each definition:

> Great in number [**MANY**] forefeet of quadrapeds [**HANDS**] construct [**MAKE**] the natural agent that stimulates the sense of sight [**LIGHT**] expenditure of energy [**WORK**].

If you come across the word 'rake' in a Restoration play, you might assume that's a man about town, and discover it's a dissolute man – but then you may need to look up dissolute, and you discover that this is a person of debauched or loose morals. So take care when you look up words that the definition makes sense. If it doesn't, look further, and keep going back to the original text, until you get the sense.

Equally, don't be afraid to look up words you assume you already understand. In *The Caucasian Chalk Circle*, the priest says 'la-di-da' (even this is in the dictionary (or at least a good, comprehensive dictionary) – it is slang meaning 'affectedly fine, especially in speech or bearing'. The translator has given you a lot to work with in such a small clue.

During Act Five of *Richard III*, King Richard is visited by the ghosts of the people he has murdered. He wakes from his nightmares with a most extraordinary speech revealing his true state of mind, the absolute turmoil of a man who knows he has done many wrongs. He says:

> Give me another horse! Bind up my wounds!
> Have mercy, Jesu – Soft! I did but dream.

One might think that he is about to swear and blaspheme because the name of Jesus stops short of the final 's' – but as you get to know more about Shakespeare and the time in which he was writing, you know that is just not possible – he would use one of the many contractions such as 'zounds' for 'God's wounds'. So you look up 'Jesus' in the dictionary; look past the first definition, and you find that 'Jesu' is the familiar or vocative form of his name

– the form of the name that one would use when asking for help. So rather than blaspheming, Richard is praying to Jesus for help. It is also the form of his name that is used in hymns, and it is a very personal form of address. This is a huge textual clue to the development of a character, and you owe it to the text and to yourself to be fully aware so that you can make informed choices. This soliloquoy reveals Richard's deepest and most truthful thoughts, and shows all his fears. After all he has done, and waking from a terrible nightmare, he asks for help. It is a turning point and one easily missed if you hadn't known this detail.

Good writers like Shakespeare do that all the time – the choice of words is not coincidental – so forage the text for every clue you can, once you have got the general sense and physically discovered the text for its feel. The great director Peter Brook talks about an actor using words that are 'strong, alive and vibrant'. You read that and think, 'yes, I know what he means'. Now you look them up and find that strong means powerful. Alive, literally, means living. Vibrant means resonating, exciting, thrilling. You say those words again, and can invest further because you are not generalising. In *Henry V*, the armourers are preparing the knights, hammering them into their armour:

> With busy hammers closing rivets up,
> Give dreadful note of preparation.

Think about the word 'dreadful' – we talk about dreadful films, for example. But look at it and you see that it means 'full of dread'. Say it now, and you begin to get and feel the picture of real fear, terror and foreboding.

Of course, you can ask for help! It is amazing how students forget to ask each other for help – when a text is being picked over in class, particularly when it is an especially dense or difficult text, it is so, so much easier to work it out in a group. Everyone has a different take on things, and we get there together. This is a collaborative process, a bit like acting. So when you are poring over a text in preparation for a class or rehearsal, help each other out and trade skills. If you are not in the habit of doing this, perhaps because you are afraid of someone's reaction, ask yourself:

how would you feel if someone came up to you and said 'You are really good at movement, will you show me that sequence?' Would you not feel good or proud? If you don't want to be asked, and you don't feel like helping, think about the role of the actor. You need to have quite an ego to become an actor, but the paradox is that that ego has no place on the stage – only the character's ego should be present. The best actors by far are the ones who are generous; they are the ones who *listen* to the other actors. And generosity has many facets.

3.10   Create a parallel text

If you are working on a classical text and you are stuck with meanings, or you really want to be absolutely sure you have understood it, a very helpful exercise is to create a parallel text – you 'translate' the text into your own words.

You can find examples of these on the internet and publications with titles like *Ben Jonson for Dummies* (I made that up) and these may be useful, but they are often a little facile. More importantly, they still won't help you to inhabit and integrate the language into your own speaking of the text, because they are someone else's translation, not your own. Make your own version – improvise around the ideas in the text so that it becomes very personal to you and gives you tactics for playing the part.

Finding your own way of writing out the lines is very useful even for the simplest of phrases. That favourite 'O' becomes many things. In Restoration plays, for example, you might get things like 'egad' – you look it up and find that it means 'ah! God!' – but that doesn't necessarily help. A student recently translated it into 'oh my stars!' – it is not a phrase I would ever use, but one that he does, so it makes sense to him. Then you put it back into the context of the speech and it begins to make much more sense – and the actor starts to sound like a real human being!

It is a bit similar to some young actors learning to speak in the accent of Standard English or RP – when improvising, they start to say things like 'oh my goodness' and 'would you care for a cup of tea?' – no one speaks like that these days, and if they do, it certainly isn't a phrase any of my nineteen-year-old students would say in their everyday life! Learn to use the accent or translate the phrase you don't understand into something that a real person today would actually say.

The 'not a tongue-twister' exercise

I tend not to use tongue-twisters very often in the work. Occasionally I put one in because people find them fun, and that is fine, but I advise steering clear of them until you are integrating thought into your text work, often not until the second year, and even then only sparingly. This is because whilst the tongue-twisters in themselves can be useful in gaining crisp and clear articulation, if this is done in isolation, you might just end up by being brilliant at the set phrases and not be able to incorporate that work into your acting and speaking. It's rather the same with articulation drills – great to be able to say 'niminy-piminy' really clearly and as quick as lightning, but if you then go on stage and your text is a muddle, you clearly haven't brought the drill into the work itself. Unless it is applied, it's almost pointless. So here is a tongue-twister:

Peter Piper picked a peck of pickled pepper.

Try it out several times. Now, begin again and I will stop you after a couple of words. Peter *who*? Oh, I see, Peter *Piper*. Please go on. He did what? He *picked*. And what did he pick? A *peck* of pickled pepper. What on earth is a peck? If you don't know, you could look it up and be really specific. Or – and this is fine, honestly! – you could just make a choice, a guess. So that you invest some meaning in the word 'peck' – you might imagine that it is a particular shape, or a particular weight (now you're on the right lines), but whatever you think it is, you commit to that thought. And have a think about pickled pepper – what is that like? It's up to you, but make a choice. That way, it won't just be a party trick. Do this with everything. And then you can sometimes work on a bit of text, and care not a jot about what it means. Do the absolute opposite.

Just play with words and sounds without any meaning whatsoever. It's quite a relief. It is very important to just let go occasionally, go against everything, just for the change, and as a relief from the tyranny of analysis.

3.12 Capacity, and more importantly, the breath–thought connection

The idea of connecting your breath to the thought is fundamental to everything you say, and pretty much every exercise has worked on this element of voice work. However, when we get to text, the reality is that we often forget all that basic stuff, and start thinking about 'acting' and creating character. If you bring all those basic craft elements to your character work, then it is really going to make the job so much more straightforward. But, of course, easier said than done.

The concept of matching your breath to the thought, and the concomitant need for greater capacity, or much more fluid and easy management of the breath, was looked at in the latter sessions of Part 1, and then taken in more detail with complex text in the opening sessions of Part 2, so refer back to those sessions.

See Part 2 for the following extracts and how they can be worked to discover the essential technique and creative possibilities of breath management: Othello in 2.2.7, Queen Margaret in 2.3.8, and Ophelia in 2.4.8. For this connection in Shakespeare, try these out and see what different techniques are needed – what does each piece require and how do they differ?

3.13 Capacity, breath and thought, pace and agility

Further texts develop your breath and thought, with the added demands of fast-paced and witty Restoration dialogue. These are explained in Chapter 2, so look again at Medley in 2.5.9, Lady Wishfort in 2.6.7, and Puff in 2.7.6. Compare and contrast these three, and then compare them with the differing demands in the Shakespeare extracts mentioned above. Flip from one period of text to the other and see if you can discover the feel of each one and how they size up to each other.

Falling inflections

Here are some very useful exercises to help the problem of falling inflections (when the end of a line or even just the end of a word is allowed to drop away).

'And another thing'

This is great for a sonnet but can be applied to any piece of verse.

After each line, say 'and another thing...' It is as simple as that! What this does, hopefully, is to help you find the next thought without dropping the end of the line. You have to keep the thought up so that the voice (and therefore the word) is still maintained right through to the end. This is very helpful for actors who have a tendency to go breathy or indistinct on the last word of a line. For example:

> Shall I compare thee to a summer's day? – *And another thing...*
>
> Thou art more lovely and more temperate. – *And another thing...*
>
> Rough winds do shake the darling buds of May, – *And another thing...*
>
> And summer's lease hath all too short a date. – *And another thing...*

So that you say this not only after a full stop, but also at a comma or just when there is an 'enjambement', or run-on line. You will find that after 'day' and 'temperate', you end the thought and the pitch may drop, but you keep that thought up and alive. After 'May', you keep up the thought and go on to the second half of that thought – with this one, say 'and another thing' as part of the whole thought. You then repeat those four lines immediately, but without the added phrase, and go on to the next section with the same exercise.

3.14b 'The little plane'

This idea came from a student a long time ago. Imagine that, as you say a line, the words are like a little aeroplane taking off from the tip of your tongue. You can extend the image so that the tongue is like a runway, the words and sounds picking up momentum and then flying off into the air.

If you guide the words with your fingers as well, reaching out and away from your mouth, that will help the line of text come from your centre and reach out into the space.

3.14c 'Click the word' – articulation and shape

This is really just a reminder that whenever you speak, it is very important to shape and fully articulate the words. If you tend towards the falling inflection as a habit, it is quite likely that you do not end (or possibly begin) words fully. So on a line ending 'too short a date', ensure that you articulate that 't' sound at the end. It does not need to be overemphatic, but it does need to be there.

To help you, as you speak each line of verse, click your fingers on the last word of every line. People who are behind the thought will click too late, those who tend to speak too fast and are ahead of the thought will click before the last word. So practise this a lot, and click simultaneously with the end of each word, or on the last syllable, on each line. It takes some practice!

3.14d Hands guide breath support right to the end of the line or thought

So often, people will drop the ends of words or the end of a line because they are simply not supporting the text right through to the end. A useful way to eliminate or reduce this tendency is to use your hands to guide your voice (the word, the line) forward and up, or move it forwards slowly all the time whilst speaking, so that the hands are still up at the end of the line, as if reaching out to someone.

With habitual 'line-end droppers', this is very instructive because they will raise their hands up and move them forwards and almost inevitably they drop before finishing the end of the thought. Even a slight hesitancy to properly finish the thought or word and you see the ends of the fingers or the whole arm flopping down – so keep them up until you have spoken the last sound! Doing this a few times and then speaking the line without the arm movement will often resolve the issue.

'And-er...'   `3.14e`

This is the exercise from Session 2.16 (2.16.14), and is really useful if you are struggling with word endings.

- Take a line of text, and where any word ends with a consonant phoneme (a word that ends in a consonant that you pronounce) you say 'er' (uh) at those endings. I have uses 'uh' so that rhotic speakers don't sound the 'r'.

   From forth the kennel of thy womb hath crept

   Becomes:

   From-uh forth-uh the kennel-uh ov-uh thy wom(b)-uh hath-uh crept-uh

- Repeat with the 'uh' several times and then say the line normally, and notice how much more weight and definition is given to each word.

Sing your text   `3.15`

This is as simple as it sounds. Singing a poem or speech or indeed any text you are working on can be a very freeing exercise. If you are having singing lessons and learning to act through song, then undoubtedly you will be speaking your song lyrics. This is a very important exercise in ensuring that you are making sense of the words, and it is not all about a 'beautiful sound' – speaking the lyrics really shows up any points at which you are unclear about meaning or intention. So the opposite can be true of spoken text – if you are struggling for any reason, then it can be very liberating to sing it. In doing so, you may well discover new notes, literally – so that when you go back to speaking it, you use your range much more fully, with clearer and deeper thought processes and greater integration.

Singing bits of text can also be a great help with some articulation issues – it's a great one for helping with the so-called 'weak r' (when the 'r' sounds nearer to a 'w'). This is not the only thing that will help this kind of speech issue, but coupled with detailed and specific tongue exercises, singing those sounds can be of enormous benefit.

3.16 Ensemble, unison and chorus – move together

Being able to speak in unison is an incredibly useful skill for actors. Obviously, if you are doing chorus work it is essential, but it is also a great way to get an ensemble working, moving, breathing and speaking together, because it inculcates a great sense of unity and belonging. It is also a lot of fun when you get it. First of all try moving as one group – this creates a sense of community/unity and enhances sensitivity within the group.

3.16a Shoal of fish

- Establish where north, south, east and west are in the room. Now someone calls out north, and you all walk towards the north wall in the room, as if you were a shoal of fish. You have to be smooth in movement, and be both very aware and relaxed at the same time. The leader keeps calling different directions, mixing it up and including directions like south-west, north east and so on, and you must move as one.

- Repeat the exercise and this time everyone moves whilst sounding on a 'sh'. You will find this makes the whole thing much easier – try it and find out.

3.16b One moves, two move

- Everyone stands in the room spaced apart. One person moves off and then comes to a stop.

- The leader calls out 'two'. Two people must move off together and stop together, without discussion and even without eye contact if possible.

- When two people have achieved that, the leader calls out 'three' and a group of three people move off, walk and then stop at exactly the same time, without discussion or looks.

This is not easy! Inevitably you find that four go. You finally achieve three, call four and then five or only two go. Some groups manage it incredibly quickly, others take longer. Practise this regularly and you may find the whole group can start and stop at will, by tapping into the collective unconscious.

As the group improves, you can just do one person stopping and starting, then two, then three and so on, without the need for someone to call the numbers.

Ensemble, unison and chorus – games

3.17

- In a circle, take it in turns to signal the in-breath and the release of the out-breath on an 'f' or 'sh', with a simultaneous movement.

- Make the signal for the in-breath very clear and very obvious to start with. For example, raise a hand for everyone to breathe in, and then bring it down for the out-breath.

- You will need to try out lots of different ways of signalling to the group – if everyone has a go, you should end up with a good few that work well.

- Repeat many times, and each time make the signal progressively more subtle. Introduce 'v' or humming or 'mah' and so on.

- Eventually that signal will be barely perceptible. If you all know it, you will then cue together as if by magic.

- You may find that when you first raised your hand, your eyebrows raised up too – a tiniest of lifts here, more a brightening in the eyes, can sometimes be enough. And one day you won't even need that because you are so in sync with each other. Listen, and feel it.

3.18   **Ensemble and chorus – breathe, sound, speak together**

Here is a lovely way to find the ensemble or unison breath and sound.

- Sit in pairs back to back. It can help if, at the beginning, you choose a partner who is roughly the same height as you. With a bit of practice that won't matter, because your sensitivity and awareness increase very quickly.

- Breathe in together and release the out-breath together on a 'sh'.

- Do this for a few minutes or until you can really feel yourselves in sync.

- When one pair is definitely breathing and 'sh'-ing together, they move to join another pair. After a short while, all four should be able to breathe in together and out together. You will be aware that some people have longer or greater capacity than others, but develop a sensitivity so that you go with the flow, as it were, and find a common breath.

- Now another pair joins, until the whole group is sitting close. Once you have established the back-to-back breathing, you don't have to actually sit right into another actor's back – you can just rest your arm round their shoulder, or you might lie down and rest on their legs – if you really listen and feel, you can sense the in-breath and the out-breath on the 'sh' as one homogenous entity.

- Take it onto a 'v'. Explore this for a few minutes (this can take anything from thirty seconds to a couple of minutes or more).

- You gradually begin to stand up, still breathing as one, and all sounding out on 'v'.

- Walk around the space and you will still be able to all come in on the next 'v' at the same time.

Practise this a few times. Sometimes a group can go on to text immediately, sometimes it takes a couple of sessions, but it does usually happen very quickly.

- So you are all on a 'v' simultaneously. Someone can now speak a short line of text over the sound, and when everyone has 'got it' you can signal the group to speak the text on the next unison out-breath. Or you can have the text to hand, and read from the page.

I have had a group of actors achieve unison speaking like this within half an hour. It really depends on the group, on the day, on how they gel together.

- Take a break and discuss the sensations.

Breathing the cue word

3.19

This is a simple technique to cue in a chorus. You all let in the breath on the penultimate syllable of the cue line, and you should quickly learn to start speaking together, on the dot.

We used this technique to cue in Macbeth's witches, and even apart and in the dark (they were hidden and crouching some distance from each other in the space) they were bang on cue every time. These were first-year students, not professionals, so it clearly works well!

Finding the individual voice in the chorus

3.20

When you have practised breathing, sounding and speaking together, you can now start to layer the sound and the experience. As a chorus, you will need to be able to speak in time. If in a Greek chorus, say, you are probably the townspeople, a community, who need to find that communal voice. Where chorus work is sometimes let down is when there is no 'layering' and there is a clear lack of intention. Just because you are all saying the same thing does not mean that you all necessarily agree with the thoughts, or that you all have the same attitude. So you can still be an individual within that chorus.

Here are some ideas to find that – either technical, creative or both.

3.20a

Choose some of you to speak on a higher than normal pitch (that works really well if some of the men speak high) and try speaking the text. Of course, there will be different pitches, tones and dynamics anyway, as all voices differ, but you can make exaggerated, conscious choices.

It is a question of orchestration, so have someone listen and make suggestions, and see how much layering you can get.

3.20b

You can do something similar with different resonances – so some people might try a very nasal sound, or place their sound into the mask of the face (to create something very 'bright' in tone), and some may be very chest-based or head-based. Experiment.

3.20c

You could then try the opposite, and aim to all use the same pitch or resonating quality and sound 'as one'. It will not then be a monotonous, dull sound because you are making a conscious choice (as opposed to accidentally landing on the same note).

3.20d

If it is a mixed-gender group, then try hearing just the men's voices and then just the women's. And then mix and match and find the best balance for the particular text you are working on – and/or choose different groupings for different lines or verses.

3.20e

Decide upon an attitude or make character choices – you could suggest half the group agrees with the thought and the others disagree, speak the text in unison and then see what happens. This does not necessarily mean that you are not all honouring the text, and if it doesn't work or sound right, then it is only an exercise in making new discoveries – which is surely what acting is

PART THREE

about. When you then try all having exactly the same attitude or thought, having gone against it in an exercise, you may find it is more richly textured.

Articulation in chorus work

3.21

This is when all the articulation work really comes into play. You may find the group is fantastically sensitive at breathing, moving and sounding together, but when text comes into play, things can go wrong. If one person is slightly woolly on their consonants, for example, it can throw the whole sound out.

So do plenty of extra articulation preparation, lots of drills, and then take a line of the text and really *use* the consonants and open out the vowels where appropriate.

3.21a

Beat it out together, making it very physical – beat the 'b's with your hands, stomp the 'd's with your feet, beat out each word – again and again.

Call and response

3.21b

Split into two groups. One group creates a short very physical sequence for one of the articulation drills (for example 'bbbbbbbbbb-ah'), which the other group copies. You then have one person signal the start and you all do it as one.

Repeat the exercise with words, then a whole phrase. Ensure that you all agree on pronunciations and on how and where the consonants sit, where the stresses are, and so on. Make a choice and work with it.

Dyslexia and sight-reading

3.22

I put these together because the suggestions for anyone who may be dyslexic should be very useful for students/actors who need to improve their sight-reading – which is just about everyone! If you are not very good at it, then you can make huge improvements with a little regular practice and good guidance. If

345

you are already good, then you can be even better. Why be good when you can be brilliant?

You cannot know what it is really like, if you are not dyslexic, but there are some great books on the subject that explain clearly what the issues are, and especially can point up the real plus points. This will help everyone, and perhaps it should be compulsory for anyone who teaches. One of the plus points is that you are in great company – Leonardo da Vinci, Einstein, Whoopi Goldberg, Robin Williams, Antony Gormley, Eddie Izzard, Steven Spielberg and Benjamin Zephaniah, for a start. Because of the nature of dyslexia, there are many actors who have it to some extent: it is incredibly common amongst creative people – actors, engineers, architects and dancers – and it takes many forms. Here, we are addressing issues relating to reading, but dyspraxia (which involves difficulties with movement and coordination, such as poor integration of the two sides of the body) and attention difficulties are also relevant. You might find that, although your reading is pretty good, you have trouble with timekeeping. Are you often late, or rushing or suddenly aware that you should be somewhere? Organisation of time is a common difficulty. I had a student who was constantly late and in a muddle, so after some discussion and basic assessment, I suggested that she get a notebook and write down a simple, clear timetable of her daily appointments. We then got into minute detail – I suggested she work out a schedule for her morning before college (get up at seven, go to the bathroom [five minutes], take a shower and get dressed [seven minutes], prepare and eat breakfast [fifteen to twenty minutes], brush teeth and wash face [three minutes], and so on). So there was a painstaking schedule which got her from waking, right up to arriving at the first class at college. A week later she came and said her life had been transformed. I doubt she still has to do that, but it gave her a start in how to organise a very muddled but bright and inventive mind.

Short-term memory loss is also a common difficulty. The most extreme I have come across is someone who would be given some information at the door, and have forgotten it by the time they got to the next room. Perhaps oddly, he could learn lines quite easily – but in daily life, the notebook became essential. Now there are electronic devices, with notepads, alarms as reminders and so on. And sometimes you need a reminder to remind you to check the reminder! Do whatever it takes, and like the tortoise and the hare, if you really take your time and do everything slowly and in detail to begin with, you will soon get much faster and more importantly, you will be more relaxed. This is very true of sight-reading.

Most teachers these days are aware to some extent about the ways in which dyslexia can affect someone, and also how to help them. The most obvious help when providing texts or handouts is to enlarge the text if possible, and/or to copy it onto coloured paper. Normally either yellow or a mid-blue will help. Occasionally other coloured papers help and, if you are dyslexic, you can experiment to see what helps you read from a page more easily. Certainly you should try and get assessed and seek professional help. This can take the form of being financially aided to buy specialist equipment, or with individual support sessions. With regard to coloured paper, you may be given coloured plastic overlays. You can try this for yourself anyway, by trying a few different coloured plastic wallets, and then cut a suitable sized piece to overlay on texts and books. This can make an enormous difference, and can be a fantastic help at auditions and read-throughs. People who are not dyslexic may also find this helps their reading, so if you ever find that reading aloud is challenging, but you know you are not dyslexic, then try this out and see if it helps.

When it comes to sight-reading, all the techniques you are taught at drama school should benefit everyone, whether dyslexic or not. But specifically, you can try these:

- Coloured paper and/or enlarged text.

- Use a highlighter pen to pick out key passages, or simply to split up the text on the page.

- Use different coloured highlighters for different sections.

- Read through a short section at a time, and mark the punctuation points (for example, with a forward slash / or come up with your own mark or symbol). This can be very helpful or it can deceive the eye, depending on the nature of your dyslexia. Try different markings or highlights.

- Try marking the end of a line in some way – if the line runs on, you can pencil in a little arrow that curves round towards the next line.

  If the next line is a new thought, then a forward slash or two (//), or perhaps a forward arrow, may be useful.

  One actor found an upward arrow helped – it certainly doesn't do it for me, but this helped him.

  You can also mark the full stops in this way, so that you know when a thought is ending, and a new thought is approaching, in the middle of a line on the page.

- Don't panic while you look at the page – you are thinking as you read and it is fine that other people see your thought process. Remember that people pause for thought in normal conversation, it is perfectly natural.

- You will make mistakes, we all do, but don't apologise – just take a breath and carry on. As the acting/sight-reading coach Nina Finburgh says, 'Real people do stumble over words!' Look at her excellent book, it is full of brilliant ideas (*Some Do's and Don'ts of Sight Reading for Actors at Audition*).

- Practise. As I have mentioned before, read aloud every day, with all kinds of texts in different styles and genres, but also read your cereal box aloud, or bits from the newspaper or magazine you are reading. If someone has a T-shirt with slogans on it, read them aloud. Even on public transport, you can silently read the information on posters or adverts – because even if you just mouth the shape of the words it can help. You may find you can speak them quietly. Wherever you see something written down, read it aloud. Little and often is always going to help. Then when you come to more formalised sessions of sight-reading, your eyes, brain, and mouth will be more used to it.

- Take your time – I think this is one of the most important lessons to learn. When a person has trouble reading fluently, they often rush, either to get it over with as quickly as possible, or to try and prove they can do it. This is also quite a common tendency in people whose first language is not English, and I just say, take the time, we will wait. That gives you the time to improve and gain confidence. We all need to take our time, and remember that, above all, we need to give our audience time to assimilate the information.

- So look up before you begin speaking off the page, take in your audience (or the space) then take a few words at a time. Practise looking up off the page as much as possible, and work out sensibly sized chunks to speak at a time. The slower you take this to start with, the better you will be able to manage. Eventually you will be able to take it all at a reasonable pace, not rushed, but pacey and relaxed.

- Ensure that you are standing or sitting with equal weight distribution for grounding and support.

- And above all, *remember to breathe.* This will calm your nerves, help you to support the word, and integrate everything into this moment.

Other suggestions for planning or paralleling a course   `3.23`

During actor training, students will be exposed to all kinds of text, in voice/text classes, in movement, and, of course, in acting. The texts used in this book have by necessity been only a small selection of what I would use over the course of two or three years in training, and are offered only as suggestions. Every course will have its own structure and place different kinds of text at different places within the training, so it is merely a guide. However, I hope it will be helpful to offer an outline plan, with some further ideas on the kinds of texts that could be used and applied to voice and speech work during this basic training.

The following are also very useful to the working actor, as so much of the suggested work is poetry, and poetry is the lifeblood of the actor.

First year

Poem – Something *you* have found and been inspired by, so that you start with your own voice and your own thoughts.

Rhetoric – Political speeches taken from the public domain, both contemporary and historical. Choose something that moves you, perhaps that you totally agree with and feel passionate about. Or you could choose something that you vehemently oppose – after all, speaking from the centre about someone else's ideas and making them your own is what an actor does.

Poetry through the ages – In another strand, I suggest a weekly poem working chronologically from Chaucer, through the centuries via Shakespeare, Milton, Keats, Owen, Plath, Zephaniah, Duffy, for example.

Alongside this is the requirement to learn progressively larger sections each week, to exercise the 'warder of the brain'. It is extremely useful to learn in new and/or different ways, for example, to learn by breath and thought, and by image (you look at a line, see the images within it and learn it by association with the image). This is the polar opposite of 'rote' learning, which admittedly can be useful, but if you only learn that way, it can let you down. Learning by thought means that, if for some reason you 'dry', you breathe, think of the last thought you said, and the next thought, image, or idea will come to you.

One can only scratch the surface of poetry from other cultures, due to the constraints of time, and indeed it is a hard enough task to do more than skim English literature! I do think it worth at least introducing other rhythms from other writings as a kind of taster. It should then be possible not to just look at other writings but also contextualise them, socially, politically and so on, which is essential to understanding. My favourites include Pablo Neruda (Chile), Seamus Heaney (Ireland) and Rabindranath Tagore (the great Bengali poet). But, of course, the list is endless.

Introduction to Shakespeare – Use a demystification process to include the physicalisation of text.

Shakespeare sonnets – Sonnets are great for working actors too. Because the form is so short and concise, they repay many, many repetitions, and are small chunks of richly condensed meaning. They are also very exposing, because there is no character to 'hide' behind, it's just you and the poem, which requires real honesty and simplicity. Try modern sonnets to locate form as well as contemporaneity in the present day.

Narrative Verse – Long narrative poems demand storytelling skills and sustained thought and stamina. They also involve rhythm, alliteration, imagery, etc. (examples include *The Highwayman*, *The Raven*, *The Goblin Market*, *The Rime of the Ancient Mariner*).

Second year

Text through the ages – A text 'trot' of dramatic literature which helps locate the changing use of language. A few suggestions might be advancing from Shakespeare through Restoration, into eighteenth-century comedies, the nineteenth century and melodrama (finding the truth without judgement in *The Factory Lad*, for example), the first so-called modern play *Woyzeck* perhaps, the later nineteenth century and Wilde, Shaw, and into the twentieth century, where you might try a bit of Rattigan, Samuel Beckett, and up to the present with the overlapping dialogue of Caryl Churchill, for example, and continuing into Mark Ravenhill, Polly Teale, Billy Roche and beyond.

This echoes the progression of poetry looked at in the first year. The value of this kind of progression in year two is that you are exposed to so many different types of language, rhythm, structure, linguistic and dramatic device, that you really have to respond and adapt your vocal range, your speech organs and the very differing articulatory requirements, as well as your mental agility to change from one to another. You can find comparisons along the way too, for example, between Restoration texts and Oscar Wilde, or Ben Jonson and Gilbert and Sullivan – not necessarily bedfellows, but this way your vocal and intellectual athleticism will be challenged. You also learn a lot about the socio-political landscape along the way, which can be no bad thing for an artist.

Shakespearean rhetoric – Applying the learned rudiments of rhetoric to dramatic text and to the classical repertoire, involving direct address in addition to the fundamentals of the rhetoric form. Joan la Pucelle in *Henry VI, Part 1*, Brutus and Mark Antony in *Julius Caesar* – these two give you the contrast of rhetoric in prose and then in verse – Richard and Richmond's orations to their armies in *Richard III*, Portia in *A Merchant of Venice*, and then rhetoric in dialogue between Macbeth and Lady Macbeth in Act One, Scene Seven of *Macbeth*.

Epic poetry – This helps to consolidate the huge range of skills that have been built up over a period of time.

Narrative prose – Reading aloud the work of Dickens, Hardy and Orwell, for example, will really stretch all your fundamental voice and speech skills, as well as making demands on your storytelling abilities. This is muscular work, requiring great stamina.

Film and television scripts – Very demanding in contrast to the big theatre voice you have been acquiring, both in terms of size, support on lower volumes, doing 'less' whilst maintaining connection and truth, and the sometimes apparently mundane element that you might have to express without judgement or pulling back. Compare televison 'soap' scripts with Victorian melodrama.

Greek chorus – A whole course on its own in many ways, because it teaches not just ensemble skills and speaking as a group, but also, though the language itself may not be complex, it is just huge in its emotional range, requiring the strongest and most released of bodies and voices. Look at translations of plays by Euripides and Sophocles, but also look to modern versions, such as Ted Hughes' *Seneca's Oedipus*, which has some fantastic choruses, and the most glorious and yet spare use of imagery and epic storytelling; or *Thebans* by Liz Lochhead, as suggested in Session 2.21.

Part 4

The Warm-up – one size does not fit all

Part 4

The Warm-up: One Size Does Not Fit All

This is such an important part of an actor's process, and yet seems such a difficult thing to understand and get right. I am not sure there is ever one right way to go about warming up the voice, but there are probably quite a lot of wrong or unhelpful ways. The least helpful way, of course, is to not do it! It is a constant surprise that some actors think they can rehearse, or indeed perform, with the most perfunctory of preparations.

Notice next time you go to the theatre, or recall a time you went and the play seemed to 'get going' after about fifteen or twenty minutes. I have experienced this quite often, where some sort of gear-shift happens a short period into the performance. Sometimes it is very obvious – you notice that the actors are starting to physically inhabit the space, or the action becomes clearer, or, startlingly, you begin to *hear* it! If an actor cannot be heard, or is not physically 'present', it is nearly always because the preparation has not been done. This may be down to a lack of warm-up, or perhaps because the actor has not done regular work on the voice and body. This might sound judgemental, but, quite frankly, if I call a plumber I want to hear the water flowing into the system they have repaired. If it doesn't work, I want my money back. Someone once asked about motivation, and for me the objective is first and foremost to be heard. I'd be a very odd voice teacher, or indeed an audience member, if I didn't have a bee in my bonnet about that one! So regular and ongoing work is going to aid you as an actor throughout your life, you know that, and a good warm-up is going to aid the work immediately about to happen. It is about being heard, and about being truthful whilst filling the space, physically and vocally.

'One size does not fit all' – what I mean is that a warm-up should be tailored to what you are doing. Make it task-specific and, more importantly, performance-specific. If, for example, the piece is highly physical and involves a lot of contact work with other actors, there's not a lot of point in only warming up by lying on the floor and humming to yourself. It'll help your voice a bit, but if the body is not prepared, then you are much less likely to be prepared for the action, both bodily and vocally, you are about to undertake. Equally, a few star jumps are not enough, or appropriate, if you are going to play Clytemnestra! Again, you know all this, but it really does help to have a think about how to make something work for you that is appropriate.

On the DVD ☉, there are several workout sequences, and at the end of the longer warm-up the actors simultaneously speak a variety of short texts so that you can join in with your own choice. If you use this regularly or repeatedly, you could use different bits of text each time, so that it is not too fixed. You could use this as a basis to warm up in the mornings, and if that sounds like a contradiction of the 'one size does not fit all' scenario, it is only intended as a guide. In fact, the idea for something, in essence, to 'hum along to', came out of a direct request from students who sometimes find it hard to do the work on their own. So they asked me to put a session on a video (that is how long it is since I was first asked).

Warm-ups generally work much better if they are suited to the day, the weather, how people are feeling, what they are about to do and so on. So, although a written or recorded routine is necessarily fixed, it should be possible to adapt it as you work alongside it. So this particular workout is just a starting point. The shorter, taster warm-up for Restoration work is intended to give you an idea on how you can make these production- or genre-specific. You can experiment from there. Additionally, there is a short workout for those days when you are either incredibly busy or you just want a 'top-up'.

Many actors much prefer to do their own thing, their own private or separate warm-up, and that is their prerogative. I do think it worth considering, however, that if you are working with other people, particularly in an ensemble piece, you might ensure that some time and space is also given to a group session. This can really help gel a company, get them all into voice in the same spirit, and, more importantly, in the same genre. So that, for example, you come up with a company routine for particular physical and vocal exercises, and group work on articulation – it is especially important to find the different demands of articulating Jacobean revenge tragedy from Mark Ravenhill, or a soap-opera script from Oscar Wilde.

The other thing I would like to mention is the feeling that you can get that you are alone, or that other actors may make fun of you warming up. I was quite shocked when graduates came back with tales of being the only ones to warm up, and feeling distinctly uncomfortable with the experience of going alone, as it were. Again, this may be uncommon, but if it exists, then you need some encouragement to get on with your thing. Actors have also reported back that they were the only one to do a regular warm-up on tour, and were the only ones to not lose their voice. If they seemed smug about it, I can only be pleased for their sake that they look after themselves. It doesn't matter what other people think of you – don't be gung-ho about it, don't comment or criticise others, just get on with your own practice and be the best you can be. And if you are one of those people who can run a marathon without warming up, then lucky you! It's a bit like smoking – we all know it's bad for you and yet some people smoke forty cigarettes a day their whole life and never get ill. I go to a smokey party and pretty soon my throat is feeling sore. It's called Sod's Law. But the voice and the body are the actor's fundamental toolkit and they simply need and deserve loving care and attention. The added attraction is that the more you do, the more you are likely to improve, expand your technical and creative possibilities, and keep on learning – which is a fantastic state to be in.

Some ideas for constructing warm-ups

4.1 **Daily warm-up**

Preceding rehearsals (can be used as a general routine). About twenty-five minutes in length.

- Preparation: will vary depending on how you feel, what the weather is like and so on. So you might begin by lying in semi-supine and doing some relaxation work. Or you might do some shakes and releases from standing.

- Do the clean-hands exercise (1.4.1), massaging the insides and outsides of the mouth, very softly.

4.1a **Begin with the body**

Integrate the breath right from the outset:

- Stand and shake with 'f', 's', 'sh', through the arms, down through the legs.

- Circle the ankles slowly, and then the knees and hips with the same sounds.

- Pat down the arms, hands, then down and up the legs, with 'f', 'sh'.

- Tap your head with 'sh' and 'f'; tap and rub the face, massage up from the jaw into the temples and up into the scalp and back down again.

- Stroke down the jaw and let it go.

- Have a few yawns.

- Begin to open up the body to easy stretching using 'f', 's' or 'sh'.

4.1b **Get more physical**

You can also use the stepping-out sequence here (1.15.7).

- Repeat the whole of the above section with an easy 'v' sound, around the middle or just above your middle pitch (warming up on a low pitch is too tiring for the voice and won't aid the vocal-warming process).

- Use any of those sequences again on 'z' and then a hum.

Wake up the spine ☺

4.1c

- Stand with equal weight distribution, feet hip-width or slightly wider apart, and think in an upwards direction. Let the head float on top of your spine – do some very slow and gentle nods and 'yes's – side to side and up and down, very delicate movements, using 'f'.

- Now gently roll down the spine (you can see this separately on the DVD) releasing the head and neck whilst releasing the out-breath on 'f'.

- When you arrive upside down, gently shake out the shoulders on 'f' or 'sh'.

- With gentle movements, bend and almost straighten the legs, and feel the connection with the sit bones and the heels, again on 'sh'.

- Shake the sit bone to heel connection on 'sh'.

- Let a breath deep into the lower-back ribs, float the knees forward and gently come up through the spine on 'f' or 'sh'.

- Repeat that several times, each time getting a little quicker.

- Repeat and as you arrive at the upright, let your elbows float up to the ceiling, then the wrists, the fingers, reach up and arc your arms out and down to the sides.

- Do this many times, going on to an easy 'v', then with a hum.

- Repeat and, as your arms reach up, release the hum into a 'mah', elongating the sound each time.

Warming and resonating

4.1d

- Bang the chest and reach the arms out with your 'mah' or 'moo' or 'moh'.

- Play with range – humming up and down on 'm', 'n' and 'ng', doing some pitch glides/sirens, ensuring an easy onset and a flowing sound.

- Do this whilst moving more through the body, stretching and reaching out.

- Bring the sound from a chant into the spoken, so going from sounding out a long 'mah' on one note, speak that 'mah' and do this with 'moh' and 'moo' and 'mee', again playing gently with range.

- Chew gently, keep moving the whole time, and start to speak some words with 'mah' and 'moo' and 'bah' and 'boo' and 'dah' and 'dey' and 'dee', etc.

- Start to warm up the articulators – keep the body moving a little and massage your lips and cheeks, gently bite the tongue, move the face around and get it as elastic as possible.

- Stroke down the jaw and let it go, let the tongue hang out and float it all back up and in again, very softly.

4.1e Bring the work onto articulation

- Get a little more muscular and go through some lip stretches and puckers, etc., and some tongue stretches, big and more precise, whilst mirroring the direction with your hands/fingers. Simultaneously, *keep sounding.*

- Using the prop if you have one, do some drills, from lip sounds ('bbbb', 'pppp', 'mmmm', 'wwww') to tongue tip sounds ('dddd', 'tttt', 'nnnn', 'llll') progressing back through the mouth/tongue on to ('tch tch tch', 'dj dj dj') to the back of the tongue ('ggg', 'kkk', 'ng ng ng'). Mirror all these tongue movements physically with your hands, feet, whole body where possible.

- Go through some sequences like 'pahtahkay peyteykey', etc. or any others that you know. If you are going to rehearsal, start to incorporate any accent or vocal quality specific to the piece.

And on to text

- Start to use some text, either a section of poetry you know, or take a few lines of text from any section in the book, or something you are about to work on. Keep moving.

- Stand quietly for a moment.

- If you don't feel quite 'there', pat again and start to bang your chest with your hands, humming and 'mah'-ing all the while.

- Hum and gently chew at the same time.

Pre-show warm-up

All of the above can work for a pre-show warm-up, but ensure that you have a think about what the show is, what genre or period or style you are working in, and incorporate the style you have explored in rehearsals, bringing that into your process. Here are a few examples:

Physical theatre

You are doing a very physical piece with lots of physical contact, maybe fights and struggles, or just hugs and kisses.

- Work with your partners, using each others' weight – hold hands facing each other and drop down and up, counterbalancing each other as you both 'f' and 'sh'. Repeat it when you are ready to with voiced sounds like 'v' and humming.

- Massage yourself and each other whilst 'f'-ing and 'sh'-ing and humming.

Restoration show

- Walk around the space right from the start with an open body, and let in the breath through the most open channel imaginable, the best breather in the world. Be terribly pleased with yourself and feel your spine lengthen and your chest open out. And when you release your out-breath on an 'f' it is the most exquisite 'f' that was ever heard at court.

- When you begin to move, you are clearly the most beautiful person in the room or the wittiest, or sexiest, or indeed all three, and your movement and your sounds will reflect that. How gorgeous do you look and how magnificent do you sound as you look into the real or imaginary mirrors in the room?

- When you start to articulate, your lip-chewing exercise is outrageously sexy; your lip exercises and stretches are simply marvellous. And as for the articulation drills and sequences – well, use the 'tha fa sa' on a whisper to tell the most delicious piece of gossip; and use the 'tha va za' sequence to tell the world how pleased you are that they can see you.

When you arrive at the use of text, therefore, you are speaking with the utmost relish and brilliance because those sensations, feelings and thoughts are already in your body, your breath, and your voice.

4.2C The setting

Think about the world of the play and start to use that as an impetus right from the outset. So you may be working on *The Three Lives of Lucie Cabrol* by John Berger, which is set in a rural community. As you begin to warm up the feet, close your eyes and imagine you are standing on the earth, or grass. As the breath comes into you, you move with the sensation of earth beneath you and breathe in the air and atmosphere of the village. The sense of the earth, dropping down and moving around on clay will ground you, which is essential for this world. Or perhaps you are working on *Tales from the Vienna Woods*. As you physically warm up and move around the space, you breathe in the elegance of Viennese squares with all the beautiful people, waltz as you release on an 'f' or a 'sh' to incorporate your body's response, or try a soldier's walk, a citizen's gait. Your sounds release but are affected by your character's thoughts, so that some of the company are sounding on easy 'sh' or 'v' sounds, some are sinister. This work will then be inherent in your voice and body by the time you get onto articulation and speaking some text.

Short warm-ups

It is possible to warm the voice (and body) in ten to fifteen minutes, when you have trained and are fit and used to regular work. There are days when even with all that experience you can need as much as forty-five minutes. But for those times when you sense that a shorter version will suffice, here's what you can do:

5 minutes

• Gentle stretches, right through the body, using voiceless sounds ('f', 's', sh', continuant sounds) – feel the body opening up and releasing. At the same time, feel the breath centring and extending its capacity.

5 minutes

• Continue to move either from standing, or rolling around on the floor and then moving to standing and walking, whilst sounding onto 'v', 'z' and humming. Ensure you begin around the middle, or just above, your middle note. After a couple of minutes, gently begin to extend the range. Three or four minutes in and begin to 'mah' and 'moo' forward into the space while patting, rubbing and releasing the sound out and all around you.

5 minutes

• Pat and massage the face, cheeks, lips, tongue. Shake it around a bit whilst sounding, then do some lip and tongue stretches with sound. Do some drills – strong 'bbbbbb', 'dddddd', 'ggggg', etc., then light and easy 'ppp', 'ttt', 'kkk', etc.

• Now use some of your sequences ('pahtakah peyteykey' or something else you've picked up) and *at the same time* do these in the accent or vocal characteristic of your character or of the text you are going to work on. Integrate the thought with the breath, with the sound, with the speech skills, and with the world of the play.

- Silently mouth, then whisper, and then speak one or two lines from the play.

4.4   Warm-ups to incorporate extreme voice

If you are going to be shouting and screaming in a performance, you are likely to need even more release work than usual so that the body, and therefore the voice, is open, relaxed and ready to work. And you also need to ensure that your support system is available and highly engaged.

So do extra work on release:

- Lie in semi-supine and simply let go; then do some pouring with and without voiceless and voiced sounds.

- When your voice is warm (you can feel it and hear it – this could take anything from ten to thirty minutes depending on your voice that day), try some easy shouts and gentle screams lying down, not using much volume. This is to discover the sensation of these sounds at this stage.

- Come to sitting and kneeling and do some revs, and bunny jumps (you can see these in the short warm-up on the DVD) and rolling around using the knees, hands, sit bones, every part of the body possible – use the floor to give your support system extra 'oomph'. Gradually bring this to standing, and then use the walls, the furniture, each other, to gain extra 'anchoring', as Jo Estill put it, to keep that 'oomph' factor going. Stand easy and open, let the breath in and sound out. Have a shout and enjoy it.

If at any point your voice feels tired or something isn't quite right, check that you are not tensing anywhere, and ensure that you are not pulling back on the sound. Keep it all forward and open.

A note on articulation – remember that very strong consonants, whether it be a really hissy 's', or a punchy strong 'b' or a spat-out 't' will give enormous weight and conviction to what you are saying, reduce the need to be too loud, and is often a far more interesting acting choice anyway.

Additional articulation warm-up 4·5

If you feel that you need extra preparation on articulation in your warm-up, either because of the nature of the rehearsal or show you are about to do, or perhaps because your organs of articulation are particularly sluggish (and it happens to us all), then go through the articulation work sheets in detail.

- Look at the lip and tongue exercises in the Appendix and work through them.

- Look at the articulation sheets in the Appendix and work through as much of it as feels useful to you. Apply any accent or other specific vocal or speech choice relevant to the day's work, at the same time or on the repetitions.

- Remember to work the articulators through the body, so that it doesn't become an isolated experience. You can do some of this stuff whilst washing your hands, or getting changed, of course. Keep moving, but then incorporate periods of rest and ease.

- Move around, and then simply stop and notice the breath, your pulse, the stillness. Let the jaw hang, let the tongue flop.

Further warm-ups taken from each session 4.6

In addition to the ideas above, if you have read through the book so far, you will see that every session (or lesson plan) has a warm-up built in, so that even though a number are repeated, there are still a great many warm-ups you can use from those first two chapters. This is particularly useful if you are engaging in work at either first- or second-year level; and if you are a working actor, then both chapters should provide you with plenty of variety, either to use the warm-up sections in their own right where appropriate, or to utilise them as a basis and inspiration for constructing your own need-specific requirements.

4.7   Warm-ups from other practitioners

If you are in training, or indeed working as an actor with that knowledge behind you, you will hopefully be aware of a whole range of voice books and methodologies. Look at the warm-ups in books, or try to devise one based on a practitioner's work and process. This is quite advanced stuff and you may want help with it, but if you were to use or construct such warm-ups from half a dozen different sources, and try one out each week, you would get not only variety, but different routines and processes – and this can be incredibly beneficial. Find what works best for you on particular days, or for specific working needs.

4.8   The warm-down

Actors sometimes forget to warm down. Athletes and dancers always do this, because they are aware that if the body has been subjected to physical extremes, it needs to warm down as well as warm up, in order to return to a good resting position, to recover and to avoid any potential injury. The same applies to the voice, particularly if you have been engaged in stage fights or have been screaming and shouting. Some theatre is very extreme, and it can be quite damaging, and certainly very tiring, to go straight from that kind of performance into the bar or outside, without making an adjustment.

You can warm down very easily – usually some very gentle humming while you are getting changed can be enough. If you have subjected both voice and body to extreme physical states, you may need to stretch gently, and especially helpful is a short period of lying down in semi-supine. It might seem unnecessary, but try it and see how your voice and body reward and thank you for taking that extra bit of care.

Drink water before, during breaks if possible, and always after a show.

A final word about vocal health and well-being

If you have a sore throat, gargling is very helpful (and always gargle without voicing) – you can gargle with salt water, but another incredibly effective remedy that is benign and quite safe is to put a drop of pure tea-tree oil into a small glass of warm water, mix it and use as a gargle. It tastes revolting but is great for kicking out bad bugs! As I am not a qualified aromatherapist, I can only recommend this based on personal experience and a lot of research of my own, but I have yet to find anyone it did not help. Ask your own health practitioner for advice, always, but if you feel comfortable with essential-oil remedies then by all means try this one.

Steaming before *and* after a show is also very good practice, and is essential if you are slightly under the weather. It is a great way to hydrate the vocal mechanism, and relax the whole system. It is also wonderful for when you feel 'bunged up'. Even a sore throat can be used in performance if you warm up (and down) carefully and steam plenty (and I mean plenty – not necessarily for a long time, but many times over a period of a few hours, for just a couple of minutes at a time, is best).

An easy rule of thumb to remember is to steam on the hour, every hour, in the evening (if at home for example), so you can get in about five steams of a couple of minutes each. Do this last thing before you go to bed and first thing when you get up – certainly before speaking or eating. Make it a habit whenever you get a sore throat and you may be amazed at how effective this can be.

Either put your head over a bowl of steaming water and inhale, or get a personal steamer. You can buy small personal steamers very cheaply and because they are small and light are very portable, so they should be an essential part of your daily baggage.

Postscript

At the end of two years, it's a good idea to come back to your baby 'f' – revisit the exercise, take that little 'f' for a walk, see how it feels, and how it is. When I completed my last group of second-year classes and we re-experienced the exercise, there were some surprising and lovely discoveries. Some just liked finding their easy sound and connection, and then I asked them to repeat the exercise, but to imagine they were back at the beginning of their first year, and also to become aware of what it was like to remember being 'new' to it. They were amazed at how different it now felt, and realised what extraordinarily different physicalities had been present before, and had therefore now transformed.

One student said his baby 'f' is now 'so high' – indicating with his hand that the 'f' is now at head height – 'It has grown up!' I ask students what their baby 'f' feels like: 'It's a marshmallow.' 'Oh, mine is bright.' 'Mine is a pug puppy.' 'I always imagined mine as a sort of blue parrot, which hopped along the floor when it was soft and then started flying if it got stronger.' 'My baby "f" was an actual letter "f" with a tiny baseball cap with dog ears either side.' 'My baby "f"s were always blue and were on a lead; they were slower than baby "s"s and "sh"s which were yellow and orange respectively and tended to fly.' '"F"s are fuzzy, "s"s are spiky and "sh"s are smooth.'

My baby 'f' is me. It is my breath; it is my voice.

Endnotes

1   W.A. Aikin was voice teacher at Central School of Speech and Drama for twenty years. Author of *The Voice* (1910, revised 1932).

2   J. Clifford Turner was voice teacher at RADA and elsewhere. Author of *Voice and Speech in the Theatre* (1950), sixth edition edited by Jane Boston (2007).

3   For more information about Annie Morrison's work and the Morrison Bone Prop™ go to www.anniemorrison.co.uk.

4   Cicely Berry is a world-renowned voice and text coach, and Voice Director at the RSC. Author of many books including *Voice and the Actor* (1973), *The Actor and the Text* (1992), *Text in Action* (2001) and *From Word to Play* (2008).

5   Kristin Linklater is an eminent voice coach working principally in the USA. Author of *Freeing the Natural Voice* (1976, revised 2006), and *Freeing Shakespeare's Voice* (1992).

6   For more information about Patricia Bardi's work, go to www.patriciabardi.com.

7   Lise Olson is an acting, voice and dialect coach, and an actor/combatant. She is currently Course Director for the MA Acting at the Birmingham School of Acting. Contact information can be found at: theatrecourage@gmail.com or lise.olson@bcu.ac.uk.

Appendices

(i) Bodyworld

Anatomy and Physiology

Anatomy (the 'what') – The study of structure: bones, muscles, cavities, etc., the body itself.

Physiology (the 'how'; results) – The study of function: breathing, resonance, articulation, phonation (speech), etc.

Here is a checklist of all body parts involved in voice in some way, either for breath, capacity, control and support of the voice, voice production and/or speech. There follows a brief description of function.

Head	*Neck*
Brain	Larynx and pharynx
Ears	Hyoid bone
Nasal cavity	Trachea
Sinus cavities	Cartilages (thyroid, cricoid,
Mouth (oral) space	arytenoids)
Jaw	Vocal folds
Hard palate	Extrinsic and intrinsic muscles
Soft palate	of the larynx
Uvula	
Lips	
Teeth	
Tongue	

Body	
Spine	cervical (neck) vertebrae
	thoracic vertebrae
	lumbar vertebrae
	sacrum
	coccyx
Ribcage	ribcage
	sternum
Lungs	
Diaphragm	
Intercostal muscles	(three sets)
Abdominals	transversus abdominus
	rectus abdominus
	external and internal oblique muscles
	pelvic floor muscles
	psoas muscles
Back muscles	particularly latissimus
	dorsi and levatores costarum

Here is a very brief description of what is involved in creating voice.

Brain – It sends the signal to speak. It's the starter motor of sound, or the conductor of the orchestra which is our voice and its component parts, and so in this context, every element of your voice and speech.

Spine – Everything is connected to and from the spine. It comprises the cervical (neck) vertebrae, thoracic vertebrae, lumbar vertebrae, sacrum, and coccyx.

Head – Sinus cavities, nasal cavity, mouth space, jaw, hard palate, teeth, and the muscles of the lips, tongue, and soft palate – for resonance and articulation.

Pharynx – The tract or area between the back of your mouth and the larynx. It acts as a passageway for food on its way to the stomach and for the flow of air to and from the lungs.

Larynx – Hyoid bone (a small free-standing bone from which the larynx is suspended, like a little hot-air balloon; it also serves as an anchor for the tongue), cartilages (thyroid, cricoid, arytenoids), muscles, including the vocal folds (the vocal cords). For the sound, the voice box itself. This is a very complex structure and, as I have mentioned, you can search out much more extensive detail if you want, from different sources.

Ribcage – Houses the lungs, the sternum, and the intercostal muscles (the muscles between the ribs, allowing for expansion/contraction and control of the air flow and vocal sound).

Lungs – For the air to breathe and speak.

Diaphragm – This is the muscle separating the thorax from the abdomen, a dome-shaped muscle that drops down when the brain gives a signal for more oxygen, and as it pulls down, ribs 8–10 swing out, the lungs expand downwards and outwards, and air is drawn into the body. This is entirely unconscious and automatic. As the diaphragm drops down, it slightly displaces the contents of the lower abdomen, hence the slight 'bulge' in the tummy when we breathe in.

Abdominals – Transversus abdominus, rectus abdominus, external and internal oblique muscles, pelvic floor and psoas muscles – these are all engaged in some way for supporting the voice, stabilising the body, and control of the sound.

Back muscles, particularly the latissimus dorsi and levatores costarum – For more 'oomph'. These muscles are more obviously engaged in heightened vocal states like shouting.

As you can see, a lot of the body is involved in creating voice and speech sounds, and I have purposely kept this information short and concise. There are great books that go into detail, but I wanted this book to be as practical as possible – which is why I have placed this brief explanation in the Appendix, so that you don't get too involved in head-based thinking whilst discovering the voice through practical exercises.

On the other hand, it is here to help you understand just how and why voice work is so physical. The old adage 'knowledge is power' can be a double-edged sword when working with voice and text. Knowing nothing at the start can be a very useful place because you tend not to bring preconceived ideas and therefore approach the work without prejudice. Allow yourself not to know. The other side of the coin is to empower yourself with the right sort of knowledge. For example, whilst you do not need to know the detailed intricacies of how the voice works, it is incredibly helpful to have a broad understanding of its functioning. If you are asked to engage with the abdominal muscles, you know that it is to provide support for the voice; or if you are doing lots of massaging and release work on the jaw, you know that tension in this area causes both speech problems, tension and constriction in the voice, and prevents forward placement. If you are having trouble with an aspect of your voice, even a little knowledge will help you troubleshoot your own problems so you can then work out what needs addressing.

(ii) TIV1a 💿
Lip Exercises

Warm-up – Have a mirror to hand.

1   First of all, see how tense or relaxed your lips are by doing some 'horse blows'.

   Massage your lips. Rub them with your fingers, and the backs of the fingers/knuckles.

   Pull the upper lip and waggle it around between your fingers. Do the same with the lower lip.

   Massage both lips again. Rub them fairly vigorously and do some gentle 'chewing' movements. Try out the horse blows again. Notice the difference. Repeat, with sounds including pitch glides.

2   Loosen jaw – massage jaw joint, stroke face down gently but firmly.

   Massage and loosen the face, cheeks, jaw, chin.

3   Make some little chewing movements with the lips, avoiding too much movement in the jaw.

   Chew a little more, so the jaw is moving too, but gently.

4   'Duck lips' – press both lips between your fingers to create duck lips.

Exercises – aerobics and ballet for muscularity and agility

1   *Pout* – and then smile into a big beam.

2   *Big kiss little kiss grin* – Blow a big kiss, really pursing your lips; then a little kiss (very light and delicate) and then grin. Do this sequence

and send it to everyone in the group (real or imaginary!) Check that, as you go round, you don't jut forward – no bobbing chicken heads!

3   *Monkey bum and cat's arse* – a charming description! Purse your lips, really pout them forwards like a big ape. Now purse them to create a tiny opening. Go between the two. As you do the ape lips, try saying 'give us a kiss' or 'mushroom vol-au-vents' or anything that comes to mind. As you do the pursed, 'cat's arse' lips, say 'oh I say' or 'oh no' – you might find your pitch goes quite high. Alternate between the two.

4   *Monkey bum and toothless* – do the big pouty lips, then stretch back your lips over your teeth – and say 'where's my teeth' or 'lime'. And try all three (monkey bum, cat's arse and toothless), alternating between them. Notice as you do these exercises and speak a phrase or two, that your voice mirrors the movements and sensations – ape lips usually produce a low pitch, limey toothless grins will often produce high sounds.

5   *Shake out* – have a little rest. Drop the head a little, loll the tongue out and gently shake the tongue and wobble the lips. Sound this.

6   *Elvis lip curls* – curl your upper lip to the right and then the left. This may take some practice. Now curl your lower lip to the left then the right, ensuring the jaw stays still. Curl up the corners of your upper lip then lower. Curl all four corners out, so that your lips make a square shape. Then bring them into a big round circle. Looking in a mirror helps you see and feel this.

7   *Square and round* – do both upper and lower corners at the same time – this gives you a 'square' mouth. Round your lips. Go from one to the other.

8   Repeat massage, then do some horse blows with and without voice ('bbrr' and 'pprr').

9   *Mexican wave* – first of all, make those duck lips again. Now trill the lips (horse blows) and this time, see if you can trill or roll them from one side of the mouth to another, creating a 'Mexican wave' with your lips.

Devise your own lip exercises – they are likely to be useful and memorable. Be creative.

(ii) TIV1b 💿
Lip Exercises

Lip sound drills with consonant phonemes 💿

1   Using the bone prop, sound out with your lips on 'bbbbbbbbb-bah'

Repeat and use the hands to emphasise the muscularity of the sound – make a fist and punch the other palm as you say the 'b' sounds, and alternate your hands.

Repeat this with 'p', but this time the fingers gently tap each other.

Repeat with 'm' and this time the hands and fingers come together and motion like waves.

Repeat with 'w', open and close the fingers rapidly as if they were 'winking'.

The hand gestures mimic the sounds, which helps by patterning the body and the lip movements together. It also makes it more fun, and you get a physical differentiation between different types of sound.

2   Go through the articulation sequences:

'oop-poo, ohp-poh, awp-paw, ahp-pah, ayp-pay, eep-pee'
'oob-boo, ohb-boh awb-baw ahb-bah ayb-bay eeb-bee'
'oom-moo ohm-moh awm-maw ahm-mah aym-may eem-mee'
'oof-foo ohf-foh awf-faw ahf-fah ayf-fay eef-fee'
'oov-voo ohv-voh awv-vaw ahv-vah ayv-vay eev-vee'

See also the sequences on TIV2b, which incorporate lip and soft-palate drills in addition to tongue work.

Every so often, stroke the jaw down gently and softly massage the face to ensure that tension is not creeping in. Then go back to find the muscularity. Flip between soft released sounds and strong released muscular sounds.

Strong sounds punch the air, so on a strong 'b' you will really hit your palm with the fist on words like 'bastard, don't dare!'

Softer sounds of 'b' would be for a phrase like 'bubbling gently'.

In other words, you find different dynamics for each sound depending on its context.

(iii) TIV2a 💿
Tongue Exercises

Warm-up – Have a mirror to hand.

1 *Massage* the tongue. Notice the difference. Repeat. Gently bite it.

2 Allow tip to *flop* onto lower lip. Flap lazily up and down between lips.

3 Allow to *roll* out over lower lip, and gently retract (not pulled back quickly). Use hands to mirror the movement.

4 *Massage tongue root* (with thumb into fleshy part under the jaw). (i) very slowly without sound; (ii) quickly with sounding – 'aaah', gently does it. Your sound will tell you if you are tensing up.

5 *Shake* head gently forward and loll the tongue, with gentle sounds.

6 *Clean teeth* with tongue, covering all surfaces, very slowly.

7 *Loosen jaw* – massage jaw joint, stroke face down gently but firmly. Massage and loosen the face, cheeks, jaw, chin.

8 Let the *jaw hang loosely* and allow to *float back* up. Mirror movement with hands. Repeat several times. Throughout this work, periodically check that there is space in the mouth, and that the neck, tongue root and jaw are relaxed.

9 Little chains and the trap door.

Exercise tongue – aerobics for muscularity

1 Press *tip into a point* against the forefinger or a thin pen.

2 *Press-ups* – press the underneath of the front of the tongue down over index finger; press upper edge upwards against the finger; press each side of the tongue in turn against the finger (left finger

left side of tongue and right finger to right side of tongue). Try using a pen too.

3 *Dart* the tongue out and allow it to slide gently back in. Hands mirror the movement.

4 *Thick and thin* – point tongue tip like a dart, then allow to widen. Repeat, resting the tongue on the lower lip (to avoid tension). Look in a mirror at the action – check the tongue is not moving in and out of the mouth. Check the jaw is still.

5 Repeat 4, this time holding the sides of the tongue between thumb and forefinger on the 'dart' position, and use the tongue muscles as you widen it to *push the fingers aside.*

6 *Tongue rolls* – put the tongue tip behind the lower-front teeth and roll out the body of the tongue. Repeat, building up speed. Try some easy sounds. Tongue movements and sound are easy and soft.

7 *Back of the tongue* – place tip behind lower front teeth and say 'ng' *then* 'ah' – check in the mirror, feeling the back of the tongue lift and the soft palate lower. Repeat, building up speed. Check in mirror that the jaw is not bouncing up and down.

8 *Big stretches* – try to touch the nose, chin, and each cheek in turn, with the tongue tip. Sound these and use your hands to mirror the movement.

9 *Precise stretches* – touch the centre of the upper lip, lower lip, and sides of the mouth, with the tongue tip – check in the mirror for precision. Change the order from time to time so you don't set patterns. Add precise little sounds.

10 *Shake out* – have a little rest. Drop the head a little, loll the tongue out and gently shake. Sound this.

11 *'Steps' with your tongue tip*, touch behind the upper-front teeth, touch alveolar ridge, then the hard palate, then the floor of the mouth. Repeat several times. Reverse the order. Integrate/sing with a little four-part tune.

12 Make a *bowl* with the tongue.

13 Make a *closure with the sides* of the tongue against the upper-gum ridge/teeth (as if saying 'y'), and then *flick* the tongue tip up towards the alveolar ridge and downwards.

14 Make the same *closure*, and this time *curl* the tongue tip back towards the post-alveolar position (further back in mouth).

Exercise tongue – balletic flow

1   Repeat massage of tongue. Check that there is a finger-width gap between the back teeth. Massage the jaw joint.

2   *Circle* the tongue very slowly around the lips, touching the outer edges of the lips.

3   *Write* your name in the air with the tongue tip, very slowly and precisely in block capitals.

4   *Write* your name again, very slowly, this time in cursive (or script) writing – be precise. Very good for control!

(iii) TIV2b 💿
Tongue and Soft-palate Exercises

Go on to some articulation – first some consonant drills and then apply to text, always with thought, breath, and connection. Make sense of it!

Tongue flicks on consonant phonemes

1   Lightly flick the tongue tip up and down on 'ttdd ttdd' and 'tttttttttta/ddddddddda'. Ensure that there is space between the teeth, and that the jaw doesn't bounce up and down – if you use the bone prop this won't happen, which is another good reason for using one. If you don't have one, gently steady the jaw with your hand. Look in the mirror to check there's no bounce.

2   Try 'tayt teet tayt taht tawt toot tawt'.

3   Repeat with a 'd'.

4   Try the sequence 'lahl layl leel layl lahl lawl lool lawl lahl'.

5   Go through the same process with 'n'; then with 'th' and **'th'** [voiced as in 'the'] sounds.

6   Repeat with 's' and 'z'.

7   Try with 'sh' – 'shahsh shaysh sheesh shaysh shahsh shawsh shoosh shawsh shahsh'.

   Repeat with 'tch' as in 'chip'.

   Repeat with 'zh' as in 'measure'.

   Repeat with 'dj' as in 'judge'.

Tongue and soft-palate work

Warm-up

1   Do three types of yawn: (i) a normal, open-mouthed yawn; (ii) yawn as if into the hard palate – it will feel slightly odd, as your lips come forward; (iii) yawn behind softly closed lips. These three yawns give you different sensations and open up the throat and mouth space in different ways – try them to discover how they differ. Notice how they feel.

2   Working the back of the tongue, try 'kkkggg kkkggg' and 'kg kg kg' 'kkkkkkkkka gggggggggga'. Feel the movement of the back of the tongue and the soft palate. Keep the jaw loose and ensure it doesn't jump up and down – using the bone prop will eliminate jaw bounce.

3   Using 'k' then 'g' go through the sequence as above.

    Try out sentences and then different texts.

    Work for precision and separation to start with, and then you can incorporate elisions – sounds flowing from one to another where appropriate.

    Keep working with a sense of ease and at the same time muscularity.

When working on text, even if it is tongue-twisters, remember to breathe, think, and speak with thought and intention.

Don't do any tongue work for extended periods of time – little and often is the key here. Tiredness can undo good work.

(iv) TIV3a 💿

Resonance and Articulation

Do these after learning the exercises physically with the DVD!

Figure of eight 💿

1   A brief reminder to physically loosen up – relax the shoulders, neck, and head by gentle release exercises; breathe into the intercostals and diaphragm; massage the lips and tongue and stroke down the jaw; do some tongue stretching and strengthening exercises.

2   J. Clifford Turner took this sequence of vowels represented in a 'figure of eight' from the 'resonator scale', which was originally designed by W. A. Aikin. I am using this for resonance, and as applied to a range of consonant combinations, it creates a comprehensive articulation course. 'OO' utilises the most extreme position of the lips (fully rounded), 'EE' the most extreme tongue position (most raised up in the mouth) and this resonator scale visits a sequence of vowels in between these extremes. For a full description, refer to Turner in *Voice and Speech in the Theatre*[2]. The mnemonic sentence goes back to at least the 1930s.

Who	would	know	aught	of	art	must
OO	oo	OH	**AW**	O	**AH**	U

learn	and	then	take	his	ease	
ER	A	E	**AY**	I	**EE**	

3   If you whisper from 'OO' to 'EE' and back again, you will hear an apparent change in pitch. This describes physically how the changing shape of the vocal tract can have an effect on resonant pitch. A longer channel for sound lowers the pitch; a shorter channel raises the pitch. The centre, mid-, and extreme vowel

positions (in bold above) are then extrapolated and put into a sequence expressed as a figure of eight.

4   Learn this physically first, using the DVD and only then go through this all on the page.

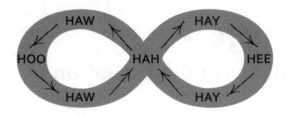

5   Do the figure of eight on the following consonants:

a)   'pah pay pee pay pah paw poo paw pah'

    'tah tay tee tay tah taw too taw tah'

    'kah kay kee kay kah kaw koo kaw kah'

    and then with 'b', 'd', 'g', 'm', 'n', 'l', 'th', 'f', 's', 'thevz'.

    You then put the three together. You will find these kinds of combinations used by many voice practitioners, because they work, and of course because there is a finite number of vowels and consonants, and the ordering of them by placement (in the mouth) is a given. We learn some of these patterns as children – 'pah tah kah', for example, is 'pat-a-cake pat-a-cake'.

b)   pahtahkah   paytaykay   peeteekee   paytaykay   pahtahkah
    pawtawkaw   pootookoo   pawtawkaw   pahtahkah

    bahdahgah   baydaygay   beedeegee   baydaygay   bahdahgah
    bawdawgaw   boodoogoo   bawdawgaw   bahdahgah

    mahnahlah   maynaylay   meeneelee   maynaylay   mahnahlah
    mawnawlaw   moonooloo   mawnawlaw   mahnahlah

    thahfahsah   thayfaysay   theefeesee   thayfaysay   thahfahsah
    thawfawsaw   thoofoosoo   thawfawsaw   thahfahsah
    [voiceless 'th' as in 'theatre', 'thing']

    thahvahzah   **th**ayvayzay   **th**eeveezee   **th**ayvayzay   **th**ahvahzah
    thawvawzaw   **th**oovoozoo   **th**awvawzaw   **th**ahvahzah
    [voiced 'th' as in 'those', 'they']

Eventually you can create a whole sequence in its entirety. Don't expect to get there too soon – it may be the second year of training before this takes hold. It takes time, so be patient, but once you have it, it is a lot of fun and is very useful. Start it all in your own accent, do it in RP, and then use it for lots of different accents. It will still work and be useful in different ways.

(iv) TIV3b ⊙

Resonance and Articulation

A slightly different combination, also based on the resonator scale. Practise the following, using the DVD first.

1 'oo oh aw ah ay ee'

Come off final consonants cleanly. Don't put in a neutral vowel ('er' or 'uh') between pairs, in other words you say 'oot-too' not 'ootuh-too' and so on.

'oop-poo ohp-poh awp-paw ahp-pah ayp-pay eep-pee'

'oob-boo ohb-boh awb-baw ahb-bah ayb-bay eeb-bee'

'oof-foo ohf-foh awf-faw ahf-fah ayf-fay eef-fee'

'oov-voo ohv-voh awv-vaw ahv-vah ayv-vay eev-vee'

'oot-too oht-toh awt-taw aht-tah ayt-tay eet-tee'

'ood-doo ohd-doh awd-daw ahd-dah ayd-day eed-dee'

'ool-loo ohl-loh awl-law ahl-lah ayl-lay eel-lee'

'oom-moo ohm-moh awm-maw ahm-mah aym-may eem-mee'

'oon-noo'	
'oos-soo'	
'ooz-zoo'	
'oosh-shoo'	*sh as in 'sheep' or 'wish'*
'oozh-zhoo'	*ʒ as in 'measure' or 'leisure'*
'ootch-tchoo'	*ch as in 'cheese' or 'chip'*
'oodjh-djhoo'	*dʒ as in 'judge' or 'june'*
'ook-koo'	
'oog-goo'	
'oong-ngoo'	*ng or ŋ as in 'song' or 'ring*

On the 'ng' sound, come off cleanly, avoid 'g' or 'k' at end – this last one is a bit tricky at first, because no words in English begin with 'ng' so we are not used to it at the start of a word, but this is a very useful exercise for the soft palate (and the brain!).

Articulation – plurals and consonant clusters

The next section is laid out so that you do a small sequence and then put it into practice words straight away. For example, go from 'oot' to 'eet' down to 'eests-stee' and then drop down to Practice Example 1. This helps integrate the articulation exercises and makes them relevant. Then come back to block two ('ook' to 'eekstr'), do practice example 2, and so on.

Vowel sequence and consonant clusters

oot	oht	awt	aht	ayt	eet
oots	ohts	awts	ahts	ayts	eets
ooss	ohss	awss	ahss	ayss	eess
oost	ohst	awst	ahst	ayst	eest
oosts	ohsts	awsts	ahsts	aysts	eests

oosts-stoo ohsts-stoh awsts-staw ahsts-stah aysts-stay eests-stee

Now do Practice example 1.

ook	ohk	awk	ahk	ayk	eek
ooks	ohks	awks	ahks	ayks	eeks
ookst	ohkst	awkst	ahkst	aykst	eekst

ookstr ohkstr awkstr ahkstr aykstr eekstr

Do Practice example 2.

ookt	ohkt	awkt	ahkt	aykt	eekt
ookts	ohkts	awkts	ahkts	aykts	eekts

Do Practice example 3.

oosk	ohsk	awsk	ahsk	aysk	eesk
oosks	ohsks	awsks	ahsks	aysks	eesks
ooskt	ohskt	awskt	ahskt	ayskt	eeskt
ooskts	ohskts	awskts	ahskts	ayskts	eeskts
ooskts-skoo		ohskts-skoh, etc.			

Do Practice example 4.

ooth-t oth-t   awth-t ahth-t ayth-t   eeth-t
ooth-ts   oth-ts awth-ts, etc.
oothts-thoo   ohthts-thoh, etc.
oot-th   oht-th   awt-th aht-th   ayt-th   eet-th
oot-ths oht-ths awt-ths, etc.
oot-ths-too   oht-ths-toh, etc.
oof-th   ohf-th   awf-th ahf-th   ayf-th   eef-th
oof-ths ohf-ths awf-ths ahf-ths ayf-ths eef-ths
ooks-th ohks-th awks-th ahks-th ayks-th eeks-th

And then do Practice example 5.

Finally:

ood ohd awd ahd ayd eed / oodz ohdz awdz ahdz aydz eedz

It can be quite a relief to come back to the simplicity and the weight of the 'd' sound after all those 's' and 'th' combinations, and brings a grounding sensation back to the tongue and voice.

Practice examples

1   *Final st(s)*:
    bequests, jests, dispossessed, guests, coasts, twists, feasts

2   *kst(r)*:
    dexterity, fixed, faxed, make'st, extra, extreme

3   *ookt, ookts*
    One must predict that it's hard to restrict but he who overacts rarely attracts contracts

4   *oosk, ooskt(s)*
    When asked why he whisked in a mask so grotesque
    He replied he but frisked and risked a burlesque

5   *oot-th oof-th*
    The eighth of the twelfth and the fifth of the sixth (eight-th, twel-f-th, fif-th, siks-th)

(iv) TIV3c
Consonant Clusters

These occur in Elizabethan, Jacobean and Restoration plays. Here are some tricky combinations with example words – see if you can think of more.

oomst   ohmst   awmst   ahmst   aymst   eemst   owmst   imst
came'st, seem'st

oopst   ohpst   awpst   ahpst   aypst   eepst   owpst   ipst
gawp'st, keep'st

ooptst   ohptst   awptst   ahptst   ayptst   eeptst   owptst   iptst
tempt'st, dipp't'st, interrupt'st

ooblst   ohblst   awblst   ahblst   ayblst   eeblst   owblst   iblst
honourabl'st

oovst   ohvst   awvst   ahvst   ayvst   eevst   owvst   ivst
believ'st, giv'st, deceiv'st

oothst
sooth'st, smooth'st

oothz
scythes, oaths

ootst   ohtst   awtst   ahtst   aytst   eetst   owtst   itst
prate'st, sweet'st, commit'st

oodst   ohdst   awdst   ahdst   aydst   eedst   owdst   idst
loved'st, could'st, chide'st, betray'd'st, should'st, bid'st

oostst
exist'st

oonst   ohnst   awnst   ahnst   aynst   eenst   ownst   inst
prune'st, join'st, discern'st

oontst
want'st, meant'st

oondst
stand'st, pawn'd'st, apprehend'st

oolst   ohlst   awlst   ahlst   aylst   eelst   owlst   ilst
smile'st, exhale'st, careful'st, marshall'st, tell'st

ooltst
felt'st, wilt'st

ooldst   ohldst   awldst   ahldst   ayldst
hold'st, behold'st, scald'st

ooldz
world's, holds, scalds, fields

ookst   ohkst   awkst   ahkst   aykst   eekst   owkst   ikst
make'st, wake'st, provoke'st, speak'st, seek'st, mixed, betwixt

ooktst
strict'st, look't'st, perfect'st, predict'st

oongst
bring'st, loving'st, cunning'st

oongkst
think'st, drink'st, rank'st thank'st

Practising clusters and then relevant words straight away helps you integrate articulation into text and enables you to feel the point of all this work.

Practical application of consonant cluster work

Here are some extracts from Shakespeare and Restoration texts, so that you put these exercises into practice immediately. It then becomes something useful and helps make the connection between class work and acting, so that you can use complex language clearly and with an easy fluency, and as an actor you have these tools at your disposal. Integrate as you go along.

> See then, thou fight'st against thy countrymen,
> And join'st with them will be thy slaughter-men.
> *Henry VI, Part 1*, Act Three, Scene Three

That honour which shall bate his scythe's keen edge,
...the huge army of the world's desires
Love's Labour's Lost, Act One, Scene One

Hadst thou no poison mix'd, no sharp-ground knife
Romeo and Juliet, Act Three, Scene Three

O, most wicked speed, to post
With such dexterity to incestuous sheets!
Hamlet, Act One, Scene Two

That thou betrayd'st Polixenes, 'twas nothing
...Nor was't much
thou wouldst have poison'd good Camillo's honour,
A Winter's Tale, Act Three, Scene Two

No, mistresses are like books. If you pore upon them too much,
they doze you, and make you unfit for company; but if used
discreetly, you are the fitter for conversation by 'em.
The Country Wife, Act One, Scene One

A mistress should be like a little country retreat near the town;
not to dwell in constantly, but only for a night and away, to
taste the town the better when a man returns.
The Country Wife, Act One, Scene One

A slander-mouthed railer; I warrant the spendthrift prodigal's in
debt as much as the million lottery, or the whole court upon a
birthday.
The Way of the World, Act Three, Scene Six

Then there is *The Art of Affectation*, written by a late beauty of
quality, teaching you how to draw up your breasts, stretch up
your neck, to thrust out your breech, to play with your head, to
toss up your nose, to bite your lips, to turn up your eyes, to
speak in a silly soft tone of a voice, and use all the foolish
French words that will infallibly make your person and
conversation charming; with a short apology at the latter end,
in the behalf of the young ladies who notoriously wash and
paint, though they have naturally good complexions.
The Man of Mode, Act One, Scene Two

See if you can work out the fundamental differences between the two
periods and styles of drama, and how the articulation differs. Think
about weight, pace, and feel.

(iv) TIV3d 💿
Consonant Clusters

Here is the entire figure of eight sequence which you can build up to over time.

1   First, read (aloud!) from left to right across each set:

'pahtahkah   paytaykay   peeteekee   paytaykay   pahtahkah
pawtawkaw   pootookoo   pawtawkaw   pahtahkah'

'bahdahgah   baydaygay   beedeegee   baydaygay   bahdahgah
bawdawgaw   boodoogoo   bawdawgaw   bahdahgah'

'mahnahlah   maynaylay   meeneelee   maynaylay   mahnahlah
mawnawlaw   moonooloo   mawnawlaw   mahnahlah'

'thahfahsah   thayfaysay   theefeesee   thayfaysay   thahfahsah
thawfawsaw   thoofoosoo   thawfawsaw   thahfahsah'

'**th**ahvahzah   **th**ayvayzay   **th**eeveezee   **th**ayvayzay   **th**ahvahzah
thawvawzaw   **th**oovoozoo   **th**awvawzaw   **th**ahvahzah'

2   Then read down each row from top to bottom, going on to the next row from top to bottom, and so on, so that you have an entire sequence that looks and sounds like this:

'pahtahkah   bahdahgah   mahnahlah   thahfahsah   **th**ahvahzah
paytaykay   baydaygay   maynaylay   thayfaysay   **th**ayvayzay'

...and so on.

This is on the DVD, and as I have explained, I find it much easier to teach (and learn) this whole thing orally/aurally and physically, so this sheet is really for reference purposes. Watch this on the DVD first and

have a go, and then use this sheet afterwards, just to look at what you
have been doing.

Here is the entire sequence written out phonetically, which may be
useful if you have learned the IPA – some people find this easier to
read (ignore it if it is confusing) and it can also be a very handy
phonetics reminder and practice of some of the symbols.

paː taː kaː   peɪ teɪ keɪ   piː tiː kiː   peɪ teɪ keɪ   paː taː kaː
pɔː tɔː kɔː   puː tuː kuː   pɔː tɔː kɔː   paː taː kaː

baː :daː gaː   beɪ deɪ geɪ   biː diː giː   beɪ deɪ geɪ   baː daː gaː
bɔː dɔː gɔː   buː duː gu   bɔː dɔː gɔː   baː :daː gaː

maː naː laː   meɪ neɪ leɪ   miː niː liː   meɪ neɪ leɪ   maː naː laː
mɔː nɔː lɔː   muː nuː luː   mɔː nɔː lɔː   maː naː laː

θaː faː saː   θeɪ feɪ seɪ   θiː fiː siː   θeɪ feɪ seɪ   θaː faː saː
θɔː fɔː sɔː   θuː fuː suː   θɔː fɔː sɔː   θaː faː saː

ðaː vaː zaː   ðeɪ veɪ zeɪ   ðiː viː ziː   ðeɪ veɪ zeɪ   ðaː vaː zaː
ðɔː vɔː zɔː   ðuː vuː zuː   ðɔː vɔː zɔː   ðaː vaː zaː

(v) TIV4
Consonants and Vowels

1 Massage and work the lips; do plenty of lip-release and strengthening exercises .

2 Massage and work the tongue.

3 'Massage' and work the soft palate with some gentle yawning.

4 Work consonant drills with clarity, precision, and release:

'bbb bbb bbb ba', 'ddd ddd ddd da', 'ggg ggg ga', etc.

Repeat with 'p', 't', 'k' , etc.

Then try out 'b-d-g//g-d-b//b-g-d', repeating each one several times.

Chew and really feel the sounds. Notice the different weights of 'b' and 'p', 'd' and 't'.

5 Work vowels for shape, length or duration:

Long vowels	*Short vowels*
ɑː iː uː ɜː ɔː	ɪ e æ ə ʌ ɒ ʊ
hah hee hoo her haw	hit het hat the hut hot hook

6 Do the same for diphthongs:

əʊ eɪ aɪ aʊ ɔɪ	ʊə ɪə eə
ho hey hi how hoy	cure here there

7   And for triphthongs:

    ʊə   eɪə   aɪə aʊə ɔɪə
    Noah's players fired our lawyer

8   Here is a progression of consonant sounds (the progression of sounds made from the front to the back of the mouth):

p	perpetually perpendicular	b	big baby bubbles
m	magnificent melon marmalade	w	will you? won't you? would you?
f	fluffy felafels	v	vivacious vivienne
θ	three thirsty thistles	ð	this, that, then the other
t	tasty testosterone	d	delia dallies decidedly
n	ninety naughty ninnies	l	lovely Lilith's lillies
s	sixty strange stories	z	zanzibar's dizzy zebras
ʃ	shall we shan't we shilly-shally	ʒ	measure leisure and pleasure
tʃ	chesty chichester	dʒ	jennie judges geraniums
j	yield your yoyos	r (ɹ)	rural rarities
k	cantankerous kangaroos	g	Gertrude's gregarious geese
ŋ	singing long songs	h	Harriet hated hops

9   'Poppy protested by blowing big bubbles while walking with Maurice and Thea, then teetered slightly, dodging drains. Yet Lilith – she loitered, as Rita and Charlie just laughed with pleasure, and giggled and cackled in the huge hall.'

Glossary

Alexander Technique Founded by F.M. Alexander in the late nineteenth century, it was developed initially to alleviate his own breathing and vocal problems and involved what he called 'The Use of the Self'. It is based on the idea that how we use the body affects the way it functions – how we move or stay still, how we breathe, indeed how we live and react to life. For more information see www.stat.org.uk.

Alignment Often associated with 'posture', I don't use the word posture as it can imply rigidity ('sit up straight'), which is unhelpful. Alignment is about finding the body's natural relationship between the head, neck and back, which helps coordinate healthy functioning of the component parts.

Connection I use this word a lot, and it means making links. These could be links within the body, as in alignment – for example, with finding the sense of connection between your sitting bones, bending the knees and down to your heels. Or you make a connection between your spine, shoulders, arms, fingertips, and the breath in between. It can mean connecting the breath to a thought – you think, you breathe, almost simultaneously, and then you speak. Connection to the word means that, as you breathe and support your sound, your physiological connection is supporting the outgoing breath and sound from your abdominal area, which is fairly 'central' in the body, and your emotional connection comes from letting the breath into that centre and speaking from there. It can mean connecting to your organs of speech – clear and muscular articulation is a technical skill but it also needs to be connected to your breath and the thought in order for it to become part of the creative process. There also needs to be a

connection to the space you are in, and a connection with your audience. I also mean that we need to find a connection between our physical senses and our emotions. If you are disconnected from a thought, it means that you are probably not supporting the voice and the word, or that your thought process is not engaged harmoniously and simultaneously with your speech, and this usually leads to an untruthful utterance – we get the sense but not the meaning; or perhaps we get the meaning but not the sense. Connection is also key to the integrated voice – integrating skills, creativity, physiology, technique and artistry.

Core skills By this I am referring to the fundamentals of voice work – alignment and body awareness, breath work (breath centring, breath capacity, breath support, the breath–thought connection), warming the voice, forward placement, resonance, pitch, articulation and shaping of the word.

Grounded Means to feel connected to the earth, to the floor, to feel support coming from the floor or ground. It gives you a sense of weight without heaviness, a feeling of stability and strength. You can feel the floor beneath your feet – try standing (or sitting with your feet flat on the floor) and notice how they – and you – feel. Now wiggle the toes, stretch the toes and feet, shake them, walk through the feet in a standing or sitting pose by undulating them as much as possible. Press the toes, then the balls of the feet, then the heels, into the floor, and then let go. Rock back and forth on them. Just stand simply (or sit) and you should really notice your feet and be able to feel the floor beneath them. This gives you a connection to the earth and a literal sense of the ground. That base will eventually help your voice free up and find weight. You can really find this grounding in a sitting position – sitting on a firm chair far enough forwards for your feet to be on the floor (if you are working in a place where the chairs are too low or too high, find a way to adjust such as placing thick books under your feet so that your thighs are more or less at ninety degrees or a bit less). Press down with your feet and feel the sit bones coming into contact with the chair. Rock slightly from one sit bone to the other and then sit through both with equal weight, using the feet to help you. This also gives a sense of weight and grounding.

Open channel This refers to the breath channel and means that the mouth and throat need to be as open as possible in order for the breath to come in without any interference and go out as freely as possible. When you breathe in, there should be no sound (if it is raspy, it generally means there is a constriction somewhere in the mouth, for example a tense tongue, or soft palate, or tension and constriction somewhere in the throat area). When you breathe in or sound out, that channel can be imagined as a wide pipe coming all the way from your centre, up the trachea into the larynx and pharynx and into the nose or mouth, with as much freedom and space as possible. The only barriers are on voicing (when the vocal folds come together and vibrate), and at the 'articulators' (for example, the closure between the lips when saying 'b' or between the tongue tip and the alveolar ridge when saying 't' or 'd'). But all this should still be as free as possible, hence the notion of the open channel.

Release　Means to let go. The emphasis is on efficiency of movement and on the breath, skeletal alignment, articulation of the joints as well as the speech organs, release of muscular tension and the use of gravity and momentum to facilitate movement. I use the idea of release in connection with relaxation. This does not mean collapse – it is really about getting the body and the voice to work through a sense of ease. It helps to create space in the body which in turn helps create space in the breathing mechanism and in the voice itself. A released voice is open, free, unconstricted and ultimately very powerful.

Index

Page numbers are generally given where an exercise or concept is first introduced, is used in the most extensive detail, and/or at key points in the book.

DVD Contents

If you are in the UK, Europe, Australia or another region requiring PAL format, please insert the disc into your DVD player with the label facing up. If you are in the United States, Canada or another region requiring NTSC format, please insert the disc with the label facing down. If you are watching this on a computer, view the PAL version in all territories.

ABOUT

About this DVD

INTRODUCTION

SECTION A

Warm-ups/Workouts/Physical

- Main Warm-up/Workout

- Short Warm-up

- Restoration Warm-up

- Angel Wings – semi-supine with arm raises and sound

- Rolling Down the Spine – with breath and voice

- Sun Salutation – with voice

SECTION B

Speech Work: *Preparation*

Lip Exercises

- Lip Warm-ups
- Lip Muscularity & Agility
- Lip Consonant Drills

Tongue & Soft Palate Exercises

- Tongue Warm-ups
- Tongue Muscularity & Aerobics
- Tongue Flexibility
- Tongue & Soft Palate Consonant Drills

Speech Work: *Application*

Articulation & Resonance

- Basic Figure of 8 Pattern
- Consonant Combinations
- Figure of 8 Accents
- Further Sequence & Articulations

The Bone Prop

SECTION C

Text & Extras

- Taking a Baby 'f' for a Walk
- *Sailor's Hornpipe* – articulation jingle
- *O for a Muse of Fire* – physicalised sections
- *There is Beauty* (*The Mikado*)
- *Poppy Protested* – articulation sentence

Credits

Note: In the speech work chapters, you can play the whole section, or select individual exercises.

www.nickhernbooks.co.uk

facebook.com/nickhernbooks

twitter.com/nickhernbooks